W9-ADU-212

Поэт. 450-300

IN HIS TRUE CENTRE

ALSO BY ARNOLD L. HASKELL

THE SCULPTOR SPEAKS (*Heinemann*)
BLACK ON WHITE (*Barker*)

BALLETOMANIA (*Gollancz*)
DIAGHILEFF (*Gollancz*)
DANCING ROUND THE WORLD (*Gollancz*)
BALLET PANORAMA (*Batsford*)
FELICITY DANCES (*Nelson*)
PRELUDE TO BALLET (*Nelson*)
BALLET (*Pelican*)
BALLETOMANE'S SCRAPBOOK (*A. & C. Black*)
BALLETOMANE'S ALBUM (*A. & C. Black*)
NATIONAL BALLET (*A. & C. Black*)
THE MAKING OF A DANCER (*A. & C. Black*)
BRITISH BALLET, 1939–1945 (*Longmans Green*)
GOING TO THE BALLET (*Phoenix House*)
ETC.

WALTZING MATILDA: A Background to Australia (*A. & C. Black*)
AUSTRALIA (*Collins*)
THE AUSTRALIANS (*A. & C. Black*)
THE DOMINIONS—PARTNERSHIP OR RIFT? (*A. & C. Black*)

A. L. H., 1950

IN HIS TRUE CENTRE
An Interim Autobiography

by
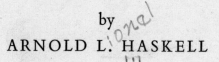
ARNOLD L. HASKELL

WITH THIRTY PHOTOGRAPHS

ADAM & CHARLES BLACK
4, 5 & 6 SOHO SQUARE LONDON W.1
1951

MADE IN GREAT BRITAIN
PRINTED BY UNWIN BROTHERS LIMITED
WOKING AND LONDON

ACKNOWLEDGMENTS

I would like to thank Mr. Nigel Balchin for having found me the ideal title for this book, Miss Edith Carlyon for her very great help in typing a difficult manuscript, and to my friends and publishers A. & C. Black for the endless trouble they have taken at every stage of the production.—A. L. H.

Nice—London—Seefeld—Bath
  1949–1951.

CONTENTS

CONTENTS

PART III

ILLUSTRATIONS

The endpapers are from photographs by Stoppelmann (Genève) *Illustration Nos. 8 (i and ii), 10 (ii), 12 (ii), 13, 15 (i and ii) and 16 (i and ii) are reproduced from photographs by G. B. L. Wilson.*

'Man is but earth; Tis true; but earth is the center. That man who dwels upon himself, who is alwaies conversant in himself, rests *in his true center*. Man is a celestial creature too, a heavenly creature; and that man that dwels upon himselfe, that hath his conversation in himselfe, hath his conversation in heaven. If you weigh any thing in a scale, the greater it is, the lower it sinkes; as you grow greater and greater in the eyes of the world, sinke lower and lower in your owne. If thou ask thy self Quis ego, what am I? and beest able to answer thy selfe, why now I am a man of title, of honour, of place, of power, of possessions, a man fit for a Chronicle, a man considerable in the Heralds Office, goe to the Heralds Office, the spheare and element of Honour, and thou shalt finde those men as busie there, about the consideration of Funerals, as about the consideration of Creations; thou shalt finde that office to be as well the Grave, as the Cradle of Honour; And thou shalt finde in that Office as many Records of attainted families, and escheated families, and empoverished and forgotten, and obliterate families, as of families newly erected and presently celebrated. In what heighth soever, any of you that sit here, stand at home, there is some other in some higher station than yours, that weighs you downe: and he that stands in the highest of subordinate heighths, nay in the highest supreme heighth in this world, is weighed down, by that, which is nothing; for what is any Monarch to the whole world? and the whole world is but that; but what? but nothing.'

JOHN DONNE: *Sermon V*
Christmas Day 1627.

CHAPTER ONE

Introduction in the Form of a Dialogue

Intruder: 'What's all this paper for? Another book? Ballet again I suppose. Don't you realize that you are hopelessly out of date? People are beginning to be fed up with "ballet books." The only writings on the subject anyone except a confirmed *balletomane*, a hopeless case, should want to read are by Gautier, Valéry, Levinson, de Valois, and of course Karsavina's *Theatre Street*; now there's a book for you.'

Myself: 'Agreed, but this isn't going to be a "ballet book." I'm interested in a number of things besides ballet, in fact I'm interested in most things, especially in people. Five of my books don't mention the word "ballet" and have gone into a number of editions for all that. This is to be a few chapters of memories; it can't, of course, exclude ballet. In any case ballet covers a number of things and has brought me many experiences. You will be surprised where it will lead in some of my chapters.'

Intruder: 'An autobiography, nothing less! What presumption on your part! What have you done of the slightest interest to anyone? You have lived a completely sedentary life, unless standing in the wings watching other people perform can be called action.'

Myself: 'Thank you. "Standing in the Wings" sounds a possible title, or at any rate a sub-title. My story may not be an exciting one. I am very definitely a coward with a perfect horror of physical adventure and a very great love of comfort, but anyone who sets down his story simply and sincerely, writing of his shop and himself, deserves a hearing. I learnt that as a publisher's reader. I've watched others perform,

13

writers, painters, musicians and dancers, and have reacted; that's the point. Even if I was perpetually seated in an armchair, I have been moved. I'm good audience, these creative people need me!'

Intruder: 'You've made out a *prima facie* case, but let me continue. You're both a busy man and at the same time a lazy one who prefers discussing things in a club or a café over a drink. Why burden yourself with all this hard work? Think of the ghastly drudgery of galley proofs alone!'

Myself: 'Well, it's expensive to live in England today and I have extravagant tastes. As a matter of fact I've already eaten into the advance.'

Intruder: 'And . . . ?'

Myself: 'Self-indulgence or vanity, if you will. I like to see myself in print. I like to keep myself in the limelight. Whether slanged or praised like most other people I feel twice as much alive when I'm talked about.'

Intruder: 'Enough of that. You'll have plenty of opportunities for bragging later on, that is if I let you finish the book. I want the real reason.'

Myself: 'Well, if you're still not satisfied, the real reason is that if I didn't write this book I'd burst. I have so many violent likes and dislikes that I must from time to time set them down on paper, whether anyone reads them or not. You might call it prejudice-letting or anything you please so long as you avoid the current psycho-analytical jargon.'

Intruder: 'Fair enough. For a start let us have a list of those prejudices to give us an early chance of returning the book to the library if, as I suspect, we find you too antipathetic. First of all, give us the likes. Set them out in true confession book style, though you can omit your favourite flower and girl's Christian name as being of even less interest than the rest.'

Myself: 'I like people in general, especially those aged between nine months and twelve years—sculpture—music, mainly French and Slavonic, and Italian opera—the painting of many schools with Giorgione as an ideal—reading with the accent on Balzac, Dickens and Dostoievski, Dumas and Scott —the non-realistic theatre and the realistic film, French in particular—the circus; the music hall, but without jazz bands or microphones; ballet, either when it is good in itself or the vehicle for the projection of an interesting personality— Saint Joan—Newman—Lincoln and Winston Churchill—the Victorian era—the Sitwell family—good leisurely conversation presided over by such a master as Compton Mackenzie, in which there is an intricate pattern of wisdom, indiscretion and nonsense—Paris at any time or season; French cooking and French wine—the smiling beauty of Austrian women—the charity of the Spaniard—sunshine in Southern Europe or Australia—Americans as individuals—Russians as individuals when not tainted by that sin against Holy Russia, the new technology; the very notion of an efficient Russian technician is an offence.'

Intruder: 'Romantically inclined, I see. Now for the dislikes.'

Myself: 'Most intensely the ideal of the little man and his plucky housewife helpmate—most modern inventions, excluding wireless, gramophone and central heating—all materialist philosophies — Luther — Puritanism — Jansenism— modernist but not modern painting, Klee in particular— modernist sculpture, modernist verse, frank "psychological" novels—the critics who trumpet these things and the dealers who wax fat on them—economics and economy—technique for its own sake, self-expression without technique—jazz, swing, crooning, tap-dancing, comic strips—psycho-analysts— the American Way of Life—the Soviet Way of Life—any un-spiritual *Way of Life* when written in capital letters—many *balletomanes* and much ballet—pantomimes and musical comedies—good (alleged) plain cooking—*obviously* efficient women and feminine men, but especially *obviously* efficient women—passport nonsense at frontiers—red lacquered finger-nails—the new portmanteau words; COMINFORM, ugh!'

Intruder: 'You sound far too much of a reactionary for my liking. But you had better go ahead and rid your system of some of these things; I nearly said "complexes".'

Myself: 'Thank you. I had intended to do so in any case.'

Intruder: 'Well, if you must, at any rate beware, I beg of you, of your besetting sin of slapdash carelessness. Why, I could quote from some of your books . . .'

Myself: 'I know. I keep one most conscientious man busy and happy noting my mistakes and informing my publisher and myself. I will try and heed your warning, but if you will oblige me by leaving my pen and paper alone, I will begin. ' "I was born on July 19th, 1903 . . . ." '

PART I

PART I

CHAPTER TWO

Around the Albert Memorial

I

BALLETOMANIA was published in March 1934. It was a great
and an immediate success. Edition followed edition, held up
only between the first and second by a threatened libel suit, and
the words *balletomane* and *balletomania* came into current use.
It was young, sincere and enthusiastic. I believe that it helped
ballet; I know that it helped me. It enabled me to make a
profession out of what had been a hobby. It prevented me from
becoming a dilettante. Not that I despise dilettanti. They are
extremely useful and hardworking members of any community,
indeed the greater their number, the greater the civilization.
However, under the present dispensation I could never have
afforded it. Creative dilettantism calls for wealth and a stable
society.

Yet *Balletomania* might so very easily never have been
written. I was spurred on in the first place by the wish to
accompany the de Basil Ballet on its first American tour. I had
just rediscovered the joys of Russian Ballet after the arid
interlude that followed Diaghileff's death, and my new Russian
friends told me repeatedly that an Atlantic crossing should
prove no barrier to someone who boasted that he was a true
balletomane. I was in business on my own, bored and frustrated,
sitting in an empty picture gallery and I knew it would be a
worth-while experience. I had always loved travel for its own
sake as well as being interested in the effect of a fresh audience
on the performer. The great thing was to find the money and
with it a satisfactory pretext that would convince my father

that I was not abandoning wife and family in pursuit of 'some ballet girl.' To him ballet still had the naughty nineties flavour. I had no need to convince my wife. She is Russian and, though a non-dancer, had long resigned herself to the great hold that ballet had over me. Moreover she liked the idea of my shaking myself out of the rut into which I was settling. She is always trying to shake the family out of ruts.

I thought of the idea of the book, its form and its title, in my bath one morning. By the time I had dried myself I felt as if the book were already written, phrase after phrase went tumbling through my mind. In this exuberant mood I rushed round to see Victor Gollancz. He had recently had great successes with Isadora Duncan's memoirs and Romola Nijinska's book, which I had brought him, and in any case he would be a sympathetic listener because he himself was such a critical enthusiast over opera.

I gave him the title and a breathless outline and also told him that, as I must leave in a week's time for America in quest of material, I would need funds. He agreed without a moment's hesitation and twenty minutes later I left the office with a substantial advance in my pocket. It was my first commissioned book.

Had he hesitated or wished to see a sample of the manuscript I am quite certain it would never have been written. I was in a state of great excitement, bubbling over with the idea of book and journey. The fact that Victor so obviously believed in it kept me that way all the time I was writing. I was never conscious of a moment's drudgery.

II

I started life with the greatest prospect of success as a dilettante. I was an only child, my father was wealthy, my mother artistic and an adoring grandmother lived with us. My father, who was years older than my mother, took not the slightest interest in any form of art, indeed he looked upon all such things with a certain amount of suspicion. A novel had to have a good plot, a piece of furniture to be solid and preferably of mahogany, a painter was only respectable when he had been made an R.A. and knighted. My mother, on the contrary, did her utmost to educate me, taking me to picture galleries, praying for a reaction when she showed me some primitives that left me cold at the time, taking me to theatres and concerts and leaving good books around where I could find them. The greatest blessing of all was her francophilia and the resulting mademoiselle who made me bilingual at an early age and thus opened a whole world of magic from Debussy and Stendhal to French bourgeois cooking.

Nearly every holiday we went to France or Italy and when my father accompanied us the drill was always the same. He grew restless until he had found the latest issue of *The Times*, then he settled down happily in the hotel lounge to read it from cover to cover. I note in passing that I now have a tendency to do the same and I include the crossword. In the meantime my mother and I busied ourselves with sightseeing. We met at lunch-time when the conversation also followed a rigid pattern. He would talk of the extraordinary ways of foreigners and the superiority of everything at home—pointing to a chestnut tree he once told my astonished wife with great pride, 'now admit you couldn't produce anything like that abroad' —and also of the latest follies of the Liberal Party and that man, Lloyd George—Labour was yet to shock him still more deeply—while we discussed some painter or the architecture of a church. My dear grandmother was all the time on tenter-hooks. In her chosen role of peace-maker, before any quarrel had arisen, she tried by a phrase here and there to reconcile the two topics of conversation; not an easy task in the case of Giotto and Lloyd George. However, in spite of her efforts we were two against one and only now do I realize how long-suffering he must have been. If by any chance he had the misfortune to admire anything, usually a neo-Gothic post office or a Palace Hotel, I invariably jumped down his throat. I well remember the day when he expressed the greatest enthusiasm for an English teashop in Paris while I was flowing over with my discovery of Ingres. I remember it with a certain shame. I must have been intolerable. I could so easily have found something appropriate to say about the crumpets and tea-cakes, while it was a bit much to expect him to react to my latest enthusiasm, *l'Odalisque*, save to comment on foreigners and nudity. I only learnt tolerance very many years later, when my own children began to find me sadly out of date, too late, alas, to repay him for his generosity and for the love he found it so very difficult to express in words.

Indeed at this time intolerance coloured my whole relationship to people. If they did not worship my gods, I had no further use for them. I was totally unable to dissemble. I was in fact pointedly rude and resentful. On one occasion a worthy old lady, a valued family friend of the kind one rather grudgingly calls 'Auntie,' revealed the fact that she had never heard of Karsavina. I promptly buried my head in a book and never spoke to her for the rest of the visit. Let us hope that she put it down to acidosis, if that was the fashionable childish complaint of those days.

Apart from my very real interest in every form of art, my opinions in general went by opposition to my father's. He was ultra-conservative, I was therefore very much to the left. He was a banker, I affected to despise all business. He refrained from pointing out, except on the rarest occasions when I had grossly overstepped the mark, that all my artistic experiences were subsidized by his banking.

My insistence on this opposition, however, while it explains the early intensity of my inclinations, must not be allowed to distort the picture or to have the Freudian significance it might be given in retrospect. Apart from occasional surface scenes we were a very united family. I loved my father, even if I did not always like him, longed to make contact with him and knew that I could always rely on his help and advice whatever the situation. Difficult in small matters, he was always infinitely patient in an emergency. I am pleased that I never gave him any major worries, sorry that I could not have given him those minor joys that add up to so impressive a total in family relationships. Had I had the intelligence or the experience to agree to differ on matters of taste, as I try to do now that I, in my turn, am a father and consequently an old fogy to others, he might have been happier. My own childhood was on the whole a very happy one.

III

I can remember far back into nursery days with a vivid pictorial memory and these early memories have a nostalgia that increases with the years. It was a world of order and security as represented by the teatime hiss and bubble of a kettle on a blazing coal fire, the guard of which threw a criss-cross pattern on the wall opposite. From outside came the percussion of horse-drawn traffic, especially when there was something on at the Albert Hall, and occasionally there would be the intrusion of a piercing whistle as a maid or a footman summoned a four-wheeler. Friendly reassuring sounds, all.

A child lived a life in a kingdom of his own quite apart from grown-up bustle and chatter. Children and grown-ups met at certain stated intervals and then (on the occasion of Nanny's day out) it was a treat for both.

My first home was but a stone's throw from the Albert Hall, my first steps round the Albert Memorial with its exciting statuary; a certain buffalo bore a striking resemblance to a family friend, that same Auntie to whom I had been so rude. Is it from these first associations that I have gained my sympathy for things Victorian?

This link with a different world, though it affects but a few

years of my consciousness, goes down deep. It is certainly of
vast importance to an understanding of my generation. How
very different the street scenes, already part of a quaint period
picture; the loads of straw laid down outside the house of an
invalid, the men and urchins running after the cabs to help
unload the luggage, massive cabin trunks then, the enormous
speed of the fire engines with their straining horses, the muffin
man's bell, the starched and beribboned maids chatting at the
area door or assisting their arch-enemy, Nanny, to pull the
pram up the front steps, the German bands, the pirate buses
touting for fares, top-hats, sailor suits, bowling hoops, especially the not so genteel iron ones with their fascinating jingle-
jangle.

Certain episodes stand out as portents: the sound of muffled
drums at King Edward's funeral; the arrest of Crippen through
wireless telegraphy; watching my first aeroplane at Ostend, I
was learning to read at the time; being taken to my first
cinema somewhere in Piccadilly near Rowland Ward's with
its terrifying lion in the window—it is still there; hunting
for one of the first taxis in Trafalgar Square; shop windows
smashed by the suffragettes.

Books, broadcasts and plays have capitalized this particular
scrapbook nostalgia and it is only worth doing when written
with great charm or a wealth of sociological detail. My only
reason for pausing to note it here is that it is a very definite and
ever-present part of myself as it must be of every child of the
1900's, whether he sighs for it or seeks to discard it. And most
of those who mock at Victorianism now do so with affection.

IV

An infallible way of stirring the memory is to examine one's
own family language. For instance, the phrase 'She's suffering
from a present' always brings to mind the Christmas season
and the nice warm feeling of home for the holidays. An old

friend of the family always asked us to chose our own substantial Christmas presents and to send the bill to his office; 'Like that you'll get exactly what you want and you'll have fun choosing.' I did have fun, lots of fun; books and pictures, a camera, binoculars, are still there to remind me of it. My mother, however, appeared to suffer intensely. It would begin like this, perhaps with a query at breakfast:

'Do you like *Empire*?'

'It all depends. I can't talk about it in the abstract.'

'Well, John's present is due and I've seen the most adorable *Empire* sofa. Or do you think I need a clock more? Or perhaps that lovely Chinese lacquer cabinet from Bodgers? In that case, I could sell those two little tables, move the cupboard from my boudoir and the tapestry stool from my bedroom; that would be a pity, though. What do you think?'—turning to my father who dryly remarked, 'Emmy's suffering from a present.'

This discussion would continue for several days and then the theoretical gave way to the practical. We would all be summoned upstairs where my mother had been moving furniture all morning.

'What do you think of that sofa, Jack?' she asked my father.

'Nonsense, flimsy stuff. One can't sit on that. Get something solid. Besides the stuffing's coming out.'

'That's the most beautiful old brocade. It can be arranged a little; that's nothing. Arnold, do you like it?'

I always appreciated my mother's taste but where furniture was concerned, especially furniture on which one sat, I fully sympathized with my father. The room looked magnificent but one could not relax. I prefer a chair into which one sinks, my mother has always liked to sit bolt upright.

The furniture moving went on at all times of day or night up to Christmas Eve, with the sofa turning into a chair, the chair into a clock, the clock into a cupboard and finally the cupboard into a Han bowl.

Today my mother still shifts furniture in her quest for perfection of line and unless I provide myself with an air cushion I still sit perched uncomfortably on a beautiful hard chair. I have inherited my father's rôle and utter his 'Nonsense, flimsy stuff,' as the beautiful chair creaks and groans under my wriggling.

'Mother's suffering from a present.' The whole of Christmas is in that phrase.

V

So far there has been no mention of ballet and ballet must wait; there is no risk that it will be neglected in these pages, but I would like for my own satisfaction to know how and when my interest started. It sounds an affectation to say that I was born interested in ballet and yet, in spite of my strong visual memory, I cannot evoke the very first performance of all, though I can remember my first visit to a theatre and also my first Drury Lane Pantomime, and the first *Peter Pan*; I fell in love with Wendy. All that I do know is that I was already something of an enthusiast by the time I went to boarding-school, at the age of eight, and could rattle off the names of dancers and their rôles as well as a list of all the boxing champions of the last decade. Photos of Karsavina and Carpentier were pinned inside my locker together with one of Winston Churchill, even then a particular hero of mine, because of the Sydney Street episode. It was almost certainly at the Coliseum that I saw my first ballet and the year 1910 that started the Russian invasion with visits from Preobrajenska, Kyasht, Karsavina and Anna Pavlova. My father often took me to a theatre or a music hall on a Saturday afternoon and we may well have strayed into a ballet by accident, the main object of the visit being to see George Robey, Wilkie Bard, Little Tich, Marie Lloyd or my prime favourite, Vesta Tilley. I remember in particular one superb Saturday spectacle

26

in which the heroine, tied to a stake, was rescued from a watery grave by the hero on horseback, and the water was real wet water and no clever contrivance of lights and gauzes. It was a blessing that the early films were considered bad for the eyes so that I gained the flesh and blood theatre habit from childhood. I was touched when Prince Wolkonsky, former director of the Russian Imperial Theatres, as a very old man told me that he could not sit in a theatre, listen to the tuning up of the orchestra and then see the curtain rise without as great a thrill as in childhood, even if the play itself disappointed. I can understand, I feel that way myself.

Still I would like to know whether it was Karsavina in *Giselle*, Preobrajenska in *Swan Lake*, Pavlova as the Dying Swan, Adeline Genée in *Camargo*, or the sparkling Kyasht who, one Saturday afternoon, by sheer chance decided my future for me.

I learnt some kind of dancing from the famous Mrs. Wordsworth, a one-eyed lady with a booming voice and an enormous connection. I was amused to learn that Ninette de Valois was also her pupil and we may have *chasséed* together. I disliked the classes intensely and they were soon discontinued. I had no ambition to become a dancer.

VI

I went to boarding-school at the age of eight, to Streete Court, Westgate-on-Sea. Leaving home was always agony; once I stuffed my trousers up the chimney to cause a delay, but when there I thoroughly enjoyed school life. That is perhaps a drawback for the autobiographer, because there is always something dramatic and interesting in the Cinderella motive of the miserable and misunderstood scholar who afterwards makes a success and so proves his masters and schoolfellows in the wrong. I have little to record of interest either to others or to myself. When I look back on Westgate

I always think of the gardens and playing-fields in bright sun-shine and it is the half holidays and the summer half term with plates piled high with strawberries and cream, and the head-master's wife appropriately dressed in a strawberry-coloured frock, and exciting excursions by charabanc that I remember.

It was at Streete Court that I met a teacher of genius, Mr. L. H. I. Peebles, who taught me more than anyone else has been able to do. He seemed a veteran then, but he has since won for both my sons an Eton scholarship and he has altered but little. He is a Scotsman with a strong personality, a man of violent likes and dislikes and a born teacher. One learnt as much from him outside the curriculum as in the classroom. He read Burns to me, gave me my love of Austen, Dickens, Thackeray and the Brontës. Although he did not teach history officially, the little that remains with me at all vividly comes from him. The great thing was to divert him in the middle of a grammar lesson. It had to be done with a certain amount of tact and cunning, but once he had started on Caesar, Alexander, Marlborough or Napoleon, the minutes flew by.

I was neither very good at anything, nor very bad. I was not ambitious. Without too much work I could keep in the first half and I could always rely on a good examination tempera-ment and a certain amount of bluff to pull me up a few places. This left me a great deal of time for private reading which, ever since those 'prep school' days, I have pursued not at ran-dom but systematically, trying to cover the interest of the moment in some detail. It was Peebles who gave me this love of reading and now that I myself am a schoolmaster I try to remember his methods.

My last few days at Streete Court shattered forever all sense of security. It made me grow up suddenly and the experience has lived with me.

Though the war had been raging for some time and on certain days one could hear the distant rumble of the guns across the Channel, life at the school was remote from the war; from time to time the death of an old boy brought it closer. War to a schoolboy of those days still had a certain romantic flavour fostered by the papers and magazines. There were no doubts either as to guilt or outcome. Every German was just a Hun and an Englishman could lick a dozen Huns; it was as simple as that. The young masters looked dashing and heroic when they came on leave in khaki; the older ones patrolled the front and hunted German spies. Everyone with the slightest accent was suspect and I still do not know if the spy scares that were the constant topic of conversation had any basis in fact. The only vivid impression that remains is of hearing of the drowning of Kitchener, a dramatic figure who was already a part of our history lessons. One day we stood on the cliffs and watched a dogfight, cheering wildly when the German plane spiralled into the sea. It was just a show, something quite impersonal that did not involve life or death.

Early one Sunday morning, my last week in school, I was lying awake thinking of Monday's Common Entrance examination and reciting to myself a mnemonic on the Kings of England, when there was a deafening thud followed by the tinkling of glass. I was half thrown out of bed, too dazed even to be scared. I ran to the broken window and saw a German plane flying over the lawn, so low that its markings were clearly visible. The bomb that had dropped, one of a score, not far from my bedroom was a tiny one of the anti-personnel type. I felt strangely exhilarated at the time. I was then one of the very few civilians with a bomb story all of my own. Many boys left that day but I stayed to take my examination. The school itself was evacuated the next term, as it was to be in my elder son's time.

This sudden shock had its effects. It left me timid, highly sensitive to noise and an uncertain sleeper. It also gave me the theme for a recurring nightmare in which I was walking up a long and narrow street with tall buildings toppling down on

29

either side of me. This nightmare persisted for many years, faded in the late twenties and then returned more vividly than ever in the thirties. It is very much with me today. It was not a good preparation for 1939.

I went to Westminster School, 'up Rigauds,' first as a weekly boarder and then, when the war made the school food quite intolerable, I became a day boy. Incidentally I missed my one chance of an Abbey burial since, during air raids, we took refuge in the Norman undercroft. It was an ideal school for anyone with my tastes, also for the first time I found them shared by a large number of the community. Among my contemporaries were Angus MacPhail, Glen Byam Shaw, Ivor Montagu and John Gielgud. I was very friendly with Gielgud. We used to cut afternoon classes and also an occasional game, with impunity because we did it with such frequency, to queue up for every type of theatrical entertainment from the Bing Boys to the Diaghileff Russian Ballet. We also visited one another. John had a wonderful toy theatre and I remember his production of *Macbeth*—on second thoughts it might have been Val's. There seemed little doubt that he would find his way to the stage. The Terry blood was a dominating influence. Even at Westminster he knew every major Shakespearian rôle. He won 'orations' with Othello's famous speech. It must have been a wonderful effort because I remember it so clearly while I have forgotten all the others during my five years at school.

Ivor Montagu was not yet a communist, no one was in those days, but then as always he was admirable company. We shared a love of boxing and visited the Ring, Blackfriars, and the Albert Hall together. Ivor was on Christian-name terms with most of the champions. Joe Beckett was a special friend of his and later I met him in Ivor's rooms at Cambridge in company, I think, with Bernard Shaw. Those were the exciting days of Bombardier Wells, Carpentier, Johnny Basham and Jimmy Wilde. The Albert Hall had the majority of the big fights but the Blackfriars Ring, one of the most picturesque spots I have ever visited, was my favourite haunt. Also it was fun contriving the visits. I would leave my conspicuous top-hat at Blackfriars Station, put on a cloth cap and muffler and then merge into the crowds outside Rowland Hill's old chapel, hoping but not really worrying that my absence from school would not be noticed. My luck held, though on one occasion I was more conspicuous than I wanted to be: the crowd taking me for a jockey who had just won a big race cheered me into my seat.

Dr. Gow was headmaster during most of my time at school. He was succeeded by Dr. Costley-White, the present Dean of Gloucester. I never had any direct contacts with him while at school, as I have said mine was ever a comfortable mediocrity, but years later when my book on Epstein, *The Sculptor Speaks*, was published he wrote to congratulate me—not only a very kind thought but a fine feat of memory. Since then I have met him and Mrs. Costley-White on many occasions and have stayed with them at the Deanery. Mrs. Costley-White is a keen theatre-goer, her husband less so. On one occasion he told her that he had just interviewed a delightful parent, a Mr. Owen Nares, whose profession he had tried hard to discover. This joke was often told against him, greatly to his own amusement.

My most humiliating memories are of the O.T.C. I am not a pacifist either by belief or temperament, but I am certainly the most unmilitary person that ever existed. During much of the war tails and toppers were discarded for uniform. Oh, those puttees! It meant getting up an hour earlier, invoking the assistance of both my mother and the maid, and even so the damned things would never end up in the right place. Another of the horrors of uniform was saluting and I have slunk down many an alley-way to avoid an officer, not through any objection to the principle, but because the whole operation was infinitely complicated for an absent-minded person. On one occasion I was awoken from a day-dream by a gruff voice asking me why the blazes I had omitted to salute. I found myself face to face with an angry brigadier-general. He soon saw from my shoulder-badge that I was a schoolboy and as luck would have it he himself was an old Westminster. 'I'm only a war-time soldier like yourself,' he said, 'I'm really a doctor.' He then took me off to Fullers and filled me with cream buns and ices.

My worst moment was when I dropped my rifle on parade and the sergeant-major likened me in highly picturesque terms to Charlie Chaplin. *Shoulder Arms* was just enjoying a great success and I could see the likeness myself. He evidently knew that I was doing my best, and ever since I have had a similar sympathy for the maid when the dish 'came to pieces in her hand.' I was sent off parade and enjoyed a read in the warm library. 1 remember the occasion well for it was on that day I discovered the delightful novels of Susan Ferrier. I came into my own on field days as I was, and am still, an untiring walker and usually managed a glass of beer in a pub while awaiting the stragglers. On one occasion Angus MacPhail and I took one another prisoner by mutual consent and then settled down to a delightful picnic, during which he introduced me to the *Forsyte Saga*.

Most games were equally trying and the walk to the playing-fields in Vincent Square was made horrible by some urchins who once accompanied me to the chorus of 'Hello Uncle Hairy-legs.' Boxing alone I enjoyed though I always had to give away too much weight to make an outstanding success.

I left Westminster for a crammer's to work exclusively at mathematics in order to get through my 'Littlego.' The establishment was about to be turned into a school for younger pupils and I arrived at the transition stage. We ragged the unfortunate crammer, excellent teacher though he was, unmercifully and with a certain amount of imagination. On one occasion after he had complained that in church we always

My Grandmother and Mother

My Mother

My Grandmother

My Father

FAMILY ALBUM

sat in the back pews, not giving the establishment its proper share of attention, we turned up in frock coats and top-hats, Edwardian style, hired from a theatrical costumiers, and filed in impressively just as the bells stopped ringing. I finished by being sacked for growing a moustache to which, with his junior school in mind, he objected. I got through 'Littlego,' a year before he said that I was ready to sit. The result was a glorious year on the Continent. I only mention this crammer episode because I believe that it was to that same school Evelyn Waugh went a few years later as an assistant master. I have found *Decline and Fall* a continual joy.

VII

As an only child I must have been lonely though I was not aware of it at the time. I know that I prayed earnestly for a small sister who could be my special friend. I lived a great deal in the books that I devoured and often their characters were far more alive than the real people around me. Each Jane Austen heroine in turn became the ideal sister, especially Fanny Price. *Little Women* also was a great favourite and I envied the lonely Laurence his discovery of Meg, Jo, Beth and Amy. This book may appear too sentimental and its morals too underlined for modern tastes but it is very real and living, the characters are splendidly observed and I can still read it with a pleasure that is not merely nostalgic.

It took me quite a time to recover from the death of Dora in *David Copperfield*. She was the first person with whom I ever really fell in love and I cannot re-read those scenes today without a pang. My ideal has always been the helpless clinging Victorian type, but thank goodness I married a practical wife. In one sense Dickens played a large rôle in giving me a happy childhood. I had read and re-read all the works with the exception of *The Tale of Two Cities* three or four times before I was

C

fifteen. There was no childhood sorrow, no pending interview with the headmaster that could not be banished from my mind by a half-hour with Sam Weller, Dick Swiveller and the Marchioness, Pecksniff or Mr. Squeers. I still re-read them all at frequent intervals.

Before I left public school I had met Alicia (Markova) and her sisters, Doris, Vivienne and Bunny, and these 'little women' did much to give me the brother-sister relationship I so much required. I saw them constantly, went to the Zoo and to cinemas with them, gave children's parties for them. Through them I realized that I had been lonely and was lonely no longer.

VIII

I am glad that this chapter of childhood is finished. It was essential as a foundation and it has been an interesting discipline in trying to see myself before writing of contacts with others. I have never been really introspective and I lack the type of imagination that can re-live childhood, though the nursery is so much more vivid than the schoolroom; before school and after one is so much more of an individual, that is unless school days have been unhappy. I am in any case far more interested in other people. It is unfortunate because I always enjoy the childhood chapters of autobiographies.

I sincerely believe that from this distance, intolerance apart, I have altered very little; and when I say 'intolerance apart,' thank goodness I can still feel violent about ideas but seldom about people. I can make no clear-cut division into phases, there are no violent inner conflicts, just an even flow that broadened out with the opportunities given me by the publication of my first successful book. The whole scene is a little muzzy and underlit. Occasionally an autumn smell of damp leaves and the bird song of late afternoon finds me, for an instant, a small boy walking up what seemed the long drive

34

of Streete Court. It is only a fleeting impression in which conscious memory has no part. Even when today I pass through Dean's Yard and look up at the much-battered school yard, I cannot really see myself as a top-hatted schoolboy or feel what must have been the strong emotions of the cadet sent off parade for dropping his rifle. For me memory starts in Brussels and in Paris, schooldays safely behind me, Cambridge yet to come.

As I plunge into these memories, I find it difficult to select. Reminiscences are only worth while when they are personal and frank. Yet, law of libel apart, to what degree can one ever be really frank? I could, it is true, be frank about myself within limits, but I have already explained my lack of intro-spection. I would have to invent a whole series of complexes and either I am not sufficiently of a novelist or am lacking in complexes. My private life has been refreshingly free from problems and entanglements. Moreover I would feel un-comfortable at too much self-revelation. When a friend of mine wrote a very frank autobiography dealing with his sex life at great length and with a wealth of detail, I felt embar-rassed every time I met him and his wife; it was as if I had been steaming open his letters or peeping through the keyhole.

Yet the other type of reminiscence, that catalogues a list of great names, giving to each an anecdote or two and a patron-izing pat on the back is even more intolerable.

I suffer also from the handicap of nearly always liking people when I meet them. I tried for my own private amusement to set down some really malicious portraits. It did not work, more's the pity. There is no better way of getting a book discussed; an enemy makes a far better job of one's publicity than a well-meaning friend.

I told Karsavina that I was writing this book and asked her advice on the question of frankness. Her formula was simple. 'Write as if you were talking to a friend who was interested in you and your doings, a friend who will understand without your having to underline every point.'

That is the advice that I am going to follow. My doings may not be of importance to any but my immediate circle, but they cover an interesting period and introduce many of the people who have played an important rôle in the arts.

CHAPTER THREE

Around the Champs Elysées

I

ON leaving the crammers I had a year in hand before going up to Cambridge. The 1914–1918 war had just ended and since it was so clearly the last of all wars the young men of my class and generation felt that they were living in the golden age. They could enjoy themselves and also plan ahead in the full knowledge that nothing extraneous would upset these plans. The Continent was open once again. I spent my year in Brussels, Berlin, Paris and Monte Carlo, falling in and out of love, dancing, learning how to order a meal and read a wine list, and enjoying every minute of the time.

It was in Brussels that I first led a grown-up life. Brussels had been chosen because of my father's friendship with that remarkable man, Emile Francqui, soldier, Congo explorer, business man and cabinet minister. Francqui stayed with us every month when he came to London for a meeting and his visit was a treat. Though he and my father could converse only with great difficulty, they understood one another thoroughly. To start with he was perhaps the only foreigner my father considered completely normal. Francqui's stories of exploration in the Congo, of the German occupation and of his efforts to save Nurse Cavell, of the politicians he met during the peace treaties and subsequent conferences held me spell-bound. He was cynical, an excellent raconteur and a mimic who could make one see Lloyd George, Poincaré and Stresemann. Even in the Locarno days he had a deep mistrust of Germany and never stopped talking of the coming war of revenge and of Germany's secret rearmament. He was the first person to treat me as a grown-up and, since I spoke French fluently, many of his stories were addressed to me.

I was sent to Brussels and placed in his charge. The idea was that after a few weeks of finding my way around the town, living in a family, I should go and stay with the Francqui's at their country place, coming up daily to work at the Société Générale to accustom me to a business career. As things turned out I went to stay with the Francqui's and started my 'business' career a little earlier than scheduled. I had managed to do the classic thing, become engaged to my landlord's daughter. As I was eighteen and she was twenty-five it was felt that I should be rescued. She was, however, very attractive; I had proposed to her one moonlight night in the Avenue Louise, and I greatly resented being rescued, the first of the many times I was rescued before my coming of age.

Although I knew that I would never be happy or successful in business my father always hoped that somehow I would take a liking to it. He wanted so much to have me where he could give me the very maximum help at the start. Francqui realized from the first that I would never do any good in business. I drove up with him every morning enjoying every moment of the conversation. I was then dropped at the office and left very much to my own devices. I found a niche in a basement room where there was a run of bound files of *The Times* and spent my days most profitably reading through the years 1900–1905. If I wanted to leave early to go to a tea dance, which I often did, there was no one to stop me. At week-ends and during the long summer evenings I enjoyed the country life, shooting or fishing with Francqui's eldest son or playing with the children; no surroundings have ever seemed complete to me without children. There were often entertaining house guests, diplomats and prominent men of all nations. One of them was the Nobel prize-winner, Docteur Bordet. His visit impressed itself on my mind because one lunch-time he held forth on the potential danger of raw lettuce and I watched the guests suddenly stop eating the salad that was in front of them; only the distinguished doctor himself and I, who was too young to care, finished our plates with relish. I wondered from his expression whether it was all a joke.

I listened to the carillon at Malines from Cardinal Mercier's garden and was impressed by that courageous and saintly man. The Germans, Huns of 1914, showed a respect for him and his position that the communists have not shown for Cardinal Mindszenty.

Without any doubt the most remarkable man I met at the Francquis', and he was a frequent guest, was the Spanish Ambassador, the Marquis de Villalobar. No one could have ever guessed the grave handicap under which he suffered. He was born a dwarf, a Velazquez figure with a normal body and undersized feet and legs. It was, I believe, the Empress Eugenie who took a special interest in him and had turned the courageous boy into a diplomat. He was stilted up, fitted with an ingenious arrangement by which his real feet served as knees. His intelligence was of a high order. He was witty, caustic but never bitter. He made great efforts to save Nurse Cavell. He told me the story of his superb retort to Von Bissing, the German Governor. 'If you think that you can tread on my toes and I won't feel it, you have picked the wrong man.'

He was a great Spanish gentleman; a grandee by descent and by nature.

My Berlin visit came during the beginning of the inflationary period. Although I disliked the city intensely, it gave me a certain sympathy for the Germans that I had never felt before. As a rabid francophile child I had loathed them to such an extent that I even wrote from the nursery one of my very first letters to a French captain who had been imprisoned on a charge of espionage and had escaped from a German fortress. I congratulated him on getting the better of those *têtes carreés*—the term *boches* was then unknown—and wished France a speedy return of Alsace Lorraine. The war and the wave of hatred that resulted did not give me a chance to revise my opinions which my stay with the Francquis in Belgium, just after its liberation, had if anything intensified. I do not know whether I expected to meet sub-humans or not. What I did see was a very bewildered people. Some of them among the *rentier* and retired classes were starving, but starving in a genteel manner with no dramatic evidence to show their plight. Their starvation was unspectacular, they would be carried off by the first chill or take to their beds and never be seen again. They were neatly dressed in clothes that dated and that still belonged to those solid first years of the twentieth century. The clothes remained, it was the wearers who fell to pieces. They had always known complete security and they could put up no fight when their entire income did not suffice to buy a single meal. What gave me the greatest shock was when I visited a Junker family and saw on the desk a signed photo of Hindenburg. To us he had been a bogey man for so many years, yet these were very civilized people who talked the same language and who shared with me an intense admiration for my idol, Karsavina. After that I have never been able to hate a people *en masse*. I have always remembered that one day again I might meet and like a family von T. There is no greater untruth than that people get the governments they deserve. People are weak, stupid and unarmed against evil and in that negative sense alone they are accessories to the crimes of a devilish minority. I had exactly the same feeling recently when I visited Austria and was completely charmed by the people. In a small café a group of young people was amusing itself, French, Italian, Austrian and English. Later in the day I visited the church and the graveyard. There were rows upon rows of fresh crosses and memorial tablets with photographs of the dead, handsome young men in Tyrolese costume, brothers and sons of the villagers who greeted us with a friendly '*Grüss Gott.*' And on each tablet there was the inscription, 'Killed in action in Russia.' Yet they were in the army of an aggressor more brutal by far than the Kaiser's or Franz Josef's.

It was in Berlin that I met, and was entertained by, a charming Russian family that was to play a very large part in my life.

II

I returned to Brussels for a further two months and then went to Monte Carlo for the Diaghileff season. I have described this at some length in *Balletomania*. Its main attraction to me was to watch the progress of Alicia Markova whom I looked upon as a member of the family. Through her I got to know Diaghileff and the whole company and was able to watch all the rehearsals and to meet the many remarkable people in the Diaghileff entourage. It was very much the atmosphere of some mediaeval principality with the Great Serge as Archduke, Boris Kochno, Anton Dolin and Serge Lifar as princes of the blood. There is little that I can add to what I have already written about Diaghileff. Time only serves to underline his record. I have never met a stronger personality. I was amused when I came to write his biography that so many of his collaborators talked of him as an impresario whose greatest merit had been to give them the chance to create. He was beyond a doubt fully creative himself, and during his lifetime not a single one of those collaborators did any worthwhile work away from his influence. He did not merely discover talent; he developed it, used it, blended it, refined it and inspired it. His knowledge was phenomenal, his taste and his daring are in many respects still in advance of the day and everything worthwhile that we are seeing in ballet today stems from him; whether it be England's Tchaikovsky classicism or France's *avant garde* shock tactics.

He understood and was highly sensitive to what one might

call the law of changing fashions. Anyone else having made a reputation with *Schéhérazade* would have kept it on, especially as there was always a great demand for it. When under pressure Diaghileff finally revived it he laughed so much at the first performance that he broke a *strapontin* and had to go outside to finish his laugh. It was not then, and is not yet, old enough to be looked upon as a classic. Young ballet-goers may for that reason find it difficult to understand the work of this extraordinary man. Companies still play such ballets as *Les Biches* and *Apollon Musagètes*. They were masterpieces, they may possibly appear as such once again, but today they are impossible. Only the classics based on the classroom technique have permanent value. They have passed through the testing time of neglect and ridicule. Kochno today realizes this truth and, as far as existing creations are concerned, he has made *Les Ballets des Champs Elysées* the true spiritual successor of the Diaghileff Ballet.

Although I was never anywhere near Diaghileff's inner circle my long friendship with Astafieva and with her pupils, Alicia and Anton Dolin, drew his attention to me and he must have found me a good listener for often in an interval he talked to me about some future plans. Diaghileff saw to it too that, however full the theatre, I never lacked a ticket. He was angry when my first book appeared commenting on his neglect of classicism; he told me that it showed '*un toupet extraordinaire*' and also a lack of gratitude, but he never withdrew the privilege.

That first book I published at my own expense, since there was then no real market for ballet criticism. In spite of a record number of misprints (for economy's sake it was set up by a French compositor) it might easily have passed unnoticed had it not been attacked in headlines in one of the Rothermere papers; I had not been sufficiently fulsome about the favourite of the moment. As a result of these attacks the small edition was sold out in a very short time.

Rothermere was a Grand Ducal figure, the protector of a number of dancers and in that sense a disruptive influence. His generosity, however, was abundant and was charmingly exercised whether the recipient had any favours to give him or not, whether she was young and attractive or past her prime. He genuinely enjoyed giving. He entertained on a lavish scale, often putting a few thousand franc notes under each plate for use in the gaming rooms after dinner. I remember his asking a young *corps de ballet* dancer what she would do with a large win. On impulse she told him that she would distribute it to the ladies of easy virtue who hung round the casino doors and tell them to go home and enjoy a night's rest. He was delighted with this reply and promptly gave her a large sum of money to spend in this way with some over to buy a couple of dresses for herself. Rothermere helped Diaghileff but only to a limited extent since Diaghileff wished to keep an entirely free hand.

I managed to finish that Monte Carlo season madly in love as usual and with plans to get married as soon as possible. I had met the girl at lunch-time, taken her to the ballet and we were engaged before midnight. It was the first performance of the revival of *Schéhérazade* and the moonlight on the terrace that accounted for the speed of this courtship. As this was the second occasion within a few months my family was less concerned than the first time and wisely decided to ignore the whole affair. They felt that a prolonged stay in Paris might prove an effective cure. They were right.

III

I had the key to a small flat in the rue Henri Martin, Passy, and several months of complete freedom ahead.

I had known Paris ever since I could remember. From the first I loved its large vistas and its narrow streets, its staccato noises and its own particular smell. The biggest impression of those childhood days, apart from the Guignols in the Bois, was

43

the draped statue of Strasbourg in the Place de la Concorde. I was a true child of the *Entente Cordiale* and felt a personal sense of bereavement.

A vision of this small boy looking up in sorrow at that draped statue was the first thing that came to my mind when I heard in May 1950 that I had been made a Chevalier of the Légion d'Honneur. Nothing could have given me greater pleasure than this charming gesture from the French Government. Anything I may have done for France has been done with love and admiration, but in the recognition of that love I feel a great warmth. I am proud of the little red ribbon.

Now I hurried from the Gare du Nord to gape at this city that was mine. '*À nous deux maintenant.*' I was awakened from my reverie by a hoot and a noise of hastily braked wheels—'*Enlève toi, éspèce d'andouille,*' shouted the taxi driver. Such was my welcome to Paris.

My Paris of this period was less characteristically French than the taxi driver's welcome. It was indeed almost strange to have hit on a French taxi driver at all and not a *ci-devant* of the Russian aristocracy or a ballerina's father. This was the time of the full flood of the Russian emigration. Within Paris there was a Russian city of considerable dimensions with an intense intellectual and political life of its own. Geographically it was centred round Auteuil, its main stronghold in the Murat district. You could always rely on hearing nothing but Russian spoken in the last *métro* to the Porte d'Auteuil. There were Russian newspapers, Russian shops and Russian cafés. It was possible for a Russian to live in Paris without speaking a word of any language but his own and without any French contacts. His children, however, would go to a French *lycée* and his grandchildren became completely French, in habit if not in thought. The Parisians were amazingly tolerant and accepted the situation as natural, though the position changed somewhat when a mad Russian assassinated the President, the mild and inoffensive Paul Doumer.

In Montmartre the more expensive *boîtes de nuit* were run by Russians. It was a current jest that every waiter was a Grand Duke and every *vestiaire* in charge of a Princess. There was a substratum of truth in this. These people had immense courage, the gift of turning night into day and a complete lack of worry about the morrow. They formed a vivid contrast to the sober and careful French. I remember hearing a practical and hard-headed French *'demi mondaine'* complaining bitterly that the Russian girls were spoiling the *métier* by giving their favours and actually enjoying themselves *'et Dieu sait si la vie est chère on vieut d'augmenter l'électricité et le gaz.'* Not only were the cabarets run by Russians but the majority of the clients were Russian. It was a period when they still had some jewels to sell. Why so many favoured taxi driving I cannot make out. They were the most reckless drivers in a city of reckless drivers and they very rarely knew the way about either their engines or the city. Yet there could be times when they knew the way surprisingly well. Once I had barely mentioned the address when the driver grew very excited. 'I know Mathilde Felixovna—you should have seen her dance Esmeralda. It was terrific, but terrific, fancy you knowing her.' He then proceeded to give me a graphic description of one of her dances, narrowly missing a tram, a milk cart and several pedestrians. He ended up by coming with me and telling our hostess exactly what her dancing had meant to him. He had been one of the highly privileged *abonnés* at the Maryinsky.

This Russian society was separated into many watertight compartments from the almost fascist right wing to what to-day would be called 'the fellow travellers.' To say that so and so was *'bolchevisant'* meant complete ostracism. Newspaper articles were analysed for wrong tendencies. There were endless varieties of radical and socialist, more even than in France, each group planning the one ideal Russia. Were they as pathetic and ineffectual as I thought them? A far smaller group in exile had planned a new Russian world and, unfortunately for mankind, had succeeded. The café talker of today might well become tomorrow's dictator. My Parisian Russians, however, were, artists apart, mostly weary and impractical, indulging in recriminations over the past. I have never understood why the Soviet should have troubled to kidnap the right wing generals, Kutepov and Miller, in daring coups from the very centre of Paris. It showed the corruption among French officials at that time that these mysteries were never fully brought to light.

My cicerone in the non-balletic Russian emigration was my future brother-in-law, Marc Aldanov, one of the most charming and interesting men I have met. He already enjoyed an immense reputation in the Russian emigration as a novelist in the great tradition of Tolstoi, but in English his works, *St. Helena* and *The Ninth Thermidor*, though they received admirable notices, had but a small sale. Aldanov has always maintained that his greatest interest lies in chemistry and he has published a volume of research, the value of which I cannot judge. A man of lavish generosity, in those days he must have found it difficult to make ends meet. His great success came during the war in America when *Before the Deluge* was chosen by the Book of the Month Club and sold over 300,000 copies. This has given him a certain liberty, but it must be frustrating to have to reach a large audience through the medium of translation. Aldanov is the most pessimistic man I know; the *Encyclopaedia Britannica* calls him a *Girondin désabusé*, but he is excellent company for all that. A socialist in the English non-Marxist sense of the word, he has never ceased to fight against communism, even when a flirtation with the Soviet was smart and lucrative. He saw his most intimate friend, Alexei Tolstoi, cross the frontier to become the idol of Soviet Russia. In his flat I met most of the leaders of the first of the great emigrations. They were charming, invariably said '*il faut parler français à cause de monsieur*' and invariably lapsed into voluble Russian.

· I understood a little Russian, just enough to get on backstage in an emergency, the usual *bolshoi scandal*, or to order a
meal. I could never have followed the complex conversation
of my new friends; philosophical, literary, political. I did,
however, have with them one point in common, a great love
of Russian literature. The Englishman will, in the ordinary
way, never quote Shakespeare or Dickens any more than the
Frenchman Racine or Molière, but the Russian, even the non-
literary Russian, will always manage to bring Pouchkine,
Tolstoi or Dostoievski into a general conversation perfectly
naturally and with no sense of parading knowledge. These
writers are their intimate friends.

Pouchkine, alas, I cannot know. Translations lose the style
and the man, serving up an inferior Byron. Tolstoi and Dostoievski survive and, as Russians are invariably fervent disciples
either of the one or the other, I have enjoyed many an argument, some of which have grown quite heated. I have even
had a violent quarrel with my wife on the subject of *The
Kreutzer Sonata*. Thank goodness the *emigré* can grow heated
about such things instead of over the deviations from the ideas
of the bad writers and still worse philosophers that trouble
the Russians of today.

Aldanov is a Tolstoyan, knowing every word and thought
of the master. Certainly, my admiration for Tolstoi as an
artist is profound and increases with the years. But it is Dostoievski who has moved me the most. He has had a strong
influence on me ever since I read him precociously in the
school library. No other writer has dealt so boldly and con-
vincingly with the great themes of good and evil, of suffering
and repentance. His portrayal of spiritual pride has never been
equalled. What other novelist has ever depicted a saint con-
vincingly? I can find in Dostoievski a prophecy and an
analysis of all that is happening today. His works for all their
imperfection of form, their exaggeration and, at times, crudi-
ties, have a wisdom that I have found in no other secular

47

writings. Though superficially more Russian than Tolstoi—more Slav expresses it better—his *Brothers Karamazov* and *The Idiot* are not pictures of a certain society at a certain time but of Man at all Ages.

My enthusiasm for these master works made me as welcome as if I had been given a very special letter of introduction.

My only close link with the political emigration was a friendship, long continued, with Alexander Kerensky. When I met him he was the scapegoat for both right and left wings, his true position revealed by the enemies he had made. Not only was his life in continual danger from some fascist hot-head, but he always ran the risk of an insult or a snub. Today there are so many Kerenskys and so many less worthy who have deliberately sold the pass that the original no longer stands out. In truth Kerensky was the type of radical humanitarian out of place in Russia but at home in the countries of the Atlantic Pact. In France such a man would already have been Premier a good half-dozen times with a career of service indistinguishable from the rest. The Kerensky I knew so well had immense dignity. I find it very difficult to reconcile the man I knew with some of the accounts of him during his short period as ruler of Russia. It is true that power corrupts but what is so usually forgotten is that failure and hardship can be equally corrupting. He was that rare being, a man who bore no trace of resentment for the vilification he had suffered and who did not try to blame others for his downfall, a downfall for which all nations are in a sense responsible and are now paying for so dearly. I have often questioned him about the past. He maintains that to have stifled the Bolshevik revolution would have involved a ruthlessness equal to theirs. Moreover to have done so he would need to have called the soldiers back from the trenches and so betrayed the allied cause. A Kerensky he was but he could never have been a Quisling *avant l'heure*. His failure has been the failure of world liberalism. He has enormous high spirits and a buoyant optimism, alas never borne

48

Kerensky and A. L. H., Begmeil, 1938

An unpublished photograph of Pavlova on tour; the Blue Mountains, N.S.W.
Efrem Kurz, Pierre Vladimiroff, E. J. Tait, and Pavlova.

out by events, also an insatiable interest in world politics. Micawber-like he always expected something to turn up. He still does. He had no small talk but ranged the world country by country. Early one morning after an all-night talk on current affairs, when even I was beginning to think of bed with some longing, he turned to me and said 'Et le Japon?' The debate continued. Later I induced him to write his apologia *The Crucifixion of Liberty*, which was published in this country by Arthur Barker.

I also met Miliukov on several occasions. He was a great savant with an academic turn of mind and, unlike Kerensky, a fine linguist. He had a profound respect for the British constitution. I found him far less human and approachable than his former political opponent. There was, of course, no reason why he should have been. I was very young, a foreigner and a non-political animal. It was Kerensky's own especial gift to make immediate and sympathetic contact and over the years that I knew him I saw him win over many of his bitterest opponents because of their liking for the man.

From time to time I met some Russian revolutionaries, among them former terrorists, men who had made history and whom history had now passed by, the Russians who had not understood Tolstoi. It thrilled me at first to meet someone who at the risk of his life had hurled a bomb at a tyrant. The reality was disappointing; not only from a dramatic point of view. These revolutionaries looked so much more respectable than the majority of my artist friends. But from that time I have always been deeply interested in revolutionary history, in the intention, the deed and the result. These casual meetings had made a history normally dull through its insistence on hair-splitting doctrinaire matters into a living reality. In any case the Russian revolution was still in being; this man holding a glass of tea had spoken to Lenin and Trotsky. The impressions that have remained with me were that hatred for the oppressors was a far more powerful incentive than love for the oppressed and that the technique of revolution had ended in attracting them for its own sake. The tyrannicide even when he sets out with the highest ideals becomes the very thing that he aims to kill. He is more closely identified with his victim than with his victim's victims.

I had one close connection with a political assassin whom I first met in Brussels and afterwards in France. He was a Polish aristocrat who had first turned diplomat and then monk. He had killed a Russian military governor and escaped by a miracle. The monastery had not completely absorbed him and at times he wore his monkly habit as if it were a fancy dress. He stood on the border-line between two worlds. He was not a Dostoievski penitent. We met on many occasions and he talked with great freedom. He told me of the fierce inner conflict between the love of his country, the hatred of the Russian conqueror and the excitement of the hunt itself, considered as a blood-sport.

'There was I, a young man of twenty, very naïf and armed with a home-made bomb. My quarry was a provincial governor always on the alert and protected by a strong police force and the military. Although through careful study I knew his every movement I knew nothing of the man himself. It was better that way. I was the hunter and it was far more exciting than stalking the game on my father's estate.'

'And at the moment you threw the bomb?'

'I don't know. I wish I knew. I am still trying to work it out. I wasn't afraid, but whether I thought of Poland or that this was the supreme moment of the hunt I can't make out. Certainly I never thought of the man I was killing in terms of humanity. You see I was acting a rôle. It was all rather theatrical, that's why I wasn't afraid. And then when I had killed him, or thought I had, because I only found out afterwards from the newspapers, there was no time to think of anything but my own safety.'

'And you regret it?'

'Yes. Not so much because of the man but because I keep on trying to puzzle out my own motives; and in any case the whole thing was wasted. I do not deny the right to revolt or to throw out an invader; Joan was made a saint. But the revolutionary should only act in purity and love, otherwise it's a negative act and everything's left as before.'

'What suddenly made you feel that way?'

'Well, I was smuggled out of Poland and treated as a hero. But, you see, I didn't feel a hero. Once the danger was over the reaction came and I began to ask myself questions. And then my colleagues set to quarrelling and suddenly it all seemed rather silly.'

The sentimental liberal, who would himself shrink from every act of terrorism, has too often looked on the terrorist as a heroic liberator when in reality he was as guilty of the misfortunes of his country as the Tsar and the reactionary. Perhaps the only reason that my particular terrorists were exiles under both regimes was that they paused for a second to think. Aldanov has drawn some remarkable pictures of terrorists in *Before the Deluge*. They are far more damning than perhaps he credits.

From that time I gained an intense admiration for Gandhi. When he was in London for the Round Table Conference I went with Aldanov to visit him. The interview is in itself in no way memorable but what I can never forget is the effect that this ridiculous-looking skeletal figure in his *dhoti* had on the matter-of-fact London bobby and on the cynical and hard-boiled American newspaper men, veterans of endless goodwill conferences. Gandhi had resolved the doubts of my Polish terrorist friend.

These experiences have made me try to use the words 'great man' sparingly and with care, to attempt to distinguish between true wisdom and worldly intelligence. They have given me an ever-increasing admiration for Lincoln that has made me read and re-read his many biographies with joy.

By way of contrast only recently on re-reading *War and Peace* I was struck with Tolstoi's masterly portrait of Napoleon. Anyone who has a tendency to put a bust of Napoleon on his study desk should read it. And if it seems improbable or far-fetched the *Journals* of Caulaincourt, a devoted admirer and loyal friend, will do more than confirm it.

I have wandered far from Paris and my youth, but everything that happened then has become a part of myself. This plunge into a new world on the fringe of history was an exciting experience for any young man, even a *balletomane*. These exiles, of the first great emigration in modern history, were going through the experiences that the rest of the world was to suffer, only the rest of the world thought itself at peace and would not listen. Through chance I had a preview that only now I can begin to understand.

IV

What struck me most about this Russian society apart from its political clique-ism was the fact that there was no division into highbrow and lowbrow. A man was either educated, in which case he took an interest in literature, music and painting, or completely uneducated. The word *intelligentsia* covered all those people one was likely to meet. Even those who were not *balletomanes*, and in spite of a popular superstition by no means every Russian is, knew all about Diaghileff and the artistic tendencies of the moment and could discuss them without being precious and risking the labels of 'Bloomsbury,' 'Chelsea' or 'Greenwich Village.'

My particular 'little Russia' was a purely artistic colony that was always more concerned with the sensational début of a Lifar or the rivalry between two of the great dance studios than with political hair-splitting between different brands of socialism. I was in a sense an honorary citizen through my association with the ballet.

The most venerable of the critics was the handsome white-bearded Valerian Svetloff. He had been the first to acclaim the young Fokine, to write of Bakst in terms as glowing as the artist's own colours, the first to prophecy that Mademoiselle Pavlova was to be the Taglioni of the twentieth century. A brilliant critical record. But now he was old, poor, and a little out of his depth in exile. He was the constant companion of the brilliant ballerina, Vera Trefilova, who had made a sensational return from retirement in *The Sleeping Princess* in 1921. In spite of that they both lived very much in the past together. She once told me how very much he had made her suffer in Russia when, as an ardent supporter of Pavlova, he had constantly criticized her unfavourably. Now all that was forgotten and it was largely thanks to Pavlova that they both lived in comparative comfort.

Trefilova was a quiet, almost mouse-like little lady who spoke in undertones and whom off the stage one might have taken for a lady companion. There was nothing in the least theatrical about her and though she loved her dancing she told me that she disliked the stage. After she had become ballerina she married a wealthy man and the marriage was ideally happy. When he died she nearly lost her reason and for a long time was so desperately ill that she could no longer walk. Then Diaghileff tempted her out of retirement and for a very brief period she returned to magnificent life. As a pure classical dancer within very narrow limits I have never seen her equal. I measure every Swan Princess by her, but I have never seen a worse performance by a great dancer than her *Spectre de la Rose*. After her wonderful two years' Indian summer she started teaching but never with the conspicuous success of her sister ballerinas. She sat, tapped with her stick, and commented in a low, monotonous voice. For a second or two when she demonstrated it was wonderful. The only pupil to whom she has given a little part of herself is that superb dancer, Nina Wyroubova. She died after a painful illness during the occupation, and I am told that her very last words were about the ballet and *Le Lac des Cygnes* in particular.

Svetloff appreciated my tremendous admiration for Trefilova and the articles that I wrote about her artistry and the classicism that she represented. It is difficult today to realize that at this time, save in the Pavlova repertoire, *Giselle* had not been revived for many years, that *Swan Lake* in one act had only been put on for one season at Monte Carlo for Trefilova, that a woman *en travesti* danced Franz in *Coppélia* at the Opéra (she still does), that the *Sleeping Princess* seen by London alone was a comparative failure and that the potted version, *Aurora's Wedding*, alone bore the standard of classicism. This was the time when the Diaghileff company, and that meant ballet, lacked the strength to mount one of the old ballets and it was necessary to wire Ninette de Valois, who had then left, to come to Rome as guest artist to make the performance of *Aurora* possible. And how brilliantly she danced that 'finger variation'! Classicism was biding its time. Diaghileff, had he lived another year or two, would have led the revival with Spessivtseva, Danilova, Markova, Lifar and Dolin.

Svetloff was my first link with the old tradition, my master as a critic.

Another link with tradition was the Quixote-looking Prince Serge Wolkonsky, an aristocrat of the old school who had been director of the Russian Imperial Theatres and who, now in exile, had become teacher of mime and theatre and film critic for a Russian paper. As theatre director he had been a failure, a man of high principle and great knowledge but of insufficient strength to handle court and company intrigue. He had early contacts with Diaghileff, in whose reforms he believed and some of whose tastes he shared but (fortunately for the Western European stage) he had let Diaghileff down at a critical moment. I was present at a restaurant one day when the bitter breach of years was healed by a handshake. Wolkonsky's own downfall had been brought about by a

MATHILDE KCHESINSKA

In the drawing-room of her St. Petersburg palace

dispute with the all-powerful Mathilde Kchesinska. She had been a close friend of the Emperor's and in consequence enjoyed his protection throughout her career. She ruled the ballet with a rod of iron, though the phrase ill describes anyone of such charm and wit. She had already run counter to Wolkonsky over the casting of several ballets and when she refused to wear a farthingale that was part of a period costume he posted a fine on the notice board. An order came from the court that the fine must be publicly annulled. Wolkonsky was left with no alternative but to obey and resign.

I first met Wolkonsky in Kchesinska's drawing-room. It was he who made clear to me the enormous extent of Diaghileff's reform.

Kchesinska remains a marvel, still able to teach all day and play cards half the night, so witty and vivacious that it is impossible to credit her age. After her marriage with the Grand Duke André and a perilous escape from Russia she settled in the South of France where they had a villa and a competence. It was there I first met her at a time when Diaghileff was trying hard to persuade her to return to the stage. She had no wish, however, to attempt to rival her glorious past, but she was full of interest in what he was doing, although it was so very different from Maryinsky classicism. In particular the young Lifar attracted her attention and they have remained friends ever since. He is the one 'youngster' to call her by her diminutive, 'Mala.' They once danced a mazurka for me. I have never seen it so excitingly performed. Alas, the casino at Monte Carlo soon made it necessary for Kchesinska to earn a living and she set up a dance studio in Paris, the studio that produced Riabouchinska and Lichine. I sent many young English dancers to her and when I came over on visits we always had the most delightful parties with Mathilde Felixovna and the Grand Duke gayer than any of their young guests. One of her pupils, Sirène Adjemova, whom I first saw as a small child, has remained a great friend of mine. A quite extraordinary beauty, a girl of intelligence and a very great heiress, she is the very opposite of the usual 'poor little rich girl.' She has everything but has retained a great simplicity, even after a successful film début. With Kchesinska there was no living in the past, all that remained were some photographs and souvenirs. During one of her visits to London I induced her to give a class at Sadler's Wells and also to make an appearance at a Charity Gala at Covent Garden. She chose a simple character dance and the impact was enormous.

The last time I saw her was after the war shortly before the celebration of the sixtieth anniversary of her début. She had broken a thigh bone falling off a ladder but she had mastered that and was as active as ever. We lunched together and discussed old times, interrupted by the sudden flight of six of her pet cats. The Grand Duke, Kchesinska herself and I, by far the least agile, chased them across the streets for an hour, calling 'pussy, pussy!' and dangling tempting morsels of fish.

V

It was at this time that I got to know Fokine, the father of modern ballet. He had settled in America and ever since his rupture with Diaghileff in 1914 had been right out of the movement. America had presented him with a unique opportunity that he had not seized. He was living on the pallid reproduction of *Les Sylphides* and *Schéhérazade* and especially on giving expensive lessons to wealthy amateurs. Ballet in America was at its lowest ebb and he did nothing to set a standard, though with his prestige he could have done so. Fortunately he was yet, thanks to René Blum, to enjoy an Indian summer career, but when I first met him he was greatly embittered about all that was going on and inclined, as the majority of choreographers, but with much more reason, to find that everything had been borrowed from him. He and his beautiful wife Vera were inseparable. She would always sit next to him during rehearsals and he would glance at her every now and then for approval. Occasionally during some comic portion both of them would chuckle with the greatest possible pleasure. Once when his wife had a bad cold he cancelled a rehearsal. 'I can find no inspiration and I cannot possibly leave her alone.' Of all the choreographers I have watched closely at work I have never seen one more masterly or inspiring, quite apart from the actual quality of his work. He started off by explaining to the company the narrative, the style of the period and the setting. Then as he worked he danced and mimed every rôle. He was not only a choreographer but also a master producer, and there is a great distinction between the two. His ballets were fully worked out before the first rehearsal and he did not alter or modify steps to suit individual dancers. He was a museum man and was also thoroughly at home with an orchestral score.

He was for the most part good-tempered and even genial when things went well but his rages could be terrible.

I once sat in a box with him during a performance of his favourite ballet, *The Polovtsian Dances* from *Prince Igor*. Watching a ballet with him was always a nerve-racking business because he could not sit still in his anxiety at what the dancers were doing. Suddenly he got up; 'I'm going to murder that imbecile of a conductor. His beat is terrible.' He strode out of the box. 'Follow him quickly,' said René Blum, '*il fera un malheur.*' I tried hard to keep pace as he took the stairs two at a time, but he had had too good a start. I saw him stride down the centre aisle. He walked straight up to the rostrum and seized the conductor by the tails. The conductor turned but went on with his sluggish automatic beat. 'How dare you murder my ballet?—you are a criminal.' Still the conductor continued, but as he waved his baton, he said, 'you will hear from my solicitor in the morning.' Fokine was nonplussed and the performance continued.

His knowledge of mime and his attention to detail were

astonishing. I once took him to watch a performance of *Carnaval* over the television. I thought that he would be both moved and impressed at seeing his creation coming across the air in this miraculous fashion. I awaited a reaction and it came. 'Chiarina's gloves are quite impossible. Telephone to the studio so that it doesn't happen again at tonight's performance.'

It is because of this minute attention to detail that Fokine's ballets will gradually die; already they are beginning to pale and *Carnaval* is the first to go. *Les Sylphides* even during his lifetime suffered from his lack of memory, his many unfortunate afterthoughts, his wish to snub the *régisseur* and from the endless pirated versions. Today it is rarely seen even adequately performed.

Some years before he died I secured the rights of this ballet, *Carnaval* and *Le Spectre de la Rose* for Sadler's Wells. Ninette de Valois found it unthinkable that these ballets should be used without the choreographer's participation. He begged me then to see that the final leap of the man, so unmusical, jarring and out of character, was cut out. 'Make a fuss whenever you see it,' he told me. I have done so.

Fokine, though he died comparatively young for a dancer, lived to see his revolutionary work regarded as classical and nothing annoyed him more. Already by 1913 *Les Sylphides* was mistakenly ranked as a classical *ballet blanc*. He continually pointed out the wide gulf between *Swan Lake*, for instance, and *Les Sylphides*. The relationship between music and movement, the discarding of virtuosity as such and the abandonment of orthodox mime marked a gulf between Petipa and the Fokine era that succeeded it. I remember Fokine's impatience at rehearsing a particular group of dancers because it underlined this gulf. 'You are so turned-out, it is disgusting. I shall have to spend the whole day in teaching you how to walk.' This is a lesson that some of our examination-ridden teachers would do well to take to heart.

Michael Fokine and André Derain, Paris, 1934

The Sculptor Speaks
Jacob Epstein and A. L. H., London, 1931

VI

It was also at this time that I first met Pavlova and though I saw her and talked with her frequently in the years that followed, and even introduced her to Frederick Ashton, I never knew her well. It was partly, no doubt, because I was identified in her mind with the Diaghileff entourage about which she had very strong feelings. Diaghileff had recently given an interview in which he had said that Pavlova and Spessivtseva were like two halves of a superb apple but it was the Spessivtseva half that had been ripened in the sun. This naturally rankled. It was a hard saying and, to my mind, quite untrue. Diaghileff could not forgive what he considered her desertion during the first Paris season. She had been one of his major inspirations when he formed his company. Pavlova also, in spite of all her fame, could be surprisingly shy, shy in the gawky adolescent's manner. In some ways she never grew up; her violent tantrums, her sudden bursts of generosity, her jealousy all belonged to the schoolgirl that had remained in the artist. I had the impression that she was a profoundly unhappy woman who would have given a great deal for home life and for children of her own. At the time that I met her she must have realized that it was too late, and also that her glorious dancing career could not last forever. A member of her company told me of her violent attack of stage fright one night in Paris, when she knew that several of the former Maryinsky ballerinas were watching her. 'I'll show them that I can still dance,' she told him, and then gave an inspired performance of *Giselle*. I often watched her from the wings and from that vantage-point one could see the sixteen-year-old girl and the tired middle-aged woman; they changed places in a flash. Her tastes were amazingly simple, her friends the dancers in her company. It was her husband, Victor Emilianitch Dandré, who shielded her from outside worries and who acted as a buffer, warning others when to keep away if

'Madame' was irritable. He became a very good friend of mine in later years and we had almost weekly luncheons. He then invited me to Australia with him in 1937 when he took out the de Basil company. He was a delightful companion. I have never met a kindlier, more courteous or more tactful man. But, of course, he lived in the past and constantly talked of what they had done in 'Madame's' company. He had been used to handling a genius who could afford to break all the rules and the aesthetic of Diaghileff had passed him by. I remember the many prolonged arguments on the way out, in which I was able finally to persuade him that it was not possible to put on the Pavlova type of divertissement without Pavlova. He was devoted to her, but living with her must in many ways have been like being the curator of a museum with a difficult board of governors. He told me after she had died that her death had averted a tragedy. From 1907 until 1931 she had danced almost nightly, never missing a single performance. She knew no other life and could never have settled down although she had saved a considerable sum of money. I only learnt later from another source the greatness of the tragedy that had been averted. During her last season she injured her knee badly and the company was laid up for a month. At first they thought it was water on the knee but the rest did not cure it and she was in very great pain throughout her last season. The trouble was a serious one and it seems certain that it would have meant the end of her career. She might even have become a permanent invalid. Her official age at her death was given as forty-eight but she must have been at least four years older. She continued to thrill one to the end.

VII

During my Paris stay I was thrown much together with a number of Russian painters. Constantin Korovin was a wonderfully handsome man, tall and white-bearded, like a boyard from one of the operas he had decorated. He had a magnificent bass voice and when he was pleased or excited he did not hesitate to burst into song, usually at the Louvre in front of some painting that had moved him. As a painter he belonged to the pre-Diaghileff period and Diaghileff's Ecole de Paris orientation found him amazed and lost. It was his *décor* for *Lac des Cygnes* that we first saw, in an old-fashioned romantic idiom that set the pace for all the future productions until Leslie Hurry introduced a fresh note. Korovin had played a large rôle in the education of Chaliapine and was full of anecdotes which with his rich bass he could illustrate to perfection. Like Doctor Johnson in relation to Garrick, he would criticize his friend heatedly but would allow no one else to do so. He often took me to see Chaliapine in his fantastic gallery of portraits. Korovin was deeply touched by my love of Russian art and wanted me to help him write his reminiscences, but they came out in such a disordered flood of Franco-Russian that I could not get down any notes. In any case to attempt to tabulate them would have spoilt my pleasure. Korovin was the complete untamed Russian. He existed in Paris but lived in a Russia of the past. The tide of fashion in theatre decoration was running strongly against him and his impressionist paintings of Paris at night found few buyers. His true art lay in his vivid conversation. I was able to sell a few sketches to English *balletomane* friends, very scarce in those days. The moment that he had any money, however, he threw a lavish party quoting the story of the Russian painter, Levitan, who after receiving a sum of money from a friend had been found bathing himself in an expensive French perfume. When reproached he had replied with absolute logic, 'When I have no money I cannot do this thing which gives me great pleasure and now that I can you say I must not; it doesn't make sense.' 'You see, it doesn't make sense,' Korovin would say, as he poured out another bumper of champagne and helped me to some sturgeon.

Later he died in tragic distress, a magnificent and heroic misfit whom I shall always remember with warmth and affection.

My other artist friends were Larionov and Gontcharova. They were well in the Diaghileff circle and their *avant garde* outlook had replaced the aesthetic of Bakst and Benois, paving the way for Picasso, Derain, Miro and Ernst. Larionov is an extraordinary man, in many ways still ahead of his time and full of stimulating ideas for ballet. Unfortunately the majority of them never get beyond conversation and like so many others he needs the stimulus of a Diaghileff to translate them into action. His knowledge of the theatre, circus and music hall is phenomenal and his room in the rue Jacques-Callot is a veritable library of theatrical art with vast bundles of material stowed under the bed and on top of cupboards. Once again the Russian character reveals himself. He is always going to tabulate and use this material for some project or other, when he finds the time. One Christmas he and Gontcharova sent me a large collection of their paintings that I had admired; Christmas cards six feet by three. Unfortunately they were all destroyed by the V1 that wrecked my house. I have seen Larionov on and off ever since those days; he turns up wherever there is a ballet season. In spite of much illness he remains unaltered, always an enthusiast, always attracted by the very latest in art, always about to engage in some great work when he can find the time. Although he is a Parisian of long residence his French is still almost non-existent, his ideas pour out as if from a siphon in a curious but always understandable and stimulating *mélange* of French and Russian. Sometimes to make a point or illustrate an anecdote he will draw on any piece of paper that comes to hand. I value many of these inspired scribblings; one of 'the typical dancer's typical mamma' gives me particular pleasure.

The remaining Russian artist and the best known, Alexandre Benois, is in sharp contrast to the others, neither a Bohemian nor a Tchekov Russian. At the end of his long life he has as much work and as great a prestige as ever. He is fluent in French, erudite, and strikes one as the retired museum official, until one sees his work. And in spite of *Petrouchka*, most Russian of ballets, the great inspiration of his life lies in France, the France of Louis XIV, where ballet was born. In Larionov and Benois you have the Russian extremes; the genial uncouth Bohemian at home only in his own language and the cosmo-politan man of the world whose capital is always Paris.

Benois, I have always felt, is a man with a grievance and that grievance is the growing prestige of Diaghileff. When the two set out on their glorious careers, Benois was the highly-cultivated man of the world and Diaghileff the enthusiastic country bumpkin. Benois largely educated Diaghileff and then, when Diaghileff had learnt all that he could, he not only broke away from this tutelage but launched Benois himself. The two men, always close together, had many violent rows. Benois still looks back to the creation of *Petrouchka* and other great ballets and feels that Fokine, Stravinsky and Diaghileff himself have received too much credit for the germ of the idea. In my search for material for the Diaghileff biography, the most interesting work I have ever undertaken, I felt this resistance strongly and, indeed, among his close collaborators as distinct from his dancers, only Larionov, Nouvel, Massine and Lifar were entirely free from the feeling that they had given more to Diaghileff than he to them.

VIII

Though I lived in the world of *ballet russe* I did not forget that I was in Paris with its admirable acting, its museums and picture galleries and its circus with those unrivalled clowns, Les Fratellini. I visited one of the three circuses every week. They were not the grand special occasion affairs like Bertram Mills' but very much a part of Paris and were the inspiration of painters and writers. The clown tradition was as old as ballet.

I had also a special love for the *chansonnier*, today with ballet still my favourite form of entertainment. The heroic days of Bruant and Le Lapin Agile were over but there were half a dozen *boîtes* where one might go to hear the latest jokes about the Government or the perennial Cécile Sorel. Fischer sang delightful songs—I can still hum *Si vous aimez les fleurs* —and others such as Mauricet improvised brilliantly on *bouts rimés* produced by the audience. My favourite songs of all were of the realistic school; Damia (La Veuve), Lys Gauty (Le Chaland Qui Passe), Yvonne George, and others; Dora Stroeva in her black dress and red scarf sat perched on the piano strumming her guitar and singing in a harsh masculine voice. The greatest of all, Yvette Guilbert, still survived, no longer the black-gloved skeleton immortalized by Lautrec. No one since has ever sung the popular *Le Fiacre* with such effect. But if with advancing age one is always apt to see yesterday's artists *en rose*, today there is Edith Piaf, one of the greatest of the *réaliste* school, an insignificant little woman until she transforms herself into a tragedy queen and becomes the greatest dramatic mime of the day. For that reason the gramophone or wireless can give one but a poor idea of the creator of *Monsieur Le Noble* and *Le Prisonnier de la Tour*. But the *boîtes* themselves have vanished and the slick American song and the microphone-huggers are gradually replacing this charming type of Paris folklore.

Indeed I was fortunate in knowing Paris really well for I soon outran my generous allowance, having by then started the vice of collecting books and pictures. The position was all the more serious by this time because I was madly in love again and wanted to take my loved one dancing. I shall never forget the first time I took her out to Ciros. The *maître d'hotel* stood by us reciting a long list that included caviare, caneton à la presse, crêpes suzette, and at each suggestion she nodded, she tells me through shyness. Not only had all my holiday funds vanished with that one meal, but I had to walk home in the rain from the Boulevards to Passy. It was also more than inconvenient to be left with one suit, the others being in pawn. I decided that something drastic must be done about this, so I borrowed from a family friend and invested the small loan in a printed card and tips to the hall porters of certain large hotels. They recommended me to families wishing to visit the art treasures of Paris. I built up a large clientèle and was soon very much on my feet again. I will not write any anecdotes of American reactions in the Louvre; all of them sound invented. I learnt to sympathize with the breadwinner whose highly culture-conscious wife and daughters made him spend many hours craning his neck at pictures to which he reacted in the manner of Mark Twain's 'talented young artist that Raphael, what's he doing right now?' and the highest praise of all: 'You say it took Leonardo eight years to paint the *Gioconda*— Why it would take me twenty at least.'

My latest and my final love was a Russian who had no connection with the ballet. I had been introduced to her by the charming family that I had met in Berlin. She was reading history at the Sorbonne and had finally settled in Paris after the long trek from Kieff via Constantinople, Berlin and Brussels. The minute I set eyes on her I knew I was going to marry her, and wrote so to my best friend, although I was still engaged to the Monte Carlo girl. We went to dances, opera and ballet together, and in spite of our having few tastes, though many ideas, in common I knew it would work. When I finally decided to propose I took her to the Louvre— she says it was to test her reaction to my favourite paintings; it may have been—then to lunch at Rumplemayers and when I had summoned up enough courage, into the Tuileries Gardens. As soon as I proposed she asked my advice and I told her she had better accept. We were both twenty-one.

I have a vivid picture in my mind of my drive to the Avenue de Versailles to break the news to my future parents-in-law. It was a hot summer's evening, the eve of 'le quatorze juillet,' and my taxi went at a snail's pace preceded by the brass band of the Quartier playing the *Marseillaise*. The interview passed off admirably with Aldanov, my future brother-in-law, uttering what I might call his theme song, 'prenez un verre d'Armagnac,' and then in a more sober tone, 'réflechissez bien, cher ami, c'est si beau la liberté.' My mother-in-law-to-be did not altogether appreciate this joke. We then sat down to a meal of bortsch and Russian cutlets cooked by the old Nyanya Nina, who approved of me in general but was rather disturbed by the mauve Oxford bags that I wore, which were new to Paris.

Afterwards Vera and I sat out on the balcony eating cherries and spitting the stones out on to the dancing couples below. Our engagement lasted a year. I had fulfilled my greatest ambition.

I have never for a moment regretted that afternoon in the Tuileries. My wife has been a marvel of patience, but to me her supreme virtue is that she has never bored me. We have given one another perfect freedom which neither has abused. My marriage has been the most fortunate and also the most intelligent thing I have ever done. Its completely happy nature cannot make it interesting to others.

CHAPTER FOUR

Dilettante's Progress

I

I ENTERED Trinity Hall, Cambridge, in 1922 and spent four delightful years there, save, that is, for two miserable weeks when my model landlady was sickening for D.T.s while I was unable to diagnose the malady. I took her at her word when she assured me that she was strictly teetotal. I usually believe what I am told. Finally she crowned her husband with a beer bottle and I was able with much luck and some cunning to turn the key on her in the bathroom and to go in search of medical aid and my tutor. The situation was complicated by the fact that I was left to take charge of her year-old twins until such time as help arrived. It was a task I would have relished at any other time save a week before my tripos. It was a tragedy, for she was an excellent cook and could lay the table for a dinner party in the grand manner.

As at school my career was totally undistinguished in every sphere. I read law to please my father and got away with a second and a bare minimum of work. Although I was interested in history, Roman and criminal law, I have never had much sympathy or respect for the non-academic legal mind and had no intention of being called to the bar. I attended few lectures, worked mostly late at night and spent a very busy time in the activities of various societies and in University journalism. I reviewed films, plays and books for the *Granta* and the *Gownsman* and wrote my first ballet criticism for an ephemeral. Film criticism was excellent fun. It was so easy to feel clever and superior at the expense of Hollywood. My free pass was withdrawn on many occasions. The industry was then as now thick-headed and thin-skinned. The Cambridge film society had just been started and proved a training-ground for Ian Dalrymple, Angus MacPhail and Ivor Montagu.

I had always been fond of children and I began to interest myself seriously in education and child psychology, forming a Cambridge branch of the New Education Fellowship and visiting their annual conferences. Here again I was preparing for my future career though I had no such idea at the time. I was still browsing, working hard at it as every dilettante must and does. Had I my time over again I would have studied archaeology and anthropology, subjects that have interested me more and more as time goes on.

For a short time I had the valuable experience of working at Cambridge House, Camberwell. My particular function was to act as liaison between the medical officer and the families of the schoolchildren he examined. I had, among other things, to persuade the parents that their children's tonsils should be removed. This was very frequently a difficult business that required both tact and persistence. Many of them had a real dread of hospitals and a strong suspicion that this tonsil business was an invention of the upper classes, some vague move in a class war. I was never actually thrown out of a house and sometimes I managed to make contact with the parents through the children. Many of these unfortunates had a breastplate of cotton-wool sewn on to them in October and this was not removed until the following May. Running ears, impetigo and ringworm were a commonplace. The greatest tragedy of all was the lack of a common language between these people and myself. Twenty years before I might have been received as a gracious dispenser of charity, but now it was with suspicion and anger. I felt that both were deserved. I once had to break the news to some parents that their son was desperately ill with tuberculosis. I shall never forget the complete silence with which my news was received nor the humiliation of my total inadequacy. The squalor of that tuberculosis-laden slum inspired me with disgust and with a feeling of guilt. I did not forget, but I turned my back on the whole thing and escaped. I am not proud of this episode. I did not attempt to work out a political or economic solution or I might easily, as so many of my generation, have turned to communism. To me the problem was mainly a religious one.

For a time I was strongly attracted to theosophy and read many books on comparative religion. It was a valuable experience, a part of the adolescent growing pains in one's search for a belief. I soon left the society in disgust at the crankiness of so many of its members, the mumbo-jumbo, vegetarianism, and the bogus mysticism that clung to it. I could not believe in mysterious Tibetan masters or in the miracles of the gross and cunning Madame Blavatsky. I found also that all those who believed in reincarnation were convinced that they had formerly been persons of great historical importance. In one year I met two Dantes, a Leonardo, a Galileo and a number of Cleopatras. While none of this was official theosophy, the aims of which are vague but admirable, people had built round it a religion to satisfy their craving for worship. Christmas Humphreys was equally interested and theosophy led him to Buddhism of which he is the leading exponent in England today. As he is also a ballet devotee we meet on many occasions. My friend Dr. Coode Adams was also a devotee and brought a scientist's mind to the subject. We still meet and argue with the same undergraduate enthusiasm. The opposite to this would-be intellectual approach to religion was the hearty rowing-cum-worship-take-a-pew-old-man attitude of so many university religious bodies with their tea and buns.

On one occasion I greatly profited by the scruples of a simple youth who burst into my rooms and, without any preliminaries, asked me in a trembling voice if my soul was saved. I must have received him rather sympathetically, and indeed he confessed that he had often been thrown out of rooms with some little violence, for he came back with a strange request. Had I got a partner for the May Week Balls? He had just developed scruples against dancing and thought that I might act as his substitute in partnering a French girl student whom his parents had wished on him. I met her first by way of precaution—I have never been a believer in 'blind dates.' She was charming and became my partner for two May Weeks in succession. I have forgotten both her name and appearance but I can still remember the good time we had, and the breakfasts at Grantchester after the all-night dance.

I do not know how things are now but in my time we were definitely interested in spiritual matters. Communism was not yet a possible religion for the young and a communist, there cannot have been many, was in continual danger of being debagged and flung into the Cam.

The immediate post-war Cambridge was very much as Evelyn Waugh has described Oxford in *Brideshead Revisited*, though apart from Kings the aesthetes were less pronounced. Most prominent among the undergraduates of my time were Cecil Beaton, Norman Hartnell and Geoffrey Gorer, all of whom began to find themselves at Cambridge.

A special friend of mine was Hugh Herklots, now Canon at Sheffield, who was editor of *The Granta* and President of the Union. He was always excellent company and fairly bubbled with enthusiasm. He has lately reminded me that he wrote a notice about little Alicia Marks, the child dancer whom I brought down to Cambridge to dance at the opening of a children's art exhibition I had organized. It must have been one of Markova's first notices. It was written a day before the event, Herklots confessed, to catch that week's issue of *The Granta*, and because in any case he knew nothing about dancing. He also acted as co-host with me at some of the children's parties I used to give at the Hall. Today one of his daughters, Silvia, has balletic ambitions and I am keeping an eye on her.

Another close friend was Erskine Childers, son of the

unfortunate author of the *Riddle of the Sands*. He was that rare thing in those days, a married undergraduate, and his delightful American wife, Ruth, was made his landlady and had to keep a tally of his times of entry. They lived in a charming attic off Portugal Street and I used to visit them frequently to talk of my fiancée and envy their married state. Ruth Childers was an altogether extraordinary person, both practical and romantic. She had learnt Erse in order to play her part in the Irish movement, she kept all her outside interests alive and yet was a wonderful mother to a large family. Alas, she is now dead, and I shall always remember her as one of the exceptional people I have been privileged to meet. She lives again for me in her eldest daughter, Ruth Ellen, whose name I borrowed in my *Felicity Dances*. It is not astonishing that though I meant the heroine to be Felicity it was Ruth Ellen who ran away with the story. In my Cambridge days she was the baby in the basket in that attic room. Today she is her mother all over again, beautiful, calm, and never under any circumstances commonplace.

Today when what is called a more serious attitude towards work is expected from undergraduates, and when youths from school go into military service under conditions that not only do not make them keen soldiers but that are educationally a disaster, some of the value of university life will have been lost. Its three years of civilizing influence and, with the exception of certain faculties, of leisurely learning provide the only time in which a man can find himself. If education only consisted in finding facts, the average youth would learn as much at night school.

The General Strike saved me from my Finals by postponing the tripos. Frank Carr, Ronald Politzer, Frank Pollard and I brought out a cyclostyled non-partisan newspaper, writing it, setting it up and looking after its distribution. It was a great success, but the distributor bolted with the money. The new tripos date was the same that I had fixed for my wedding. My tutor, a bachelor, supported my appeal to be allowed an honours degree without examination on the grounds that a desire to marry showed undoubted symptoms of mental illness. I received my degree on an aegrotat.

At first when I returned on visits to Cambridge I wished that I had had the ability and the ambition to become a don. It seemed a wonderfully insulated life. I shall never forget my first return when a number of Fellows were discussing the Hall men who had achieved something in life. There was a bishop and a judge, a colonial magistrate and a Henley champion. I mentioned J. B. Priestley, thinking I had produced a trump card; his *Good Companions* had become a household word and I was a member of his publisher's firm, and its first reader. Only the mildest interest was aroused and that was immediately damped down when someone produced a county court judge who had once rowed in the college eight. But after a few years it would be impossible to slip back into that gentle world of vintage port and learning.

II

After a honeymoon in Corsica, Sardinia and Provence we returned to London and to the many problems of married life awaiting us. The problems really started at Arles, where over a dish of *tomates farcies* and a bottle of Chateauneuf we discussed finances and I found that we had nearly run out of money. I had thought that our wedding present cheques were inexhaustible. From that meal time my wife took charge of the accounts. It has been an admirable arrangement. My wife says that she found our house on Campden Hill with a hundred pictures on the walls and not a single chair or table. That is a slight exaggeration but it does depict my attitude at that time. I was definitely not practical and I had a tendency to dramatize this fault and to regard it as a virtue. The immediate problem was to find some occupation. After an expensive education there was nothing for which I was particularly fitted. Once again my father proposed banking and as I could not counter it with any better suggestion and as pride was pushing me to earn a living as soon as possible, I agreed.

One Monday morning I took the Underground to Bishops-gate with my father and we separated outside the Bank of which he was chairman and I raw recruit. And this was different from Brussels; I was expected to work. Masses of scraps of paper were put down in front of me filled with figures and meaningless abbreviations. I never quite knew what I was expected to do with them. There in the gloom, surrounded by melancholy but highly efficient men-machines, I sorted and added. This lasted less than a week. The head clerk of the department came to me one morning and suggested very politely that in future I bring a novel to the office with me. It appeared that since my arrival my unfortunate colleagues had been kept doing overtime nightly checking my many mistakes. I had even committed the classic one of adding in the date. For the next six weeks I arrived at the bank promptly at nine and stayed until five-thirty in order to read *A La Recherche du Temps Perdu* rather uncomfortably perched on a hard high stool. Finally my wife broke the news to my father who had been half expecting it and who took it remarkably well. The search for ideas continued, interrupted with great frequency by ballet seasons and visits to Paris. I had begun to write a book on ballet to lay down for myself some standards of criticism so as to add to my pleasure. *Balletomania* was still an eccentricity that only my Russian friends could understand. It could certainly at that time never have appeared as the start of a career. The book was published at my own expense and as I have already related met with considerable success because of the attention of the Rothermere papers.

That small success did not, however, answer my problem of choosing a career. I had made seventy-five pounds on the venture and there was neither material nor a market for further work. I was now a father so that the urge to find work was a pressing one. For a year I worked in a press agency ghosting articles by sports champions, writing film criticisms for Scandinavian papers and even a series of fashion articles that I compiled with scissors and paste. Very occasionally there was something to be written about ballet. You can be certain that it kept intruding in all my written work. My patience failed at about the same time as the agency. I had gained a certain experience in putting my thoughts—or more often those of others —on paper and about enough money to pay for my lunches.

I also wrote, unpaid, art and ballet criticism for Orage's *New Age*. Orage loved to stir up controversy and an article of mine on the Royal Academy brought about a ding-dong battle with Will Dyson. We were both exceedingly rude and even personal in print but met on the friendliest terms. I expressed myself with great violence in those days. The Academy was fair game, especially Munnings, whom I selected for my main target, but I might have been more subtle. Dyson brought up the popular argument that only an artist should criticize art. I retorted with the obvious one that, as a political caricaturist of great savagery, he constantly criticized functions he did not practise and then went on to quote the number of times great artists had been wrong on the subject of other great artists. Such controversies prove nothing and convince no one, but it was great fun and also an admirable education in keeping one's temper, and in writing in a way that did not leave one wide open to attack. I have never written controversially about anything personal, not even when the greatly lamented James Agate, reviewing a book of mine, quoted as mine and ridiculed a certain section that I had quoted and ridiculed. It was so obvious that he had just opened the book at that page and written. When, on one occasion, we did meet, in spite of his violent dislike of ballet, I found many points of contact and a number of common friends in the characters of *La Comédie Humaine*. I sadly miss his Sunday article.

It was while writing for Orage, always a stormy occupation, that I became embroiled with a number of animal defence and anti-vivisectionist societies. I had written a series of articles on the *corrida* as a spectacle. I cannot call what happened a controversy, though it raged for weeks, for obviously I had not advocated cruelty to animals; neither had I ignored it. The letters that I received—only a few of the milder ones could be printed—very clearly advocated, and with sadistic gloating, cruelty to all bullfighters, all who watched the *corrida*, all who permitted it and not least myself. I came to realize that the 'professional' animal lover, not to be confused with the person who is fond of animals, is in truth an idolater with a real hatred of humanity. It was as if I had told a priest of Bubastis that the cat was a dirty animal. If the vast sums of money given and willed yearly in this country to the welfare of animals were used instead for child welfare it would show not only greater sanity but the correct understanding of the word *love*. The anti-vivisectionist is either compelled against all the evidence to deny the benefits to humanity brought about through vivisection, or to say that the end does not justify the means and that it is just too bad if a large number of babies die of diphtheria. I very much doubt whether the anti-vivisectionist is consistent when personally involved.

If I have written this with some violence it is because I am still under the impression of the number and brutality of these letters. I could not have received more had I been fined the customary £10 and costs for cruelty to a child.

CHAPTER FIVE

Publisher's Reader

I

PUBLISHING was an obvious and a pleasant profession for a
young man of artistic inclinations and no positive creative
talent. In those days the films meant exile in America, the
B.B.C. was not the vast employer of today and did not cater
for the Third Programme public, and the British and Arts
Councils did not yet exist. It would have been wonderful to
start right away as a dramatic or an art critic but the papers had
more sense than to engage a complete tyro; that only happens
in ballet. Publishing it had to be, and moreover it was a profession that my father was prepared to sanction, since publishers
were in business and issued balance sheets. Through a friend
he got me a letter of introduction to Theodore Byard, chairman
of William Heinemann. The day before my interview I
developed a bad attack of laryngitis with the result that I could
only speak in whispers. Byard was an imposing white-haired
figure, and as he sat behind his desk he looked like those actors
who play the more respectable senators or district attorneys
in Hollywood films. I felt nervous and had no idea which of
the two interview techniques to adopt; the confident, if-you-
engage-me-your-troubles-are-at-an-end manner, or the very
modest I-know-nothing, I-am-nothing, give-me-a-chance-I-
am-keen approach.

He whispered and croaked a welcome, and I whispered and
croaked back. He stared at me and then we both said 'laryngitis' and burst out laughing. The ice was broken and I had
gained a sympathetic listener for a start. He called in his

partner, the managing director, C. S. Evans from the next room and I immediately realized that this was not the type of man I could bluff with interview technique. I happened to have very much the same taste and outlook on books as Evans and was engaged for a trial as reader, replacing as I afterwards found out an unfortunate man who had been caught napping over *The Bridge of San Luis Rey*. I immediately asked him on what principle he wished me to report. 'No one can tell if a book will please the public or not,' he said. 'I want a straight-forward personal opinion on the book's merits, that is the only type of reading that is any good for this firm.' His reply was in sharp contrast to the American publisher, George Doran, to whom I was loaned for a London visit. When I asked him the same question the reply was, 'Will it ring the bell?' and when I looked puzzled, 'Will it pay the rent?' He then went on to tell me of a dinner party he was giving that evening and of the eminent guests who were to be present. Yet he must have had some flair for his list was a fine one.

The following Monday began a five-year period with Heinemann's at their Kingswood office that was a happy and invaluable start to a career.

My work at Kingswood made it necessary for me to learn to drive a car. I became the most dangerous and absent-minded driver on the road. It was only by sheer good fortune that I escaped a major accident. On one occasion when I was giving Edmond Segrave a lift to London we came into collision with a lorry. The car was crumpled up but we climbed out unhurt and sat down on the pavement roaring with laughter. We were suddenly called to order by an old lady. 'You heartless creatures laughing like that at such a nasty accident. I saw it all. There were two young men in that car; the Lord knows what's happened to them.'

We were just able to say, 'We're the young men and that's why we're laughing,' before going off into fits again.

Apart from knocking over a lamp-post while backing, and

other minor mishaps, I was never in an accident again. But on leaving for America in 1933 I sold the much-battered car and I have no intention of ever driving again.

C. S. Evans was a remarkable man, whom I learned to love and respect. He had an insatiable curiosity for everything around him, flair, a thirst for knowledge, an intense zest for good living and a large heart that made him an admirable employer. He had the imagination to understand the other person's position, and was at his best when anyone had got into trouble whether it was a pilfering office boy or an author's personal problem. He was highly temperamental which made him difficult on occasions, but being calm myself I have always loved the temperamental people with whom I have had to work. If he flew off the handle as he did on occasions, a talk after business hours over a glass of sherry soon restored matters.

He had started life as an elementary school teacher, and with a growing family must have had a dreadful struggle to make both ends meet. He joined the firm in a comparatively subordinate position, but soon mastered every side of publishing, and when the 1914 war broke out, and his health kept him out of the army, he was carrying on almost single-handed. It is a wonder how with his bad health he managed to work and to live as intensely as he did. Many times he looked as if he would not last another month yet he always continued until he collapsed and had to be carried out. During one enforced rest in Egypt he took up the study of Egyptology and did it with a thoroughness that was astonishing. Had he had the time he would certainly have written well. His book, *Nash and Some Others*, gives a delightful series of pictures gathered from his experiences as a teacher.

Theodore Byard I scarcely saw again. He looked dignified on suitable staff occasions and that was all. Once he poked his head into the office and asked, 'Can anyone tell me where is Baham?' No one could until we saw it written, 'B'ham,' the abbreviation for Birmingham.

Publishing then was in an extremely interesting position. Victor Gollancz had just left Benn's to set up on his own and was full of ideas that were to revolutionize the trade. He discarded the timid list of new books that was considered dignified and went in for large two-column advertisements and imaginative sales campaigns that forced the other publishers to follow suit. Gollancz was building a list and attracting authors; Heinemann's had a long list, was famous for its discovery of new novelists and had, as most large publishers, to increase its pace to compete with Gollancz.

After a long experience of the theatrical temperament and jealousy I still think that authors, especially women novelists, are infinitely more difficult to handle than stage folk. As I have said, Gollancz set the advertising pace and immediately every author started with a tape measure to examine the space allotted to him and the size of his name, while at a literary cocktail party when advertising, sales and royalties are not under discussion the general conversation reaches an all-time low. The average novelist should be read and not heard.

The firm had recently started its own printing works at Kingswood, Surrey, on a model inspired by the American associates, Doubleday Doran's Garden City. The idea was to attract the employees to live in the country round the works which were magnificently designed by Gerald Wellesley and resembled a Georgian manor-house in its own spacious park. The printing works meant a great extension of programme.

Old Doubleday ('Effendi') used to come over frequently on visits to watch the success of the experiment he had inspired. He had been the friend and the American discoverer of Conrad and Kipling, and was a remarkable man. At this period he was suffering from a particularly distressing form of paralysis and most of the interviews with the staff took place in his car, driving up and down the Surrey countryside. The phrase, 'I'm being taken for a ride this morning' was in current use.

The other partner, A. S. Frere, was a much younger man who had been at Cambridge just before my time but after war service; he is now the firm's chairman and managing director. Frere and Evans not infrequently took different points of view over a manuscript, and this occasionally placed members of the reading staff in a position which called for some diplomacy, though at the same time it was undoubtedly stimulating. I remember reading *The Specialist* with Frere and both of us roaring with laughter at that superb piece of 'folklore.' The sequel was that I had to read it aloud to C. S. over the traditional glass of sherry and try to explain to him why it was funny. I did not succeed and the firm lost a money-spinner. Frere and Evans were equally charming and their widely different qualities were complementary, a fact to which the sustained and often brilliant success of the firm owed a great deal. Evans looked on publishing as a one-man business in which the books published reflected his own particular taste. Frere looked ahead as a business man and was also more in touch with the younger generation. His uniform edition of D. H. Lawrence, put through against great opposition, was a magnificent piece of publishing that has justified itself. Frere was always interested in foreign books and brought in his friend, Warren Shaw-Zambra, to read them. If it was only my meeting with Shaw-Zambra, who has the best balanced mind of anyone I have ever met, my stay in Heinemann's would have been worth while. One of the happiest days I can remember was when after having read what I thought was his obituary in a casualty list and mourned him bitterly, I ran across him in St. James's Street. The obituary referred to a cousin of the same name. Both Shaw-Zambra and Frere were continually thwarted in their wish to publish translations since C. S. had a way of dismissing every foreign book as 'that Hungarian thing you've just reported on; interesting but not worth the bother.'

At this time also, I saw something of another thwarted young

publisher, Allen Lane, who was dreaming of the mass publication of good books to be sold for sixpence. He was not taken
very seriously. When he finally did start his great Penguin
venture it was on six titles and an overdraft. He completely
revolutionized publishing. I know Allen well these days and
wrote the first specially commissioned Pelican for him, *Ballet*.
Everyone thought I was mad. It has sold magnificently and
done me a great deal of good. Yet when he proposed the idea
he had never seen any ballet and the subject was not yet really
popular. I have no idea to this day whether Allen reads books
or not. His flair, however, is tremendous. His sudden inspirations have built a list that altered the reading habits of the
nation. He has a lively sense of humour and does not take
himself seriously so that success has not changed him. He
maintains that his real interest lies in farming.

II

The editorial department was situated at Kingswood and,
much as I disliked the Russell Street main office with its
unsuccessful masquerade as a private house, I loved the calm
of the works and the amenities of a spacious office from whose
windows I looked down on a lily pond and could, in season,
see a profusion of bluebells. In Russell Street it was quite
impossible to read with much concentration. Some author
would always intrude. On one occasion it was George Moore
who could always be relied upon to upset a whole day's work,
buttonholing anyone he could find, delighted to pinch a pretty
typist as he brushed by her on the stairs. Once the pretty typist
objected and was told that it was a great honour to be pinched
by such a celebrity and that she could tell it with pride to her
grandchildren. She was not convinced. 'What a list!' he once
told me. 'These men don't know how to write. Fancy advertising Galsworthy like that. This book,' pointing to a large
MS. he had brought in, 'is one of the peaks in my small range.

Will you advertise it like that chap Galsworthy's? Will it sell in the same way? Do you know who writes the best English at the present time? Ernest Newman.'

On another occasion a sad and bewildered young Russian, hugging a large portfolio of drawings, was found wandering in the corridor in evident distress.

'I have never been so insulted. I go into that room and a strange man, one of your directors no doubt, asks me who and what I am. I say a Russian artist. "Impossible," he replies. "There is no such thing, only the French are artists. I knew Manet, *there* was an artist." And then he practically turns me out of the room.'

It took some time to explain to the Russian that it was a distinguished writer and not a member of the firm that he had met in the waiting-room. Apart from the eccentricities of the distinguished, one could always be the prey of some maniac with a message to save the world. On one occasion a woman threatened to undress if C. S. Evans would not agree to publish her manuscript, and she began to implement her threat before she could be hustled out by a secretary. Before my time, C. S. Evans told me, Hall Caine had practically lived in the office when a novel of his was due for publication. He was an absolute master of publicity. He once told C. S. Evans, 'Do you want to know how to make a fortune with a novel? Mix sex and religion, it simply can't fail.'

Kingswood was ideal for reading, and it had to be, for in the five years I spent with the firm I reported on just over five thousand manuscripts. That sounds an impressive number and on the whole it was hard work, but not quite as bad as it sounds. I had always been an exceptionally rapid reader. There was the day when I polished off twenty-one manuscripts before lunch and spent the rest of the time trying to do *The Times* crossword puzzle. An actual and typical report of a five-minute reject reads:

'Badly written novel with a Cinderella plot. Heroine,

who is named Cassiope, marries wealthy race-horse owner
after his filly, named after her, wins the Derby at its third
attempt.'

The main trouble is caused by the very many border-line
cases competently written, publishable but rather dull. C. S.
Evans was marvellous with these doubtfuls, able to gauge
whether the author's next book would be really worth while
or if he had put everything into this first attempt. He backed
Margaret Kennedy on *The Ladies of Lyndon*, an average good
novel, and was not surprised when *The Constant Nymph*
followed it. Once when I reported enthusiastically on a novel
he took it home for the week-end and returned my report with
the comments, 'I agree with you; an excellent book *but* if
you examine it carefully I think you will find it has been
translated from the French and someone is trying to pull a
fast one.'

He proceeded to set out the data and afterwards I was able to
confirm it. The whole episode gave him enormous pleasure
since he adored detective stories.

I was exceptionally lucky, for in my very first week I read a
manuscript that impressed me enormously. It was a first work
by a young man, Graham Greene, and was afterwards called
The Man Within.

I believed that reading would always give one this warm
glow of discovery especially as the very next week I came
across another first novel of great charm, Lorna Rea's *The Six
Mrs. Greenes*. After that it took over two thousand deadly
manuscripts before I got as much as a nibble. I would probably
have chucked the whole thing but for the fact that I liked my
colleagues, got on admirably with C. S. Evans and in any case
had not the slightest idea what to do if I went away. The
bank episode had left me thoroughly scared.

There were also many other aspects of publishing that were
interesting. Heinemann's did not work in watertight compartments but relied greatly on the personal enthusiasm of the

staff. If anyone had a special feeling for a certain book, he could nurse it carefully from the moment that it came in, suggesting its catalogue description, jacket and publicity. There was a wonderful feeling of collaboration and no trace of inter-departmental jealousy. In this way, too, practically every book had its sponsor and there were few that were just published as a matter of routine.

I remember in particular the case of Henry Handel Richardson. She had written an admirable novel in *Maurice Guest* that had enjoyed a real vogue among a few devoted admirers. Years later there followed the first part of the now famous trilogy, *The Fortunes of Richard Mahoney*. It hung fire badly. Australia was not a popular setting, and the second two volumes were more or less taken on sufferance so as not to split the trilogy. The second volume was almost a permanent feature of the editorial, gathering dust on top of the manuscript safe. I always found some kind of excuse for not reading it. Then Arnold Gyde, who looked after the publicity with the great gusto of an impresario, and did not usually read, unless the subject appealed to him, picked it up, I imagine out of a sense of fair play. He became enthusiastic, boring us all for weeks with the wonders of this novel. He laid out a clever publicity scheme, selling it first to his own colleagues. The result was the great and deserved success of what is now recognized as an Australian classic.

The majority of accepted books came sponsored by an agent or by one of our own authors. There were cases when an author had been carefully nursed for years in anticipation of something big to come. Such was the case of J. B. Priestley, a friend of Frere's. I had been at Trinity Hall with him and though I knew him but slightly there was always the feeling that this Yorkshireman had it in him to succeed in a big way. I came across his name again in Heinemann's as a good critic and essayist and the author of two novels, *Benighted* and *Adam in Moonshine*, that deserved a better success. Then one day when

I was up in Russell Street, C. S. Evans handed me an enormous manuscript and said, 'This is *The Good Companions*, Priestley's latest. I think this is it. Write me a report.' I dislike overtime as much as the average trade unionist, but I did not stop until I had read it right through and written a lengthy and enthusiastic report that ended on the naïf note that 'this should sell some 30,000 copies and should have a large first printing'!

An important factor in the selling of books at that time was Arnold Bennett's *Evening Standard* notice. A mention in the midday edition was good for an immediate reprint. It was enormously exciting to wait for this notice, and when Bennett died no other critic took his place.

We had always to be extremely careful in reading for any possibility of libel, especially as there were always shyster lawyers waiting, knowing that most firms would settle for a small sum rather than go to the trouble of a lawsuit. One novelist lost a heavy case through mentioning that one of his characters 'threw his foul-smelling weed away.' Elsewhere in the book he had mentioned a brand of cigar. We had several alarms and one book was stopped by sheer chance when already in the packing-room. It was an American book taken in sheets that no one had troubled to read till the very last moment. I also remember a suppression from a book of viceregal memoirs where a delightful incident was mentioned; that of Lord Curzon having the lavatory in the vice regal train lowered so that he could still retain his top hat. After Gollancz had been caught with a libel that he could not possibly have foreseen—the resemblance of a fictional school to a real one—most publishers had their doubtful books checked by a solicitor. But until the antiquated laws are altered the most innocent writer and publisher may, in spite of all precautions, fall a victim to heavy damages.

Reading could be a nervy business because, if a book met with an enormous success under another imprint, Evans would always call for the reader's report. I turned down two very big best sellers, but fortunately in each case my report bore the words, 'Have read and agree, C. S. E.' My worst scrape, of which I have often thought, came about when I was writing the 'blurb' for one of those very dreary books about European politics. I could not trouble to plough through it. The papers had just begun to write about Hitler, the name was sometimes misspelt, and in my blurb I wrote ' . . . this book tells all about the origins and political activities of the German agitator, Adolf Hitler.' When it was published someone in the office pointed out that there was not a single mention of the name. I had several weeks of anxiety, but the man seemed so insignificant that no one else noticed. Perhaps, like me, no one had had the patience to read right through the book. However, we always read the many manuscripts sent us by lunatics which were of considerable psychological interest. One, I remember, was written in a copper-plate hand on three toilet-rolls; the author said that it kept his ideas revolving.

As a result of my five years' reading I have suffered from novel indigestion ever since and, with the exception of my Victorian favourites, Stendhal, Flaubert, Balzac, the great Russians, the Edwardians and Evelyn Waugh, Graham Greene, Nigel Balchin, C. P. Snow, Marquand, Hemingway and a few others, I can only struggle through a novel with the greatest difficulty.

III

Another interesting side of publishing that kept the manuscript indigestion within bounds was to think of books that should be written and then to contact and convince the potential authors. This type of creative publishing made the publisher into a patron, and brought back some of the excitement lost when the agent began to make publishing impersonal. We had a weekly staff conference on Wednesdays and I always tried to put up some suggestion, however far-fetched, to relieve the monotony. To follow up even the most scatter-

brained idea meant an escape from a desk littered with manuscripts that were mostly variations on the theme of Cinderella.

Whatever happened, these weekly conferences were always
good for a laugh as when one of our travellers informed the
dignified Byard that the sales of a certain book could be said
to *flunctuate*, or when one of our bright young men suggested
that the one-volume six-novel edition of Jane Austen be
advertised as "The Austen Six." C. S. E., I remember, in his
search for a word strong enough to express his feelings,
finally came out with 'ghoulish,' which seemed to relieve him.

My first suggestion was for a book by Epstein whose every
work caused a violent sensation. I had met him on a few
occasions and found him sympathetic. I broached the idea but
without getting very far until one morning Mrs. Epstein
telephoned me, told me that she was very much in favour of
it and suggested that I call immediately. Epstein then said that
he would agree, if I myself would write the book in the form
of a dialogue.

I thoughly enjoyed the work. We had no fixed plan. I
would come in two or three times a week over several months,
talk, listen and watch. The visits were always of value because
of the extraordinary mixture of people gathered round the
table, beautiful exotic models, writers, painters, musicians and
politicians. Epstein spoke well and with vigour on a number
of subjects and never under any circumstances acted the
celebrity. The room was always littered with interesting
objects, casts of his latest works, sketches, paintings by
Matthew Smith and others or some fine example of African
art that had been added to his large collection. Mrs. Epstein
was an admirable hostess, only roused when it was necessary
to protect Epstein from some unwelcome intrusion. The
dramatic occasions were the private view times when the
popular press would seize on Epstein as news and try every
possible device to interview and photograph him. Rightly he
resented these intrusions, and the publicity was highly damaging

since it frightened away not only sitters but the architects who might have employed him. One or two of his guests betrayed his hospitality by giving interviews, one, a woman author, in particular aroused the usually gentle Mrs. Epstein's wrath by writing about dirty teacups, a picturesque detail that happened to be untrue. I think that Epstein suffered the most from certain intellectuals who discussed his work in the art jargon of the period and dismissed his modelling because it was not carving. He was polite with fools but very careful not to be at home when they called again.

Most beautiful of all the models was the Kashmiri girl, Sunita, decorative and charming, with a sense of fun one would not have expected from anyone so statuesque. I went out with her a great deal, and was always flattered by the attention that she caused. She was the first of a large circle of Indians whose friendship I have enjoyed. No fashion will ever equal the sari; it hides imperfections and embellishes true beauty. Alas, the two loveliest women I have ever seen, Sunita and Pearl Argyle, died young. Epstein wanted to do a bust of Pearl and the sittings started, but they were so interrupted by her rehearsals that the project had to be abandoned.

The book I wrote, *The Sculptor Speaks*, gives a true picture of Epstein and his opinions. It was a little naïf in its insistence on misunderstood genius and also unnecessarily violent since it only required time for Epstein's acceptance as a great sculptor. Today with the freakish forms that are the vogue, it is doubtful whether any work could ever again cause a sensation similar to *Rima*, unless it be a general's horse or the treatment of his uniform. Yet between the desperate mediocrity of the Grosvenor Square *Roosevelt* and the meteorite-looking bits of stone that pass for creation, there is a whole field of activity that is in danger of being overlooked. Epstein, the one-time sensation, today raises his voice against the pretty but trivial fantasies of Klee.

IV

Another of my Wednesday morning suggestions brought me a friendship that I value more every day. 'Why should not Karsavina write a book?' C. S. E., who was not especially interested in ballet, was immediately struck with the idea. He remembered in his poor days queueing up for hours to see La Karsavina and the enchantment she brought. My suggestion was well received and I set off to persuade her.

She had at first a great hesitation about becoming 'a literary bloke,' but was willing to have a try and to leave it to me to decide whether it would do. I fully expected to have to edit the book and also to have to do a great deal of the writing myself. I did not yet know Karsavina, or fully realize that she would have made a success of any activity that she undertook. There was, however, one great difficulty about submitting anything she had written. I simply could not read her writing. Whenever she wrote me a letter I had to ring her up to ask for a translation. The writing looked like words until one examined it carefully and then one was completely lost. She never wrote in clichés and as she had an extensive vocabulary it was no use looking for the obvious sequence of words; it might be a quotation from Pouchkine or a simple invitation to tea.

She therefore decided to read me the book as it developed, which always meant a delightful afternoon or evening listening and, of course, looking at the most gracious creature that ever existed. From the very first reading of the first chapter of *Theatre Street* I knew that the book would be a classic. During all those months I never helped with a single line or intervened in any way. No, I am wrong, for there was one memorable occasion, an evening after dinner with the suitable background noise of the roaring of the lions in Regent's Park. Tamara, who had by now become the complete 'literary bloke' and was thoroughly enjoying her work, was in a very ebullient mood, particularly proud of a certain paragraph which she was about to read us. She prepared us for something wonderful. And then came the paragraph. All that I can remember was the word 'kaleidoscope.' I looked up at Benjie, her husband, and asked him if he could understand what it was all about. He seemed doubtful. 'I am afraid that it'll have to go,' I said, 'kaleidoscope means something entirely different.'

'But I must keep it in, I like the sound so,' and she repeated 'kaleidoscope' several times with evident relish. However, Benjie backed me up and the paragraph was deleted, to be regretted by Tamara ever after, as I was to find out. Nearly twenty years later I was taking the chair for Tamara at the opening of an exhibition. 'I have a wonderful surprise for you,' she whispered to me, and she was shaking with suppressed laughter. I introduced her, always a difficult thing to do without appearing fulsome, and having got it safely over sat down to enjoy one of her always excellent speeches. She was in full flight with a long and carefully constructed sentence when she turned straight to me and uttered the last word, 'kaleidoscope,' in the fate-heavy voice of a sibyl. I cannot imagine what the audience must have thought of my instant and violent reaction, made worse as she continued her address by my catching Benjie's eye.

Tamara's worst experience as an author came when the book had been completed. She 'phoned me in agony to tell me that something had gone wrong with the book. When I arrived she was sitting on the floor like a snake charmer, surrounded by serpentine galley proofs that she could not get into sequence, and small wonder. Joey, the sealyham, who thoroughly disapproved of the whole business, was busy in the garden savaging a few chapters.

The completion of this book left an enormous blank in my life, though it ended with a delightful episode. I suggested that Tamara gave a series of dance recitals at the Arts Theatre Club and arranged the season. For a week she danced Le Spectre de la

Rose and a number of delightful divertissements one of which, *Mademoiselle de Maupin*, was especially memorable. The romance of the rose was very nearly shattered when an inspector called during the rehearsal and asked me if it had been fireproofed. Harold Turner was engaged as her partner, his first important piece of work. Phyllis Sellick played the piano and Sophie Wyss sang.

Though Tamara was at the end of her dancing career and I remembered her great days, I have never seen her dance and mime the young girl's rôle to greater perfection. The moment of awakening as interpreted by her, its creator, twenty years later was a complete study of adolescence.

V

There were many other Wednesday suggestions, not all of which succeeded, but they served as an excuse for days away from routine and, if I spent the time on various ballet activities, no one was any the worse or the wiser. These were the Camargo days that I shall describe in the next chapter, and there was a great deal to be done both in committee and in the theatre.

I have spoken of the pleasant atmosphere at Kingswood and of the really friendly community. I have kept in touch with most of my colleagues of those days. Isolated as we were in the country with directors only visiting us once a week, discipline was by no means rigid. As long as the safe did not remain too full and the reports were satisfactory when a harrowing post mortem took place on a novel that we had rejected and that was selling well elsewhere, we were left entirely free. We forgathered for long undergraduate discussions on every subject under the sun, rehearsed for amateur theatricals or ragged, sometimes noisily. A great feature of the editorial was a steeplechase track under chairs and over tables. Everyone was expected to compete and I believe that

Zambra held the record. On one occasion we carried out a highly complex practical joke that took a great deal of organization. But here it is necessary to introduce one of the leading characters. One morning a 'new boy' arrived and was dumped into the editorial. New boys were always dumped into the editorial and added an interest to life. They were fairly frequent, too, because it was difficult to refuse a prominent writer's protégé. They rarely lasted long. One of them, a lanky lad, had the amazing gift of being able to balance a tumblerful of water on his head and to dance round the room singing as he did so. We kept him at it for a fortnight and it never failed to delight. It must have been his only gift for he left suddenly. This particular new boy was extremely young, apple-cheeked and ingenuous. He had an encyclopaedic knowledge of the classics, which found him a job proof-reading the Loeb series, and a complete ignorance of what was going on in the world in general. His name was Edmond Segrave and he had just left a seminary shortly before he was to take holy orders. He had discovered a lack of vocation and was very wisely advised to go out into the world. It was in the height of the slump, but Edmond did not know enough to be frightened for his future. People who wanted jobs went to London and got them, so with his unusual store of knowledge and ignorance he went to London and got into touch with his eminent co-religionist, G. K. Chesterton. Chesterton rewarded his faith by giving him a temporary job on G. K.'s Weekly, and then arranged for him to join Heinemann's. That was the beginning of an important career in which hard work and knowledge backed up very great charm.

I saw a great deal of Edmond and, I fear, taught him to drink. Certainly I took him to his first cocktail party, and was horrified to hear him say, 'I've drunk a dozen of those little lemon things. Who said they were strong?' He collapsed in the street and I had a difficult time for the next few hours. Matters were complicated by the fact that my wife, whose first cocktail party this also was, had made the same mistake. I ran between the two with ice-packs.

Today Edmond Segrave has a fine palate for claret and most certainly avoids offending it with the crudity of cocktails.

This particular joke came about through Edmond's gift as a calligrapher. He could copy any handwriting without difficulty. Arnold Gyde had been boring us all about the marvels of Henry Handel Richardson. So we sent him a letter signed by her name saying that her niece, Lottie Ostrahan—I take an author's pride in the name—would be coming down to visit the works on a certain day, and would he kindly entertain her. As the whole office was in the secret we were able to intercept his reply without much difficulty. Gyde set off to the station in a staff car and Lottie, an excellent actress, arrived. The joke proper began at tea when I set out to be deliberately rude to her, upsetting a cup over her dress, laughing in the wrong place, contradicting her flatly, and so on. Wherever Gyde piloted his honoured guest some mishap or other occurred. He tried to tell her that I was quite a decent chap as a rule but had recently taken to drink, but it was of no avail, and finally she left in a great huff saying that she would tell Auntie about our lack of hospitality.

We deserved a violent scene for the dreadful afternoon we had given him, but his invincible good humour and his relief at hearing the truth made him enjoy the joke as much as we did.

At one Heinemann party a magnificent but unrehearsed scene took place, when late in the evening a hired waiter slapped Clemence Dane on the back, saying, 'And do you write too, dearie?' He was discovered long after office opening the next morning, fast asleep under C. S. E.'s desk.

When I think of those parties, especially the garden parties at Kingswood, I always call to mind the conscious picturesqueness of Cunninghame-Graham, a fine stylist and a much-neglected author. He knew so well how to stand when others were seated or how to pose by some tree as he lit one of those straw-wrapped Brazilian cigarettes. He had the courtly manners of his appearance. Only on one occasion did I see him fail in dignity, when he fell through the seat of an antique chair in the Russell Street waiting-room and I had to give him a hand up. He took it with great good humour.

VI

After I had been in Heinemann's for five years and written 'this is the usual variation on the Cinderella theme' for the five thousandth time, I decided that I was getting into a rut and that, if I did not leave at once, I was there for good. For some time, largely on account of my failure at Cambridge House, I had been thinking about taking up medicine and later of specializing in pediatrics, which would give me plenty of opportunity of being with children, with ballet my other interest. There was not yet enough ballet to make a career of it, either as writer or administrator.

I broke it to my father, who was sympathetic to my leaving publishing though strongly opposed to the idea of medicine, to my wife who backed me as she always has, in spite of the difficulties of having a student husband, and to C. S. Evans who was as always magnificently understanding.

I should in the end have been able to win over my father to the idea of subsidizing me for another long period had I been persistent enough. But after buying the textbooks necessary for the first M.B. I found not only that the physics and chemistry for pre-medicine were entirely beyond me but that what little arithmetic I knew had so completely vanished that I could no longer do a sum in long division. It would mean the delay of a precious year or even more before I could work at anything connected with medicine. That blunted my enthusiasm. I still think I would have been good with children, and if I could have my time over again I would read medicine as a student, whatever I did afterwards. Law has been a com-

plete waste of time as an education for the non-lawyer. All
that now remains is a vague reminiscence of the more sensational cases of murder, arson and rape.

My publishing was in every way a wonderful education and
a happy experience since it gained me so many friends. It had
lasted just long enough.

CHAPTER SIX

Last Appearance as a Dilettante

I

POSITIVELY my last appearance as a dilettante was the founding of the Camargo Society. True, I was living a double life, working and working hard at Heinemann's who were paying me, so that my extra work for the Camargo and our many meetings were partly subsidized by them. Though the Camargo proved of such importance that the British ballet of today is its direct outcome, I had at the time so little vision that I cannot recall any of the details with precision and my records, minutes and programmes were destroyed during the war. I have, however, many vivid memories, often of the inessentials. As this is a personal record and the Camargo story has been written many times, I have not tried to refresh my memory by research. This account is more impressionistic than historical. Whenever I see *Job* or *Façade* many memories are reawakened.

It was shortly after Diaghileff's death that I had lunch with Philip Richardson. He edits *The Dancing Times*, the only paper then that dealt with ballet and still its leading journal. Richardson has done more for dancing, both ballet and ball-room, than anyone else. His is a precise and tidy mind so that the minute he sees a situation that looks promising and where some action is needed, he proceeds to act. Committees are formed, he is appointed to the arduous post of honorary treasurer or honorary secretary and something happens, as in the case of the Royal Academy of Dancing. I know nothing of his activities in the ballroom world; his boards there are

DIAGHILEFF MEMORIAL SERVICE, VENICE, AUGUST 1949

Back row: Colette Clark, Sir Kenneth Clark, Georges Reymond.

Front: Pierre Michaut, Director of the Fenice, Sr. Reyna, A. L. H., Serge Lifar.

legion. In meetings he is practical, knows the rules of the game by heart and if anyone queries some proceeding as being *ultra vires* and can quote the exact subsection of the bye-laws proving the point, it is P. J. S. As I write I can hear him say, 'Just a moment, Mr. Chairman, are we quite in order?'

The restaurant chosen was Taglioni's in Gerrard Street, a favourite of mine. The proprietor was, I believe, a direct descendant of the immortal Sylphide. The setting was propitious but when we met there was no idea in our minds except an exchange of views and, of course, a little gossip. I can remember the main dish, *Poulet Pembroke*; it was accompanied by a bottle, or possibly in view of the result, a couple of bottles of *Pouilly Fuissé*. We had reached the *café flambé*, a speciality of the place, Richardson had lit his inevitable Grey's cigarette, and I my equally inevitable cigar, when I produced a sheaf of French newspaper clippings commenting on the death of Diaghileff. They all struck the same depressing note: 'The great animater is dead, ballet dies with him. . . .' 'The puppet-master is dead, the puppets must be put back in their boxes. . . .' 'Former Diaghileff dancers to appear in cabaret and revue.'

At the end of these depressing accounts we called for some Armagnac and began to discuss the situation in England, where we had an increasing number of experienced dancers and a growing public for ballet. My companion was roused. Here was an untidy situation where something could, and indeed must, be done. He started to make a list of names on the back of an envelope, and then dragged me back to the depressing old office, high above the fruit and vegetables in Wellington Street. The first thing I did was to telephone Heinemann's to tell them that I was delayed by an important potential author —I always had a few up my sleeve—and that I would not be in that afternoon. We brought our list to completion and drafted a circular letter suggesting that those interested should meet us for dinner at the Moulin d'Or, Romilly Street, in a fortnight's time. Meals play a very important rôle in this story, as indeed they did with Diaghileff.

In the interval we approached that prince of *bon vivants*, and musical expert, Edwin Evans. The order of his attributes is deliberate. He once told me that his proudest moment was on being accepted as a gastronome by an exclusive French club. And well do I remember his anxiety at having to entertain one of its members in London; what should he give him that was not merely an imitation French meal? The final result included Whitstables, Dover sole and a mixed grill. Evans had long been musical adviser and maid-of-all-work for Diaghileff, and he looked the rôle with his enormous girth, his long beard and the broad-brimmed black hat that he always wore. Wherever he sat he brought with him the atmosphere of the boulevard café or the *bier halle*. He was in complete agreement that something must be done. Moreover his great gifts were being wasted; apart from a little editing and an article for one of the weeklies, he had no real platform. Years later, when he became music critic for the *Daily Mail*, he was able to earn a living wage but still he had no platform. Even in those far-off days of unlimited newsprint, the space available for this remarkable man's criticism of an important musical occasion was about one inch. He was far better known on the Continent and in America than in his own country. Musically, he always said, England was a German colony while he was a champion of French, Slav, and of contemporary English musicians. He was the obvious chairman for any society that might be formed. I think the name, Camargo, was his, and I cannot remember an alternative suggestion. It was admirable in spite of the fact that compositors are inclined to favour CARMARGO.

Scarcely anyone refused the invitation, already a most hopeful sign. I found myself sitting next to J. M. Keynes whom I was meeting for the first time. Keynes as a master economist I had to take for granted. I knew him only as a superb writer.

I gained an immediate contact through our common admiration for Vera Trefilova. Later I found that Keynes was the most complete man I had ever met, almost a figure of the Renaissance. Whatever the subject, he was thoroughly at home and not in a dull encyclopaedic manner but creatively, with discrimination and rare taste. As a very rapid thinker and a man of quick decisions he could be trying in committee, but he bore no grudges for a sharp difference of opinion. In any case, when such differences arose he always proved to be right. Many years later his conception of C.E.M.A. (the Arts Council), coming at a time when private fortunes were non-existent, has given a new lease of life to the arts. All the time he was in America at the Bretton Woods conference, he managed to keep in the closest touch with artistic affairs. If ever a man was killed in action, knowing full well that to live he should relax, it was Keynes.

But on the occasion of which I am writing it was Mrs. Keynes—Lydia Lopokova—who held the limelight. She has a genius for coming out with the unexpected, of being the *enfant terrible* who will shake some staid gathering with the booby-traps of her humour. She has also an intense sympathy for experiment and for all young endeavour. She immediately showed it that evening. She had, I know, more faith in the outcome of our endeavours than anyone else round that table. She was immediately urged to become choreographic director. Her reply is fixed in my memory. I can even remember the voice and the look.

'I am not a committee woman. Joining a committee is a serious step, like losing one's virginity. It requires the most careful thought.'

Fortunately she was persuaded. Her reputation, her enthusiastic high spirits, her experience and the charm of her dancing in *Façade* and *Coppélia*, played a major rôle in establishing us.

There was to be still one more banquet before we set to work, a grand dress affair at Grosvenor House presided over by

Adeline Genée. The only thing I remember was our efficient secretary, Montagu-Nathan, struggling over the seating-plan, indeed he was never free from seating-plans, and a characteristic postcard from Bernard Shaw, telling us to stop eating and get on with the dancing.

Dear Edwin Evans,

These people are idiots in business. My joining their Society will—my own subscription apart—make not one farthing difference on their takings. Tell them to kick out all their Press agents and publicity experts, amateur or professional, and stick to their job, as Diaghilev did. He succeeded by delivering the goods, not by celebrity-hunting and post-prandial speeches. I can do nothing for them, as I neither dance nor compose nor plan ballets; and I have enough sense to keep out of the way under such circumstances. The notion that a dinner can act as a send-off to a ballet season—unless they can make the Lord Mayor drunk enough to dance a hornpipe on the table among the walnut-shells—is beyond my patience. Intimate the same as violently as you can.

Ever,
G. B. S.

The performances themselves belong to the history of ballet. What an extraordinarily high standard they reached with no trace of growing pains! Two choreographers gained immediate reputations, Ninette de Valois with *Job* and *La Création du Monde*, and Frederick Ashton with *Pomona* and *Façade*; four completely adult works for a nursling undertaking that followed on the heels of Diaghileff. Constant Lambert immediately established himself as the great musical leader of our ballet. Then there was the season at the Savoy, with memorable performances by Spessivtseva in *Giselle* and by Markova and Dolin in *Swan Lake*.

The Camargo Society resulted directly in establishing Marie

Rambert's delightful Ballet Club, the Vic Wells Ballet, and in improving the standard of dancing in musical comedies and revues.

II

At the same time as the Camargo Society, and in a sense as a result of it, I worked with Marie Rambert and Ashley Dukes in founding the Ballet Club. My rôle was an honorary one and I really do not know what my contribution was except to bring unlimited enthusiasm and to save the committee from being a purely husband and wife affair. We had no set meetings and our discussions were frequently interrupted by what Ashley Dukes called 'vinous uplift,' when he uncorked some exciting bottle that he had bought in a mixed lot at a sale. Ashley has always protested that he is not interested in ballet, but I still have my doubts. His taste and practical knowledge of the theatre made the venture possible. Marie Rambert showed immediate results though for a time the public was so slow to react that, on occasions, I formed one-tenth of the public. Marie Rambert is one of the most interesting people that I have met, intelligent, vital, generous in her appreciation of others, and with considerable taste. I enjoy a discussion and a difference of opinion with her more than with anyone, and it can be done with no damage. Although her position as a pioneer is assured, she does not like it stressed. 'You are trying to make me into a museum exhibit,' she says, 'and I still have a great deal to show.' I agree; yet one must face the fact that she has not advanced as far as she might. I think the reasons are many. She started before anyone else and showed the first results, but she started on a small scale and found it difficult to expand. She perfected 'chamber ballet' and sighed for the big classical production. Also she is an enthusiast and at times her enthusiasm may prove too heady for her dancers, so that they become disheartened and feel that they have failed both themselves and her. This enthusiasm is a priceless asset and at the same time a great handicap in an art that depends so greatly on long-term planning and on infinite patience. The ballet in England needs Marie Rambert, and I feel that her rôle is to produce the experimental work of, let us say, the Champs Elysées' ballet, leaving aside the large-scale classicism that must have an important stage. She must be given the chance to have the time to develop and benefit from the talent that she recognizes with such flair.

My chance lunch-time conversation with Philip Richardson had had the most far-reaching results, not only for ballet but for myself. It brought me self-confidence, a wide new circle of friends and the possibility of making a career in ballet, although I did not realize this at the time. It also taught me the rules of committee procedure and the invaluable knowledge that if a thing is really worth while, somehow or other the funds will be forthcoming.

CHAPTER SEVEN

From Hobby to Profession

I

HERE was I out of work again and annoyed with myself because, after all these years, I could not keep my wife and growing family, more especially annoyed because I did not like to confess to my father that I had made yet another false start. It is true that I had a little more self-confidence since I had an excellent record as a publisher, had gained many friends and had seen the Camargo Society grow into a success. Also, I was bored with no precise job to do and only really enjoyed myself on my frequent visits to Paris where I could persuade myself I was on a holiday and where anyhow one could be more busy doing nothing agreeably than in any other spot on earth.

Then very rashly I went, not into one business, but into two. With some friends I decided to start a picture gallery and a literary agency, knowing absolutely nothing about either job.

The literary agency bored me from the start. I never realized how dreadful manuscripts could be before they had passed through one elimination and how dreary could be the many interviews involved. I believe we placed a book or two but I lost all interest when I became our only best-selling writer.

The picture gallery was great fun even though no one but friends ever bought anything. We specialized in drawings and had some really interesting exhibitions of drawings and watercolours by Rouault, Matthew Smith, Henry Moore, Epstein and others. The trouble was that if I liked an exhibit I could not bear to part with it and so I added to my collection and did no good to the business. It was exceedingly difficult to sell pictures during the slump and the amount of work it took to make a pound or two was utterly exhausting. Some days no one came near the place at all and I had to write a number of names in the visitor's book so as not to discourage the painters. It was very like playing at shops in the nursery. My great consolation was that Shaw-Zambra was with me in the gallery and the absolute calm gave me the opportunity of enjoying endless discussions with him on every subject under the sun; discussion with him was and is a treat. We made and remained friends with our artists and learnt a fair amount about painting. But I was faced with another parental interview, another confession of failure and the search for some kind of work that would pay without boring.

It was then that Colonel de Basil came to the Alhambra and my true career began. I have described my first meeting with him the previous year in *Balletomania*. Our association really began over a cocktail party I gave for Toumanova in the gallery. It was she who, in *Les Ballets 1933*, first gave me the certainty that Russian Ballet was still a living art. I had grown friendly with this wonder child as with the little Alicia years before and she spent much of her scanty spare time in our nursery where she could really relax. When de Basil came to London without her I felt I was missing something and began to build her up. Then she rejoined him and I gave this party in her honour and coined the name 'the black pearl of Russian Ballet' which stuck.

De Basil was annoyed at the fixing of attention on one of his dancers and told me so one day. 'Why don't you work for ballet as a whole, as you have for Toumanova? This way you are helping to destroy instead of creating.'

He was perfectly right and I have never forgotten the lesson that the ballet is more important than the individual. It was the concentration on individuals by American managements and press agents that was to destroy de Basil's work. As his was then the only ballet that counted, working for ballet meant working with him.

From that moment I joined de Basil's staff without pay or well-defined position, but with travelling expenses provided. I turned my hand to endless jobs in the theatre, writing programme descriptions, tackling mothers, arbitrating difficulties, taking notes during the performance and attending all conferences and auditions. De Basil was quite prepared to call an urgent meeting, then cook an excellent meal which took some hours as he refused to allow anyone near the kitchen, and only begin to discuss the business on hand at 1 a.m. He was then at the beginning of his meteoric success and every moment was exciting, every meeting showed immediate results.

No wonder I wanted to continue to live in this atmosphere, to gain a practical experience of an art that I loved and that I already knew so well from the front of the house. I decided that it was essential to leave the art gallery and agency to my colleagues and to go on the American tour where I could learn more and at the same time do some really useful work with the company. But how could I keep myself? Every available bit of spare money had been put into the gallery. It was then that I thought of *Balletomania* and set off to sell it to Victor Gollancz.

II

I am deeply grateful to Colonel de Basil on two counts, in general because he gave *ballet russe* and through it all ballet a new lease of life, and personally for the start he gave me and the opportunities of studying the work of such an organization at close quarters. Also, I have a very great affection for the man himself though I am far from agreeing with many of the things he has done. His reactions will always be something of a mystery. He had inevitably made a quantity of bitter enemies ready to attack him on such irrelevant grounds as to whether he was entitled to the rank of Colonel or to the decoration that he wore. His great services as a soldier are irrelevant, but they are established beyond all shadow of a doubt.

Let us look closely at what he has done for the art of ballet and try to see what type of man he really is.

There can be no doubt that the pre-war revival of the fortunes of ballet and its world-wide popularity are entirely due to his drive and initiative. Nothing can alter that fact. He headed his company through Europe and America like a conquering general, but as he occupied more and more territory the quality of his army began to deteriorate until little but the name and the memory remained. Three to four years of near perfection; one must be deeply grateful for that. Was the failure due to de Basil himself or to circumstances over which he could have no control?

De Basil himself is an organizer, a driving force but in no sense creative as was Diaghileff, neither has he a really critical outlook. That is not to say that he has not a very strong dose of that definite but intangible quality, theatrical flair. He started with a team of the finest creative minds in contemporary ballet: Boris Kochno, Leonide Massine and Georges Balanchine, and with the late René Blum as co-director. Blum was an artist to his finger-tips, something of a dilettante, an amiable man of the world, but weak when it came to a struggle for control and liking to avoid trouble. His artists loved him but did not respect him in the same way as they did de Basil. They looked on him rather as a good-natured uncle in whom they could confide their little worries. Only in his death did he prove truly heroic, returning from complete safety to share the suffering of his beloved France. He was murdered in a German gas chamber; the son upon whom he doted was killed fighting in the Maquis.

With de Basil to drive and this team to create, the ballet could not fail to suceed. But the Colonel has never been a good collaborator. He has always surrounded himself with second-rate people, amateur impresarios and the like, who helped to create the comic opera atmosphere of Balkan politics, whispering in corners, distracting the dancers and working up cliques where a team was essential. Blum, Kochno and later Massine all left because of these conditions. Creation ceased and the company lived on a series of Diaghileff revivals. Thus when outside circumstances presented difficulties the whole fabric of the company was weakened from within.

Some of these balletic hangers-on were really extraordinary. There was tubby little Z who spoke not a word of anything but Russian but who was entrusted to take the company to Australia. The company had also been entrusted to X, a lawyer, who was no more a theatre man than Z. Neither had been told about this dual control and both were horrified to find it out on board ship. A woman impresario also had some rights about which Z and X were in complete ignorance. 'More bloody directors than company,' said Ted Tait when we landed. The cost in cables and travel was fantastic and the tour, though a major success, was badly damaged through a strike in Perth that anyone who knew how to handle artists could have quelled in five minutes. Poor Z. On the occasion of my last night in Melbourne, knowing that I would soon be seeing de Basil in America he invited me to what he called a 'grande soirée' in my honour. I did not particularly want the grande soirée, but went to the address indicated and found a magnificent private house with an army of footmen standing in the hall. I felt embarrassed by this unnecessary cost in entertaining an old friend. I had not been there five minutes before I found out that it was a charity affair with the company as the main attraction. That was Z all over. He could not resist a pathetic little bluff for its own sake. He lived in a world of intrigue. He was on the whole the least harmful of these comic opera collaborators.

X was equally futile and fantastic. He started his career with the company on board ship by calling one of the Polish boys to order. As no one had been told he was a director he was very roughly handled. He soon got on the wrong side of Ted Tait, the Australian impresario, a great man of the theatre with a boisterous sense of humour. One day when I was sitting with Ted trying to cover up one of the usual ghastly mistakes, in walked X. Ted solemnly strode across the room, picked up an antique pistol off the wall and pointed it at X. 'Get the hell out of here. If you're not out of the door by the time I count five I'll shoot you in the pants.' X bolted and I had a hard time preventing him from going to the police to give information that his life was in danger. But such scenes were almost of daily occurrence and my friend, Caryl Brahms, might have invented the whole tour for one of her Stroganoff fantasies.

The theatre unfortunately is full of rogues. Your grand scale rogue does at any rate get results; he may rob a company within limits but he does at the same time carry the company to fame. These little men—and how many there were—were not only an expense and a dead weight, but caused mischief and material damage every minute of the day.

The Colonel was a shrewd man, he knew perfectly well what was going on and he positively enjoyed pulling strings and saving the situation at the last minute by some bold stroke. He was a master of tactics brought about by a deliberately faulty strategy. He was constantly let down by people he should not have trusted or allowed within a mile of the theatre. In fact I only saw him really glum when things were going well. He was restless and enjoyed moving from place to place. Moreover his physical endurance was, and still is, phenomenal.

In Paris in 1934 he had what seemed a bad heart attack. He was removed to a clinic and two famous doctors told him that he had better put his affairs in order. We were all warned and I even discussed plans with Grigorieff. But before I had time to pay him a visit he turned up in the theatre.

'I'm bored with staying in bed, *au travail*.' And he danced a jig on the Champs Elysées stage in defiance of the Faculté de Médicine.

The next year when he crushed his finger to pulp in the door of a car, he came to the theatre immediately after the operation. 'The doctor says I mustn't move the finger,' he said, and took it out of the sling, banged it on the table, and laughed.

He ran away from hospital in London after he had broken his arm in a lift accident and turned up for his first night at Covent Garden followed by a distracted nurse. I shall not forget his doctor's expression when he walked into the box, gave his arm a smart tap and said, '*ça va bien.*' And of course he suffered no ill effects. In all he does he seems to invite misfortune and then to set out by sheer will power to conquer it.

De Basil is not fond of money and has saved far less than many of the others have made out of his enterprise. In any case he is too generous to save. He is not given to ostentation and has simple tastes. His greatest pleasure is in entertaining his friends to a meal cooked by himself; and he is a *cordon bleu.* I know him too well to think that he is vain in the film star manner in spite of much evidence to the contrary. Personal publicity and the building of his name into a trade-mark are both indispensable weapons in his fight. The key to his character is the love of coming out the victor in a struggle where the odds are against him.

His career in South America during the war really merits a book on its own. He brought ballet to the most fantastic places, flying the company through the jungle in relays in a rickety plane. At times a number of his dancers were recruited on the spot and Grigorieff was faced with the task of rehearsing *Les Sylphides* with girls of no experience and of all shapes, sizes and colours. Yet the work he did on opening up new territories and in planting a love of ballet all over South America is of great benefit to others. I wish that I had been by his side then, when every day brought a new adventure and a fresh conquest. I can imagine his joy with a river in flood, a depleted cast and a revolution taking place in the town, because that is exactly what did happen on one occasion.

III

In December 1933 we left for our first American tour which I have described in some detail in *Balletomania*. We were met at the quay by that spectacular impresario, Solomon Hurok, with the traditional Russian welcome of bread and salt; an occasion naturally seized upon by a battery of waiting photographers. Hurok, who has written in a highly romantic fashion of a life that is romantic enough without any frills, is without doubt a tremendous personality of a type only possible in America. Everything he does is on a generous scale; he is a master of publicity and efficient organization. To meet, he is genial, expansive and lovable. I believe he loves music and ballet sincerely and has a fellow feeling for the artists who have made him famous. They nearly all like him immensely, as indeed I do. He has enormous gusto, but the impact of such a system on a delicate art is a disaster even though he made it popular from coast to coast. Something was bound to happen when the Colonel and Hurok did business together after their first brief honeymoon.

The first night supper was held at the Waldorf Astoria where white-gloved butlers served very excellent hot dogs. I remember the occasion especially well because Toumanova was missing and we were worried about the poor child in a new city. We need not have been, for she made a sensational late entry with Otto Kahn on one arm and Paul Cravath on the other. Her extraordinary beauty and great talent made her the sensation of the first season.

Hurok's publicity machine was one hundred per cent effective and it was based on the desire of the public for glamorized 'stars.' This would not have mattered much, if the 'stars' had not, with very few exceptions, been taken in by their own glamour, but, of course, they were. As we had nineteen mothers, three fathers and one sister-in-law in tow it can be imagined how each paragraph was scanned and discussed.

One could see the damage caused day by day, and the unfortunate Colonel had his work cut out to cast his ballets in the way he wished. Pressure often proved too strong. On one occasion I saw the mothers of two young ballerinas engaged in a tug of war with the Aurora costume, each crying out the claims of her daughter to the coveted rôle as the costume came apart. Then, to counter all this, the Colonel decided that publicity must be centred on himself, not unwise from a business point of view since dancers came and went while he remained. Photographers found it more amusing to catch the girls in poses showing plenty of leg rather than to snap the tall bespectacled Cossack. After a time they used blanks. On top of this feverish rush to pose for the cameras there was the terrible fatigue of continual train, stage, train, stage, performing on one-night stands to a public who had no idea of ballet and who turned up because Mr. Hurok's publicity was telling them that they must not miss THE BIGGEST AND BEST IN RUSSIAN BALLET. It was so then, but afterwards the slogan became a trifle far-fetched and Russia was sometimes represented by St. Petersburg, Fla.

After a year or two of this with such notable records as 'one million gross taken at box office' it was a very bedraggled company whose performances would have shocked London, Paris or Monte Carlo. Enough 'stars' were arising to make a second milky way, but not a production of real significance was being put on. Then began a complete disruption. Some dancers dreamed of Hollywood, others of Broadway musicals. Some wanted their own concert groups. Even Massine was to form a 'Highlights of Russian Ballet' company with a handful of dancers. That was the inevitable outcome of a system that converted artists into quotable stocks and shares. Perhaps all this is an inevitable part of the American way of life and Hurok is playing the American game brilliantly in the only possible way. Frankly, I do not know. Certainly the Unions have made the cost of new productions so prohibitive that experimental work is out of the question; they have done the same to our film industry and are having a very good try at ruining the orchestra.

Apart from my very real affection for Hurok I have always respected him because though when we first met I had not yet written a best-selling book and could be of no great value to the ballet, he was as kind and attentive as in after years; such an attitude is rare and endearing. It has been a pleasure to meet him again over the Wells tours of America. It has also shown that when working with a superbly organized venture he has no equal as an impresario.

The war might have dealt a death-blow to *ballet russe*, a branch of theatre that cannot live too long away from Paris. But it was moribund before the war. It may be that only the security given by state-supported organizations will allow such an expensive art to flourish. 'But then,' as my wife says, 'the state company tends to take on the solid unimaginative virtues of the legitimate wife, while the travelling independents are like the mistress who is all the time seeking new ways in which to make herself attractive!'

THE RUSSIAN BALLET OF COLONEL DE BASIL
Setting out on board the *Lafayette*, December 1933, to conquer the U.S.A.

CHAPTER EIGHT

Problems of a Critic

I WAS not worrying over-much about the future of Russian Ballet that first exciting year. I was far too busy working, learning and enjoying myself. The success of *Balletomania* had certainly helped the company and given me added authority. On my return from America I took on the job of reviewing ballet for the *Daily Telegraph*.

On my very first visit to the office I made a friend whom I value more and more with the years. Bernard Mortlock, journalist, dramatic critic and university lecturer, was then vicar of Epping and I had come to displace him as ballet critic. Apparently the proprietor had felt that it was not seemly for a clergyman to be a dramatic critic in spite of the archbishop's opinion, when consulted, that he wished that all dramatic critics could be clergymen. Bernard Mortlock took charge of me, confessed that he bitterly regretted having to give up this department and ended up by asking me to Epping for the week-end. It was the first of almost monthly visits until he transferred his living to London shortly after the end of the war.

What happy memories I have of those Epping week-ends. First of all Bernard has the right ideas about wine and food and his devoted Mrs. Binder was and is an admirable cook. Then his range of conversation is a formidable one and he is an admirable listener. There was always a vast pile of new books for review and a stack of gramophone records. I did an immense amount of reading at Epping, both sacred and pro-fane. I do not think I have ever seen a more untidy desk and working table, unless tidiness means the ability to find things so long as other people do not tidy them. Many a time have I helped him smuggle in some large picture or an attractive piece of junk upon which the tidy Mrs. Binder might frown.

Today Bernard Mortlock is a Governor of Sadler's Wells School and Chairman of its General Purposes Committee. It is Mortlock who made the wise remark on seeing a candidate for headmistress, 'no woman with a hat like that would be of any use in our type of school.' He is a tower of strength, understanding those extremes of complication the Burnham Scale and the kitchen range.

I enjoyed my *Telegraph* days up to a point. I could write with speed and it was necessary. Also in those spacious days sub-editors treated one with great consideration. Where I was less happy was in forming an opinion then and there, even though I had generally seen the work in progress and was familiar with the background. Often repeated visits would lead me to a contrary opinion, revealing defects or new beauties. All this is inherent in periodical criticism, hence the fear of so many critics to express a decided opinion. How those critics unfamiliar with ballet can, after a single visit, write anything of value I find it impossible to conceive. At present I greatly enjoy the time for reflection given me for the writing of the events of the year in *Ballet Annual* and the year book of the *Encyclopaedia Britannica*. If enthusiasm or disgust can survive the long wait, the correction of galley and page proofs, it is worth recording.

Now I come to a personal problem, the difficulty presented of criticizing the work of friends and people with whom one is in daily contact. There were no real rival companies to de Basil at that time, otherwise my contact with him would have made the work impossible, even though I worked with him in a purely honorary capacity.

In any case I have never taken sides and am on good terms with the most bitter opponents this gentle art can produce. I am solely interested in performance and all friction between artists damages the result, as we have seen and are still seeing.

Even when de Basil was at Covent Garden and René Blum at Drury Lane I was admitted without a shade of suspicion to the confidences of each and naturally those confidences were never betrayed.

It is almost impossible to criticize ballet and not to know dancers and choreographers; for that matter it is equally impossible to be a literary critic and not to know writers, or a music critic and not to have at any rate a nodding acquaintance with contemporary musicians. I have, however, never found it in the slightest degree embarrassing and as I have always tried to keep my criticism constructive, and have never gone in for the brutalities sometimes indulged in by French and American critics, the dancers have always realized that I am on their side. And that is a very important aspect of criticism. The experienced and trained eye does not only comment on the performance for the benefit of the audience, but also for the sake of the performers. Dancers never see themselves, and they seldom have much opportunity for studying other dancers outside their company or their particular tradition. The chief criticism that they hear is in class, and that is rightly of a technical nature. The critic is concerned with interpretation, musical and dramatic, with attack, with the impact of personality. He has a watching brief for ballet itself as distinct from the arts that compose it. There is a constant tug of war between these arts and the critic must keep a level head. Today when, with few exceptions, the choreographer rules because there is a lack of artistic leadership the critic has a real function to fulfil. In my own case I was fortunate enought to have studied in a school that produced a Pavlova, Karsavina Trefilova, Spessivtseva, Nijinsky and Lifar, and to have assisted at the classes of Cecchetti, Legat, Preobrajenska, Egorova, Kchesinska, Volinine and others; to have watched Fokine, Massine, Balanchine, Nijinska, de Valois, Lifar, Ashton, Petit, Charrat and others create, to have talked with Svetloff and Levinson. I have rarely commented on technique unless it was glaringly inadequate; it would never occur to one to dissect the technique of a Karsavina. Technical questions belong only to the teacher of dancing or the complete tyro who likes to roll the picturesque terms round his tongue with an easy air of familiarity. I have found that if one can only discuss a dancer in technical terms, and there are many such, it is because there is nothing else that one can say. In such cases I prefer to say nothing.

It is personality and quality that really count; by personality I mean movement that is an expression of the individual and not merely a mechanical reproduction of what has been imposed from without; by quality I mean complete fluidity of movement and perfect phrasing as distinct from the basic necessity for rhythm. Quality also implies a feeling for line, the avoidance of clipped movements, the concealment of technical preparation. Today quantity is all too frequently the aim, also there is a *faux classicisme*, the desire to superimpose brio, like varnish, by a finicky and mannered finish, a far worse fault than to lend to the classics the neo-romantic interpretation of Fokine. The Continental dancer has a tendency to the first, the English dancer to the second. These are the extremes into which most dancers fall; Fonteyn, Chauviré, Wyroubova are magnificent exceptions. Genuine attack is not something added to the completed step as an embellishment, it comes from deep down, from the artist's feeling that she is absolute mistress of the situation, from the sheer physical exhilaration of movement. It comes also from an understanding of the music; Tchaikovsky lends himself to attack, to a sense of the truly dramatic in movement. Attack means a feeling for climax, but if the climax is added by a toss of the head or a flick of the wrist without there having been any build up, the result is ridiculous.

The dancer rarely provides a complete surprise. One can tell almost from the start what she will give when mature as an artist. The only truly doubtful element is as to her ability to absorb technique, and to last the pace. The young Markova in Astafieva's studio, the débutante Fonteyn; Toumanova and Baronova at Preobrajenska's *barre*, each clearly foretold the direction that she would take. It required no prophet to divine such talent in spite of seasonal ups and downs. I happened to spot them earlier than others, only because I was one of the first to see them and to know by experience for what to look. The first teaching instils a discipline that is both mental and physical; it can very easily damage talent and aptitude beyond repair; it can never make a dancer even out of the perfect body if the necessary temperament is lacking. There is such a thing as 'the dancer's face' that any connoisseur will rapidly recognize, and it has nothing to do with popular conceptions of beauty. It has a range of expression from serenity—and serenity is something positive, not just a bovine lack of interest—to extreme animation, which does not mean restlessness or the negation of repose.

I have in my time made some reckless judgments and have been proved wildly wrong. A timid critic is a useless critic. Middle age may find me a little more cautious because of increased experience, but no less of an enthusiast when I feel that I am really seeing something genuine and outstanding.

The most vivid and humbling lesson in criticism that I ever received came from the Sakharoffs, about whom I wrote one of my earliest notices, my very first in fact. I did not appreciate their work or understand their aims and indeed, at that time, anything outside the classical ballet tradition was suspect. I felt that it would be an admirable way of attracting attention to use some cutting phrases; it was easy to do and seemed great fun. All young critics pass through this phase; some remain young too long. I did not think any more about the matter until at Aix les Bains in 1939 I saw them billed for a series of recitals. I went to the first, was greatly interested and felt rather small as I remembered my heavy-handed attempt to be witty at their expense. I felt still more uncomfortable when, after the performance, a mutual friend said that they would very much like to meet me. I could not refuse: I wanted very much to meet them, I could only hope that they would not identify me as the writer of those stupidities. The very moment that we sat down at the café Alexandre started, 'Tell me frankly what it is you don't like in our work? I must confess that what you wrote was wounding. I agree with so many of your opinions that I really want to know.'

We talked it out on the friendliest terms and continued to meet daily throughout the week. Alexandre, who had known the Diaghileff circle well and was a penetrating critic, opened several fresh windows, but what he really taught me was never to criticize for the sake of being clever or to express opinions that one could not justify in calm and friendly conversation.

I met them again in Paris eleven years after and we resumed our friendship and our discussions. Clotilde remains one of the most beautiful women I have ever met; hers is the perfect beauty of the artist in which a fine and sensitive intelligence lights up a face of superb structure, making her ageless.

I still feel that Alexandre's immense artistic culture, his musicality and his choreographic research should have been employed in the main development of the dance instead of in the splendidly picturesque backwater that he has made his own and that will be lost with him and the wonderful Clotilde, a dancer who could have held her own in any company. I feel that this is ballet's loss.

Alexandre was a painter in Munich when Duncan first drew his attention to the dance. He continued to paint, however, until he saw Sarah Bernhardt. He did not know French well at the time and so concentrated on her mime and to a new conception of movement. This turned him into a dancer, his plastique being developed over the years through museum study. There is much that he could teach ballet especially in the use of hands and arms and in style as distinct from technique. The Sakharoffs have never met with success in London, but then London likes classical ballet almost to the exclusion of all other forms of dance.

There is no ballet criticism worth the name in our popular press. Even when the *Daily Mail* had such an outstanding expert on the subject as the late Edwin Evans and the space of pre-war newsprint, he was given at the most four or five lines to cover an important event. And the position has become steadily worse through the plea of lack of space. When one sees how the available space is used no one is going to take that excuse very seriously. Mr. Stanley and his tailor, Rita and her Aly, can all find unlimited coverage. Editors may argue that art in general and ballet in particular are of no interest to their readers. This is of doubtful truth—I myself have sold well over a million copies of a popular book on ballet—but even were it true there are certain obligations that cannot be ignored in a civilized country.

Yet some of these papers have had the effrontery to attack the British Council for doing indispensable work for our national prestige, work in which they themselves should be collaborating. I feel this particularly, for not only am I closely familiar with the work the British Council has undertaken in arranging the Sadler's Wells Ballet tours, and the repercussions from these tours, but I was one of the people invited to meet the very charming Argentinian, Victoria Ocampo. The few hundred pounds spent on her entertainment in this country have been brought up on countless occasions, and with really damaging effect, 'Why,' say the Barbarians, 'use our money on entertaining a poet?' Apart from the fact that one might do a good deal worse, they would willingly spend the money on a footballer; Madame Ocampo is the owner of a large-circulation journal, a staunch friend of this country's when we needed all the support we could raise, and someone who has spent far more than she received in entertaining English visitors to her country.

All of this is a digression, but a relevant one. The papers

that do give more space to ballet entrust it to their music critics, who can only look at one particular aspect of a complex production. Often the musical critics in England are emotionally unsympathetic to the stage and to the French or Slavonic music used in ballet. If a ballet attempts to deal with a serious subject such as Tudor's *Pillar of Fire*, they say that it is unsuited to the medium; if it is mere froth such as Petit's *Oeuf à la Coque*, they dismiss it as flippant. The result is that four-fifths of a short notice is usually confined to a criticism of the music and orchestra while invariably the scenery is completely ignored. However, their great advantage that outweighs their specialized angle is a really sound knowledge of the rules of criticism. For years *The Times* and *Manchester Guardian* have been outstanding.

In France ballet criticism is entrusted to men who have a knowledge of all the arts and who have a feeling for the artistic movements of the day. They may be cantankerous, they inevitably disagree with a certain violence that stimulates one's interest, but they have a right to their point of view. While here, most of those who cover ballet for the popular press know considerably less than the youngest gallery girl, who at any rate feels intensely. Our many new critics of ballet who write in specialist publications are sometimes inexperienced and often tend to be partisan, and the family atmosphere in which they live gives them no scope to expand, but they do write with the great incentive that comes from a love of their subject. Unfortunately they are jealous and distrustful of one another, and are over-inclined to believe what some individual dancer tells them. It is fatal to listen to a dancer friend, however honest she may be. It is equally dangerous to listen to a choreographer on choreography. By his very nature he must be a strong individualist who is continually thinking of how he would have tackled the problem. In that sense friendships in the dancing world are harmful to the critic.

Yet never has ballet needed more informed opinion. Contrary to the general belief, which is entirely superficial, the British public does not care for ballet as such—it never has. It is passionately and uncritically devoted to dancing in those long familiar classical ballets about which it is no longer necessary to make the slightest mental effort. Had this not been the case the public would have flocked to see the works of Roland Petit, the most important and stimulating creations, in spite of many shortcomings, since Diaghileff, however one may view them. *Les Forains, Le Jeune Homme et la Mort, Les Amours de Jupiter, Le Rendezvous* and *Les Demoiselles de la Nuit* are all works about which it is possible to argue at length, works over which the press should have been prepared to give a lead. To take only the last-mentioned, *Les Demoiselles de la Nuit*: this is a collaboration between Jean Anouilh, Jean Françaix, Lenor Fini and Roland Petit, each one an artist of European reputation in his own line. It may be praised or attacked, it cannot possibly be ignored. Yet few newspapers criticized it, most of them ignored it completely, a few made flippant mention of a 'cat ballet.' Our great dance public, and its numbers are considerable, preferred to stay away rather than to make up its mind about something new. Only *Carmen* woke them up, mainly, I suspect, because it was daring and 'sexy.'

There is also at the moment a tendency to excessive chauvinism. Our ballet has made gigantic strides, and is in some particulars second to none, but only in some particulars. It is doing it an ill service not to examine with care what others are creating and to judge impartially in what we excel, and where our visitors have the upper hand.

I feel that I can say all this with a clear conscience and without the suspicion that I have an axe to grind, since I am working actively for the future of our ballet and have long recognized its great achievement, refusing to follow the clique that could only see the Russian companies and continued to do so when nothing but the trade-mark remained.

At the time with which this present chapter is concerned, those early de Basil days, I criticized the Russians for their mark-time policy with an energy that surprised them, since their houses were full, and praised our débuts, not on any patriotic lines but judging them by the highest standards. To quote Ninette de Valois, the great architect of our national ballet, 'He has always had the English Ballet at heart—but he did one very clever thing at the commencement of its existence. He absolutely refused to become its patriotic godfather. I am afraid he did exactly the opposite. He went on praising the organizations that were flourishing abroad, until he aroused a fighting spirit in us and made us feel that we had to do something to improve our own standard and live up to that avalanche of praise which he bestowed on those foreign companies which so richly deserved it. To us he was "Mr. Arnold Haskell," or "that Arnold Haskell" according to how we felt at the moment. We know now that he was genuine and sincere, and the fact that he would not praise where he did not feel it was due at the beginning was really responsible in the end for making us put our house in order.'

My point of view remains unchanged. Even though 'the house is magnificently in order,' it must remain so and the furnishings will certainly need changing from time to time.

I went both to Covent Garden and Sadler's Wells. I saw in Ashton from the earliest Rambert days a future master, and drew the attention of Pavlova to his work, I saw in Fonteyn a ballerina that equalled and would eventually excel the brilliant young Russians. I gave a practical expression of my belief in becoming one of the founders of the Camargo Society, and a director of Marie Rambert's Ballet Club. I do not set these things down in this place out of pride, though I am proud of them, but as a necessary background to enforce the argument.

Once we begin to applaud our ballet as an isolated phenomenon we take it for granted and it becomes, together with the Royal Academy, an institution that ceases to have the slightest meaning. Its young talent will rebel and it is from the rebels that we will have to look for good work. All this is in the future, but it is inevitable unless press and public wake up and assist. I shall deal with this further when I come to write of my close association with our national ballet.

CHAPTER NINE

Ballet Russe before the War

I

WHAT a joy those pre-war Covent Garden seasons, and what a complete escape from what we knew was bound to come! Though the ballet was popular it was also something of a family affair that revolved around the personality of Bruce Ottley. Truly he was Maecenas; though the money was not his, the time, skill and patience he gave to the affairs of the ballet were beyond price.

Bruce Ottley was a great artist in life and friendship; the very type of highly civilized man that is rapidly disappearing in this present-day world. He was captain of Eton and a classical scholar who carried his love of the classics with him throughout life; Horace was a bedside favourite. In business everything that he touched was successful, not through luck but through a first-class brain. He once said to me: 'I think you might have liked business if your father hadn't dinned into you that one must start at the bottom. The secret is to have a good education and start at the top; details can soon be picked up, but not the wide overall view.'

Business alone, however, could never have interested Bruce exclusively. There was music, and he was a sensitive natural musician whose piano playing and song arrangements could give immense pleasure to others besides himself.

I have never heard anyone more adept at musical caricature. We would keep him at the piano until the early hours playing *Sweet and Lovely* in the manner of a dozen different composers. I can never hear that tune without a numbing sense of

124

loss. He would also on occasion play impromptu character sketches of various people; one represented a heated argument between de Basil and a choreographer, with myself trying to keep the peace. But it was Bruce who was the greatest peacemaker of all.

Erlanger's Bank, of which Bruce was a director, had a literary and musical tradition and Baron 'Freddie' enjoyed great success during the last years of his life with *Cent Baisers* and *Cendrillon*, real ballet music, orchestrated with great skill.

The Russian Ballet was to Bruce an absorbing hobby. From the moment that he saw it at the Alhambra in 1933 he was determined that it must come to Covent Garden as an annual event. He arranged its finances—another might have done that —but what he did supremely well was to give it the right *ambiance*, that untranslatable word that means setting, atmosphere and something more besides. He literally hand-picked the audience, making new converts from among his wide circle of friends, many of whom booked seats for the entire season. This gave the ballet a friendly but a critical audience that it had not had since Diaghileff and offset the damage done by the American tours. Wherever we went on tour someone was bound to say 'We can't do this in London,' or 'Covent Garden will never stand for this.' London saw by far the finest performances.

In addition to this he acted as informal welfare officer—fairy godfather is too whimsical—on a gigantic scale. He knew every dancer and every dancer's background and assisted them in all their personal problems, whether X was wondering where she could get a new dress, Y was wishing to see a lawyer about a divorce, or Z's passport was in a muddle; it was usually Z's passport. Just as Bruce was willing to go out of his way to do anything for anyone, everyone who knew him was eager to oblige Bruce.

He loved the ballet for its art, but he also loved it as a manifestation of personality. He liked to watch the politics of the company, whether personal or external. He was shrewd and saw through all the little tricks and intrigues but was never harsh in his judgments. When some plot was ripe he could intervene with telling effect, but his strong words never left anyone with a sense of grievance.

He was definitely less interested in the English effort because he felt that it was all too correct and well behaved and that this could be felt on the stage. He had, however, become a governor of Sadler's Wells School and the part he played in the only meetings he was spared to attend showed how great his service would have been.

I met him frequently during the war when he was working so hard in the Economic Welfare branch. Characteristically he still found time to live.

Lunching one day at Wiltons he was shocked to hear that this old-established restaurant might have to close down. Acting on impulse he asked the price and before he had paid the bill he had bought the restaurant in association with a friend. Like everything he touched it turned out a good venture, but its value to him was as a place where he could entertain his friends to the very best. I would meet him there from time to time to talk of our absent ballet with nostalgia.

When they did return Bruce was there, looking in at the rehearsals and listening sympathetically to all the difficulties of the day; by now Z's passport difficulties had become catastrophic! I last saw him at the Savoy, surrounded by his old friends eager to dance for him again. He was taken ill that evening and died on the day of the first performance at Covent Garden.

Today it is his friend James Smith who nurses our ballet and opera with the same touch of joy and disinterestedness.

II

The dancers of pre-war Russian Ballet received a hospitality that was altogether Russian in its extent and its warm-heartedness. A whole group of friends entertained for them, some-times in a restaurant, usually the Savoy Grill, but more often in private houses. During certain week-ends two charabancs would call at the stage door to take us all down to some country home. I remember in particular the parties given by Lady St. Just, Mrs. Pollen, the Saxton Nobles, the Oswald Birleys, my good friend Bobby Jenkinson, and those won-derful outings at Hall Barn, the home of the Lawsons.

Ballet hostesses understood the dancer's needs for absolute rest and the fact that they did not like to meet strangers and to have to answer questions as to whether dancing was tiring or if it hurt to stand on their toes. The recipe for a successful ballet party was to assemble as many dancers as possible, the very minimum of outsiders and to have a well-stocked buffet. It was then all very simple: the guests made a bee-line for the buffet and then sat about on the floor talking ballet gossip with their colleagues. Occasionally they would enjoy ballroom dancing, performing with a zest and vitality that could only be equalled in Harlem. In the country bathing was the favourite pastime and most of the dancers were fine swimmers.

The favourite parties of all were at the Ottleys', simple family gatherings with Claudia Ottley as slight and as beau-tiful as any of the young dancers. There was almost a ritual about these gatherings. At about 1 a.m. Colonel de Basil would look at his watch and say, '*Allons mes enfants, il faut partir. Répétition demain très tôt.*' Everyone would begin to make a move, though with Russian goodbyes it took a good half-hour, since vital conversations and sudden phone calls to Barcelona or New York were nearly always held in the hallway. The dancers then walked round the block for five minutes until they were sure that the Colonel had left and returned to con-tinue the party with Bruce improvising at the piano until the early hours. Once to his improvisation the lovely Sono Osato made up an Oriental dance that was movingly beautiful.

Working as they were, these late hours cannot have been

too good for them, but it was always difficult to relax after a performance and even in their own lodgings they never got to bed until two or later. These entertainments were simple and most of the dancers went in for soft drinks.

Bloomsbury was the ballet quarter, the small private hotels around Montagu Street, and any night one might see someone standing outside a hotel whistling a few bars of *Schéhérazade*; a key would then be thrown out of a window. It was the late-comer's signal.

During their first season I was once rung up in the very early morning from a police station and asked to come along in a hurry. There I found a distraught ballet mother who had been out late at a gathering of *emigrés* and had drunk a little too much vodka. She had forgotten her address and when found by a policeman whistling the pass tune outside a number of houses had only been able to reply '*Moi ballet-russe, moi ballet-russe.*'

'She wasn't what we would rightly call drunk,' he said, 'just excitable as foreigners are apt to be, so we put her up for her own protection.'

After a certain amount of detective work I returned her to a distracted daughter.

But it was not only the privileged few who enjoyed the ballet's visits or who met the dancers. There was the ever-faithful gallery who queued half the day and who stopped to talk to the dancers as they came in and out of the stage door. They often struck up friendships, taking the dancers into their homes or to Lyons. The Covent Garden porters also were exceptionally friendly and would throw fruit through the dressing-room windows; very welcome during the heat of a summer matinée.

There was one little man in particular—no one knew his background or how he managed to live for he spent his entire day and half the night haunting the stage door to the great annoyance of Jackson, the stage door-keeper. He gave the girls little trinkets, tracts, a homily on good behaviour and an occasional cup of tea and a bun. For a long time the Colonel believed that he was a very important person, none other than the *chef de claque*, so familiar in Continental opera houses, and upon whom the gallery applause depended. He was sometimes given first-night tickets and turned up in full evening dress. He was also allowed to watch an occasional rehearsal, shown in by the Colonel himself, but the moment the Colonel's back was turned Jackson would throw him out.

Jackson was a great character, the friend of every visiting artist, and for years I spent hours in his box yarning with him about the great ones of the past. It took him no longer than a day or two to memorize all the complicated foreign names. He was a magnificent judge of character and was never influenced in his opinions by the extent of a tip. I do not imagine that he ever got to see a performance but he always managed to sum up the chances of a season with amazing accuracy. 'Not up to our standard' was a phrase he often used. Only the 'fans' could spoil his geniality and some of them were very persistent, one or two completely unhinged. I once saw him chase a tall woman who was brandishing a large gamp half round the building. She in her turn was chasing Massine, whom she said had stolen her idea for a ballet. I myself was pestered by another elderly amazon for over two years until I had to threaten police action. She claimed that I had used my influence against the acceptance of her Inca ballet. Jackson rescued me from her clutches, literally clutches, on innumerable occasions. Neither he nor I were ever able to solve the mystery of what the fans did with the autographs they collected, since the same people would ask for the same autographs every night of the season; they still do. Is there a market in late Massines and are they swapped for an early Fokine or a middle period Nijinska?

It was a great loss to the Opera House and to me personally when Tom Jackson died in 1948.

III

After the de Basil peak period when the company had begun to split it became highly embarrassing for the friends of the ballet. He expected absolute loyalty, but one could not drop friends in other companies, and in any case all that has ever mattered to me has been loyalty to good ballet itself. One season saw de Basil at Covent Garden and René Blum's Monte Carlo Ballet almost next door at Drury Lane. The dancers naturally fraternized even if the managements kept in touch by solicitor's letters only. The London friends always tried hard to bring all factions together, but even Bruce was defeated. It was tragic to see so much talent in violent opposition, with the Massine ballets deteriorating while he was but a hundred yards away, and the same thing happening to Fokine's work.

I sat in court one day and watched the tragi-comedy that resulted. What judge could decide about copyright in choreography? What expert could swear to the degree of exactitude between two works? What exhibit could be brought in evidence? How unenviable the position of an expert witness! Thank heaven I was never called. In this case many of the jurists involved started with the idea that the dancers made up the steps as they went along. I do not remember the actual award, if I ever understood it, but the result was that the scenery and score belonged to one party, choreography to the other, and the public lost an enchanting work. Why will ballet companies spend money on lawyers? No court of law will ever take such cases seriously, no decision is ever regarded as binding. Most theatrical contracts are a complete waste of paper and dangerous at that, since an unwilling artist is of no use at all and can in any case always manage to produce a contrary opinion. In the early days Diaghileff never put his artists under contract. In a long experience of ballet behind the scenes I have never seen a lawsuit that benefited any but the legal profession, that did not interfere with the work of both parties equally and that did not leave increased bitterness behind it.

It can be imagined that with rival companies in town the press representatives worked overtime. I remember a press conference that was held to launch the ballet on Beethoven's Seventh Symphony. All the important music critics were present and the affair was conducted by an American business man, who harangued them as follows—I do not think I exaggerate:

'Well boys, it was just like this; Beethoven was playing away at the piano when Wagner heard him. "Say," says Wagner, "that's the apotheosis of the dance"; of the dance, mind gentlemen. And what Beethoven was playing was his Seventh Symphony, the one the ballet's about.'

This same agent came up to us at the Savoy Grill and when Bruce asked him if he enjoyed the new ballet, he said:

'Enjoyed it? Was I moved? Feel me, I'm sweating.'

A great press occasion was also made of the marriage of one of the dancers at Marylebone Town Hall. She went to the ceremony in ballet dress, walking up the steps *sur les pointes*. No wonder Igor Youskevitch that same season kept his wedding a great secret. 'Otherwise I would have had to appear in my *Spectre de la Rose* costume,' and I am convinced that this was so. The rot had set in.

IV

In one way alone the New York approach to ballet resembled that of Paris. In London once a dancer had become established she was always sure of the same warm reception. She might return almost a cripple or the size of a beer barrel and still hear the shouts and plaudits she had earned years before in *Les Sylphides* and *Aurora's Wedding*. The first night ceremonial of *Aurora's Wedding* gave the audience a chance of saluting its favourites as individuals. And it was the same with the ballets themselves. Any established Diaghileff repertoire piece drew an enthusiastic crowd, especially the fast-fading *Schéhérazade*, while new creations were received with suspicion at first and took some time to play themselves in, sandwiched between two old favourites. Diaghileff, always in search of novelty, was able to dictate to his public but then it was a restricted public of sophisticates. In New York, as in Paris, it was the novelty that counted above all, the success story of a young dancer or a new choreographer. For London the scenery could be shop-soiled and the costumes the worse for wear, while in New York everything had to be fresh from the costumier's. The New Yorker was in many ways more sophisticated than the Londoner, less sentimental, and changing his outlook from season to season. Paris looked rather for the expression of the contemporary artistic outlook, cubism, dada-ism, surrealism, and not for novelty for its own sake. A ballet *première* in Paris could and often did lead to fisticuffs and to acrimonious press controversy between studio groups. When the Russian Ballet left Monte Carlo and Paris it lost touch completely with contemporary artistic thought. It could have carried on in London with its 'bread and butter' reper-toire, but America needed novelties and these had to be sup-plied with no genuine source of inspiration and no time for reflection. The ballet took to Dali when he was a dead letter in Paris, with the result that the novelties were far more old-fashioned than the genuine antiquities that had stood the test of time.

Outside of New York, San Francisco and Los Angeles, success depended on the skill of the press agent. Chicago alone showed a public that was faithful in the London manner, though its roots went far less deep in time.

There was also a natural contradiction of sentiment; the great public applauded the 'exotic' *biggest and best Russian dancers* while a smaller and more vocal group turned chauvin-istic and said, 'So many of these Russian dancers are really

Americans. We have a fine folklore and our own artists and musicians; it is American ballet that we want.'

In England we had been through all this years before and had found the solution of compromise that the Americans are finding today; a native ballet guided by those with Russian training and experience. The French, the most chauvinistic of peoples as a general rule, have always been able to dub foreign artists Parisians, and have greatly benefited thereby.

V

During all our American tours the most sensational of all news episodes fortunately remained unreported. It is a detective story that still remains unsolved.

It was New Year's Eve in Chicago and the company gathered in a big hotel had just been celebrating in the traditional manner. In the early hours the ballet executives were awoken by a house detective and closely questioned. A leading male dancer had been found in a corridor, lying in a pool of blood, stabbed. He was removed to hospital. Fortunately the blade had missed his heart by a fraction of an inch. In true Chicago fashion he refused to talk. Officially the mystery was never solved though every member of the company turned detective and advanced the most complex theories. It must have required masterly skill on the part of Mr. Hurok to keep this wonderful story from breaking; also it must have been a most expensive business.

Such melodrama, was exceptional; most scenes belonged purely to farce. One I remember in particular; I think it happened in Boston. One of our dancers was a great Don Juan. His wife had put up with this for many years and, as long as he gave her a piece of jewellery or some furs whenever he strayed, she was well content. But this time it had gone too far and looked serious. Quite apart from the fact that she was genuinely fond of her husband, she was not a very good

133

dancer and her position in the company depended very much on her remaining the wife of a *premier danseur*. The triangle was watched with great interest; indeed it was the only subject of conversation on a very dull tour. Don Juan and his innamorata had certainly caught the train by the skin of their teeth while the wife waited anxiously, looking up every now and then from the pin-table at which she was playing in an attempt to disguise her feelings.

The next night at the hotel at which the whole company is staying, the office is rung up. 'This is Madame Z speaking, please tell my husband, if and when he comes in, that I have just taken poison. Goodbye.' For once the telephonist did not reply with the usual 'You're welcome.' She plugged into all the rooms and explained the situation. Soon there was a queue outside the room marked X. One of the musicians threw the door open. The beautiful Z, clad in a flowing negligée, was leaning back in an armchair, eyes half closed, clutching a small bottle. The musician made a rugger player's dive for the bottle and for a time they both rolled on the floor. Then he grasped the bottle, smelt it and said, 'Brandy, as I thought,' and the disappointed watchers melted away to their bedrooms.

I do not want to give the impression that the company's morals were loose, because that would be inaccurate. There was no time or energy left for any fast living and there were no 'stage door Johnnies,' and indeed no liaisons outside the company. Within the company there were the usual number of romances. But mainly there were those couples who had not gone through the formality of marriage mainly because of the expense and the idiotic formalities that made it difficult for a Pole to marry a Nansen-passport Russian during a series of one-night stands.

Otherwise the story of these tours is one of deadly monotony; lack of sleep, tasteless food, inane interviews and creative frustration. One rarely realized in which town one was appearing and in any case it made not the slightest difference. Only the warming charm of Sol Hurok and his masterly organization and the comfort and warmth of railway stations and hotels made the whole thing possible and, but for a cancelled or late performance through snow or flood, the ballet was like a circus; arrived on time, gave its show and departed.

In nearly every town there was an audition of local talent after the performance and occasionally a new girl was taken on. Doubtless she gained useful experience and the label 'late of the Russian Ballet' for what it was worth. Only a very few gained rôles except on the night that they revisited their native city, when the local girl was sometimes allowed to make good in a small way.

What struck me most in these auditions, and I have seen them all over the world, was the perfect physical condition of the candidates, their vivacity and also their remarkable technical aptitude, especially in the more sensational type of movement. From the point of view of personality they resembled one another to quite an astonishing degree, adopting a similar style in dress, coiffure and even in their smiles. In England it is safe to say that only one candidate out of forty—these are actual figures—is able to make even a *prima facie* case for taking up dancing as a career. The girl with the correct build and the right legs and feet is excessively rare. Talent can, of course, only be discovered after a long probationary period. Making a decision in America was far more difficult, and from a purely physical point of view we could have taken a dozen or more girls every week.

CHAPTER TEN

The Dance of Death: Part I
Background to the Twenties and Thirties

IF I am to present a true picture of the writer and the age in which he writes, I must delve down far deeper than I have done. Ballet is my *métier* and I love it, but I cannot rest content with the label *balletomane*. I cannot remain on my tiny brightly lit stage full of dancing figures in a darkened world and truthfully say I thought of nothing else, this is the real, the essential me, these are the times in which I live. As things are today, it is even possible that I write this for myself alone. In a sense I do so whatsoever may come—this is a wonderful opportunity for facing myself in the mirror; yet what I write is in the minds of most of us, especially those whose lives have been fortunate enough to be spent amongst beautiful things and who are always seeking to analyse and explain the nature of that beauty. I have already insisted that ballet is not merely a technique, but a manifestation of personality and that it is its humanity and not its mechanics that gives it a meaning. I have already insisted that the dance in its larger sense has been used by man as a means of self-expression, from the magic ceremonies of primitives to the jitterbug caperings of modern man seeking an escape into the womb of time.

Ballet today is, to many, an escape, an escape from those things that I am about to set out, and as I write in the privacy of my comfortable untidy study, puffing at my pipe, there is the roar of an engine overhead.

The 'amusing twenties' lacked the robustness of the 'gay

nineties'; the bright young things were brittle compared to their parents. We were so horribly afraid of silence and of ourselves. The night club and not the family circle was our ideal. Modern psychologists, the witch-doctors of our day, told us that our parents were the true enemies, that mothers did not know the first thing about their children and that God was merely a father image. It was as simple as that. Freud and filth entered into general conversation, but that was a good thing, it banished those horrible complexes. And, if any still remained, they could be dealt with at three guineas a session. The village priest and the family physician knew more and gave more for less.

It is true that we had just emerged from the war to end wars, and that another world war was unthinkable, but 1914 had shattered all sense of security, the wicked hum of aero-engines invaded the calm of nurseries and classrooms. The motto 'An Englishman's home is his castle' could now only be uttered in irony. We, who had been reprieved by the date of our birth, snatched eagerly at the joy of living. There was an enormous gulf between us and those four or five years our senior. It was disturbing to hear them talk. In the schoolroom we had been fed on heroics while they told us of mud and futility. I was never a 'bright young thing,' just because I did not happen to belong to that particular social set. But I can feel as they did. Evelyn Waugh's *Vile Bodies* has forever recorded the mood of that period. To most of my generation it is surely one of the saddest books ever written; it seemed so amusing when published. I have no doubt that my obsession with ballet —and it was an obsession at a time when there was no chance of a career—was also brought about through this same feeling that it was painful to face reality. There was about it a feverish quality that I tried to express in my story of that obsession, *Balletomania*, the constant fear that such beauty would disappear. And when, finally, it did wane with the disappearance of Diaghileff, I truly found my vocation if not myself. I was no more a spectator, drugged by what Lucian called 'this sweet poison,' but an active worker whose aim it was to keep ballet alive at all costs. I am convinced that *balletomania* is a dangerous and paralysing influence. It is certainly destructive of the art of ballet itself, which thrives on criticism. I have seen too much of it and have been too close to it myself not to realize its neurotic aspect. Ballerina worship, film star worship, are among the many modern substitutes for religion. Of the two, the first is the saner since it deals with reality. Certainly the practitioners of both films and ballet are themselves eminently sane, hard-working people. The dancers are continually grappling with an essentially logical technique, and play no conscious part in provoking the unbalanced admiration of which they feel themselves the victims.

Another symptom of the time was the steady growth of homosexuality, not necessarily in its more unpleasant forms but as a paralysing mental state, as if there were the realization that it was futile to continue the race. Many of the most sensitive and intelligent fell victims to this state of mind, often with a feeling of conflict, so that repressed they became misfits, victims of many types of neurosis. Then they went to the psychoanalyst after which they rested in an asylum, took to drink or committed suicide. If they were fortunate they ran out of money first. Such things were not infrequent at the universities. Modern art and poetry, too, not only expressed this uncertainty but at times consciously fostered it, returning for inspiration to forms of tribal magic.

It was in this paralysed state that we entered into the thirties and the end of those twelve years of anaemic Mafeking, totally unfit to understand the suffering of others or the evil that was abroad, unable to react save by a hiccup or a yawn. Against that positive evil we were only able at the worst to oppose a callous and flippant indifference or at the best the feeling that it simply wasn't cricket, but that foreigners could not be expected to understand.

I had never held any strong political convictions. None of my set was politically minded, though most of us held sentimental and vaguely left wing sympathies, which meant that we felt sorry for the unemployed but went on with our pleasures. The others, who shocked us and made us feel superior, told stories about working people who kept coal in the bath tub and talked about unemployables. I did, as I have told, work for a time in an East End settlement. I should have stuck it, but I was not a saint and the things that I saw hurt; besides, the smell was dreadful. We believed ourselves to be among the highly civilized because we could grow more violent about a *décor* or a score than about a political pronouncement. A general election was exciting as a dramatic event; a municipal election did not penetrate into our consciousness. We wanted to go on living in a world of artistic stimuli, but we were not prepared to face the ugly reality around us. A strike was a nuisance, a damned nuisance, but then so was a pea soup fog. Both kept one away from a first night or an amusing dinner date.

It was my second visit to Australia that brought me face to face with reality. I journeyed out with the ballet like a hermit crab carefully taking my shell with me. Once out there, 14,000 miles from home, the great man-free spaces and the fantastic nature of the scenery began to give me a sense of perspective. The September crisis had broken and I was in a panic at being separated from my family. A tumblerful of whisky was not enough to dull the ache of hearing of the trenches in Hyde Park. One cannot be flippant about one's loved ones. I did not, of course, think of the Czechs, I had never met one. Selfishly I welcomed Munich, applauding Chamberlain and Daladier for one of the greatest betrayals in history. I am still ashamed of my feelings, and my irresponsibility. My wife saw and felt more clearly, writing to me letter after letter to explain what had happened. She even paid a special visit to my eldest son at school to impress on him the full enormity of the crime.

I imagine that he was a little disappointed that the excitement had died down and that the normal routine had engulfed him once more.

A prelude to the immense effect that Australia had on me was my meeting on the boat with a Marist missionary father, an ex-poilu, an explorer and an anthropologist, a man of great learning who could have succeeded in any branch of life. He was the friend of painters and writers and intensely interested in the ballet and its dancers. He was fully conscious of the sacrifice he was making. We were constantly together and talked long into the night. He made no direct attempt to convert me, but he did warn me against over-rationalization. He said that in Australia I would have time to think, to feel and to listen. His understanding of people was extraordinary. There was one tough Parisian girl, an avowed atheist who went out of her way to antagonize and to shock him. He saw the good that was in her and told me that, if ever she came up against a serious problem, not only would she not fail but that she would show more positive goodness than anyone else in our community. And it came true, two months later, in her unselfish devotion in nursing one of our dancers who died.

When he left us in Adelaide, on his journey to the interior of New Guinea, I felt I had lost a close friend. I asked him for his blessing. His last words to me were, 'Get away for a time, here you will have an opportunity to listen. Out of the cities there is space and simplicity.'

I left the ballet and travelled. I met people and studied the history of this vast old continent and new nation. These people were direct and uncomplicated, naïf and wholesome and sufficiently detached from Europe to give me a new horizon. Moreover I was not neatly labelled *for ballet use only* and allowed no other interests. Both the press and the radio gave me a wider scope than at home. As few people had seen much ballet, discussion was free to wander.

It was only after my return to London that the experience

came to life. In spite of my joy at seeing the family again I had the feeling of being walled in from the moment we docked at Liverpool. Hitler thundered, his disciples cheered whilst we triumphantly held up our gas mask cartons in defiance, marvelling that every member of the community was so well protected against the contamination.

I shall never forget my return to Covent Garden. It was the first interval and as the house lights went on I glanced up. Suddenly I had an overpowering feeling of panic, the impression that the roof was caving in, filling the auditorium with rubble and dust. I almost ran out into Floral Street only returning after a breather to the crush bar where I was joined by the friendly figure of Bruce Ottley. The ballet had begun again and I could hear the music of *Aurora's Wedding*, punctuated by the usual applause. I told him of my momentary feeling of panic. "It may well be true before next year," he said, and we both lit cigars and turned to the barman to order some drinks.

That imaginary explosion finally blew away every vestige of those 'amusing twenties.' It left me restless. Its impression remained with me throughout the real explosions, it remains with me as I write.

Most depressing of all, however, was not the physical impression of panic but the terrible sense of futility and frustration. What could one do but light a cigar and order yet another drink? There was the crushing sense of a personal responsibility. What should I have done? What could I have done? Was voting any use? Should I have felt more compassion? Was I right in going about my little affairs? The position in Germany, Italy and Russia was different. The majority there believed in something, they had the sustaining strength of conviction. Few people in Britain could have the slightest faith in a government of very stupid and, on the whole, well-intentioned men who uttered platitudes about peace, who dismissed Eden and kept out Churchill because they had offended the evil-doers and had the imagination to feel the true nature of evil. Yet this is being wise after the event. Had I not from the distance of Melbourne applauded Chamberlain and—God forgive me—called him a statesman?

I began from that moment to realize that there was no such thing as politics, that its discussion led nowhere, that Tolstoi was inspired when he said that you could not alter governments without first changing men. Every political problem was not merely a moral problem, but a question of religious belief and discipline. The moral man without religious belief is like a soldier without a gun. He can only exist in isolation. 'My religion is to do good as I feel it,' he says. 'Mine is to do evil as I feel it,' is the retort. And if he does not believe in the divine revelation of good, he is too weak to continue the argument. Your moral man will see the nature of the problem, but he is not armed or disciplined to deal with it.

This point of view might at first sight seem to be leading me to Buchmanism, and its well-advertised Moral Rearmament, but reason, temperament and taste kept me far removed from that exuberant and extrovert activity. I had seen something of it as an undergraduate and had been as shocked by the public confessions of petty sins and the evident pleasure in the telling of them, as by the insistence that a true understanding of it would keep the wheels of industry moving to everyone's advantage. Neither had I any need to be convinced of the spiritual and moral truths of Christianity. The doubt was as to whether it was practical or for saints alone, and which of its many interpretations was nearest to the truth. The easiest way out was to say that every Church was based on the same teaching and had a facet of the truth so that there was no need to make a choice. It is the way of the majority, of the liberal-minded men I so admire, but who have proved so weak before the onslaught of so-called ideologies just because they believed that their opponents were misguided, but fundamentally reasonable and reasoning beings like themselves. It takes a mystic rather than a liberal to understand evil in its many forms. It was impossible, too, not to believe in the Devil, in an absolute evil, the perverted religion of Fascism, Nazism or Communism, based on a purely materialistic and opportunist outlook that denies the dignity of man.

These things have not been written in haste or on impulse alone. The simple are fortunate, their doubts are resolved more rapidly, they know how to listen. The would-be intellectual is too bemused by his own chatter, too fascinated by his sophistication. Dostoievski has shown us that great truth.

My path has led me to Rome, to a Church that is wise, experienced and infinitely understanding; terrible only in its fight against evil. And it is well armed. The writing of this book has helped me to know myself.

From childhood I had been attracted to Catholicism. When I began to reason I feared that my attraction was prompted by my aesthetic sense, by the same motives that had led me to ballet. And partly for that reason Rome itself drove me farther away from its Church. The feeling of Pagan Rome predominated over Christian Rome, the concordat and the politics of the Vatican ran counter to my convictions. I wanted a saint to show me the way. I hoped for the miracle of St. Joan. Instead I saw more politics. I had yet to realize that one could reconcile a certain anti-clericalism with Catholicism, believe in the Church yet have doubts about the men who compose it at certain periods in its long history. I should have realized that the Church has survived the leadership of mediaeval banditti and inspired great saints, great scholars and great artists. That while some bishops may have been worldly, a Sainte Thérèse in the calm of her convent gave evidence that God still speaks to the humble, that religion was not something that had happened in ancient times, but was no longer a living force. Later a visit to Lourdes moved me deeply. There I found what I had missed in Rome. For all its flamboyance and vulgarity, the crudely painted stucco saints and madonnas, the commerce in the healing water, the shops with their religious tourist souvenirs, Lourdes had an atmosphere both of mystery and holiness. One could not doubt that Bernadette had been touched by God, that millions had flocked to the spot believing it, that some had been healed and that many had been comforted.

Not only did I gain an especial affection, call it a cult if you will, for this simple village girl, but I have since then come more and more to regard her as one of the most significant figures of modern times. Bernadette suddenly appears at a period that prides itself on its rationalism, that believes there is a concrete answer to every problem, that science is the only truth. With great courage and simplicity she stands up to exhaustive cross-examination as did another village girl and succeeds in shaking many of the complacent rationalists as Darwin shook the complacent theologians. In a lecture that I heard recently a distinguished non-Catholic physician said, '. . . fifty years ago a physician would have been ridiculed by thinking people for saying that things happened at Lourdes that could not find a rational explanation. Today he would make himself ridiculous by affirming the opposite. We have become more humble.'

Bernadette, incapable herself of philosophical argument, has forced many of us to think and to become more humble; her very strength lies in her complete simplicity. Aquinas and Bernadette; what wealth and variety they represent under the same wide roof!

But by the time of my visit to Lourdes I was learning to distinguish between stucco and reality, and to know myself well enough not to mistake the impulse of an emotional enthusiasm for a faith that may come to some fortunate ones in sudden rapture, but that others can only find after a long pilgrimage. I had still to undergo many experiences before I would admit it.

The position of my children is far worse than mine. I have

known security and many good things that once seemed secure for which I shall never cease to be grateful, most of all for a wonderful wife; I could never have lived alone. But they have never ceased to hear the sirens' wail. They must seize their pleasures so rapidly that they scarcely have time to enjoy them. They are pitchforked from schoolroom to army with no time to pause and think. With every prospect and every project the thought intrudes; is it worth it?

What are they to believe? The just war ended in victory, but the weapon of victory, the atomic bomb, was by any standard of morality—religious or purely ethical—a monstrous crime, a callous crime, an impersonal crime, a crime without hate, but nevertheless horrible beyond words. Hiroshima and Nagasaki are already exacting their punishment as bewildered and frightened men sit round a table; and we tried war criminals. The heroes of the resistance of yesterday against the Nazi tyranny are today's oppressors, tomorrow's fifth column. The democrat who gave the Nazi his deserts becomes a rabid witch-hunter, the soldier who fought the exponents of racialism refuses to travel in the same compartment as the negro. Must our young man choose between Soviet materialism or the suaver, more decent, but equally soul-destroying materialism of the new world? Or, like myself, can he only light a cigar and order another drink? But then, I was a failure, and here I am setting this down in bitterness and fear. Today, I am mortally afraid of living, and of dying, without some meaning to life and death.

If there are sinners there must be saints, whose aid we can invoke, if there is evil there must be good for which we can pray. If there is nothing but a blind madman trampling his creations at the dictate of a whim, then the sooner we end it all the better. There would at any rate be logic in suicide.

But neither instinct nor intellect can allow me to believe in life as a dance of death.

CHAPTER ELEVEN

Record of an Unheroic War

I

I HAD, as I have already written, a terrible fear of bombs, a hang-over from the last war, and this fear had become an obsession. I was equally afraid of being afraid and of showing it. In order to try and overcome this I enrolled myself as a warden in the pre-Munich days. It was all so unreal that I found it almost soothing. We talked of 'incidents,' a beautiful euphemism for mass carnage, calculated the thickness of brick that would serve as a barrier against blast and the amount of brown paper and cellophane necessary to make a gas proof room. I took my training as a kind of mental discipline, tried to familiarize myself with the picture of what would happen and to see myself not as an individual but as part of a disciplined machine. My reason told me that war would come, but at times I indulged in elaborate day-dreams in which, by saintly inter-vention, Hitler would suddenly be converted. Some nights I woke up in a sweaty panic just listening and waiting for a bang and the caving in of the ceiling. It was made worse by the fact that I confided in no one. I felt that I could not tell my wife who has never in her life been frightened of anyone or any-thing and who despises physical fear. But then so did I. Today I am prepared to admit it; the strain of concealment is too great.

The Hitler-Stalin pact found us at Pilat Plage near Arcachon. There was no doubt of its meaning. But the final warning came from the hotel management. After I had rung in vain for breakfast the porter came full of excuses. '*Je regrette le retard, monsieur. Il est arrivé un petit accident au cafetier,*' '*Quoi donc?*

146

On vient de le mobiliser.' He then assured us with true concierge-optimism that there would surely be no war and that we could rely on the good weather and the management's consideration for the rest of the season. Our departure was simplicity itself. My wife, three children, a governess and I bundled into a taxi and told the driver 'Boulogne.' At any other time the drive through France in full summer would have been a joy. We spent a night at Tours, a sleepless night, since tanks and gun carriages rumbled over the cobble-stones and the tramp of soldiers' boots had become the music of the streets. There was no glamour, no bravado, no singing. Just the sober phrase, *'Cette fois il faut en finir.'*

We finished our holiday at Buxton, and in the very same hotel that I had been staying at in August 1914, and there heard Chamberlain's grim speech telling us that we were at war.

I felt that the very best thing that could happen to me would be to get into the army where I would have no personal decisions to make. I volunteered, but it was some months before I was called for my medical and an interview. The interview stands out in my memory, it was so magnificent a piece of fiction.

The interviewing officer was old and exceedingly deaf. I shouted at him and the message was transmitted by a junior officer at his side who bawled straight into his ear. I said I thought I might be of some use in Education. When finally he heard me he yelled at his neighbour, 'Have we got anything of the kind? I never heard of it.' Finally, they said that they would let me know. I never heard another word until my calling-up papers came with my age group. That was during a cold winter. I was crippled with rheumatism and failed to pass my medical. The army had a narrow escape, but I personally would have been happier as part of a disciplined body.

After Dunkirk when the raids started in Bournemouth I joined the A.R.P. and eventually became Deputy Chief Warden.

I enjoyed those two years. My colleagues were all delightful and I had a definite job to do with some responsibility attached. There were endless alarms and not too many bombs, and even during the unpleasant moments, one of them a very close shave, I was surprised at my own calm and lack of fear. I think it was the space all around, the sight of the vast expanse of sea that prevented the dreadful feeling of claustrophobia that I had had in big cities. The thought of invasion never for a moment entered into my mind.

II

After two years of civil defence in Bournemouth in which I lectured on gas and had the greatest difficulty in keeping ballet out of it I moved to London. From there I was sent out by the Ministry of Information, on the recommendation of my friend, Sir Charles McCann, to lecture in factories and schools on an Englishman's impressions of Australia. Those long tours turned me into a professional lecturer, by making me dispense with notes, the only way of holding an audience not very interested nor well disposed; and that describes most of the factory audiences. I had to speak in the din and clatter of the canteen during the recreation hour on a subject that was by no means popular save with the very few who happened to have a 'sister in Melbourne,' and who always asked me if I had met her. Strangely enough there were times when I had. There were some who played table tennis in a corner, as quietly as they could, and I sympathized with them.

My very first lecture in an ordnance factory at Aintree was nearly a disaster. The organizer had collected an enormous crowd and, after introducing me in dramatic fashion as the author of *Waltzing Matilda*, he pointed to an open piano and announced that I would sing my own songs and tell stories I was in such a blazing fury with this unfortunate official and showed it so openly that I gained some sympathy from my listeners. That incident did one good thing for me: I have never since felt nervous of my audience. I also took part in a series of Anglo-American Brains Trusts in American hospitals and those I thoroughly enjoyed. It would be difficult to imagine a more appreciative audience and the questions chosen showed the difference between our points of view and were always stimulating. The English members were often asked if they did not feel themselves downtrodden by the Lords and whether they would not rather live in a democracy. The 'oppression' of India always came up in some form or other and one had to exercise the greatest restraint in not mentioning America's colour problem. One of my colleagues when asked about the Indian question said with great innocence, 'Do you mean the Red Indians?' He made his point with an audience always ready to laugh at itself. Even when we spoke in the wards where the seriously wounded were confined I never heard a single word of complaint. There was one exception, a G.I. who cursed and groaned, but then he was suffering from a bad attack of lumbago.

Especially stimulating were those meetings presided over by my friend, Professor MacInnes. 'Mac,' who is professor of Imperial History at Bristol University, has been blind from an early age. He read out the questions with rapidity from a series of braille notes and before very long he was surrounded by G.I.s admiring and interested. Their attitude was wonderful, none of the hushed and sentimental pity or the obvious avoidance of the subject that passes for good manners. They asked questions openly and laughed at the professor's rich Canadian humour.

I have kept up a close friendship with Mac since those days. I can think of no more invigorating company, no one with whom I prefer to crack a bottle of good wine, and indeed we nearly ruined two lectures, his and mine, both to women's clubs, by lingering too long over our lunch-time wine at Bristol. Mac once paid a girl the most moving compliment

I have ever heard. She was one of his pupils, a nun, who had come to say goodbye to him. He patted her gently on the cheek and said, 'I hope that God knows what a prize he is getting.'

As a teacher and lecturer he had the most extraordinary grip over young people. On one occasion he was lecturing to some A.T.S. when he was disturbed by constant low whispers. 'I took advantage,' he said, 'of the fact that people imagine the blind to have extraordinary powers of hearing, a superstition of course, and I said, "Unless those two young women stop their animated conversation I shall tell everyone what they are saying, and believe me it's very silly."' He gave the rest of his lecture in dead silence.

One of my plans for the future is a wine-tasting tour in France with Mac, when neither of us have any lectures to cramp our style.

My most irritating audiences were without exception the worthy Rotarians. The formula was an exceedingly bad lunch with hearty conversation across the speaker, followed by some minutes of business and the unctuous introduction of visiting brother Rotarians from other clubs. Then twenty minutes of speech, taking great care not to overrun the time since the Rotarians, being busy men, had to be back at work by two-thirty and so looked at their watches from time to time. They were always gracious in their thanks and applause but, poor dears, they were so talk-hardened that I wondered if they knew what the subject was about without consulting their lecture lists. A member once told me that he had heard an excellent talk the week before by a missionary on China, or was it Japan? Anyhow it had been most enjoyable.

My one amusement was to read from the printed discs that each one wore his name and profession and to try to make up my mind whether the wearer was properly cast for his rôle. The fact that there is definitely a Rotarian type of face made this difficult.

Much as I enjoyed schools, the best audience of all, youth clubs were usually intolerable. Pimply youths with dangling cigarettes and girls imitating the latest screen favourite, presided over by a worthy but timid teacher who 'hoped' that they would listen attentively. I saw to it that they did, even if I had to turn one or two out of the room as a start. How cold and gloomy are those church halls, covered in dust with an occasional text, oak-framed in vicarage style and hung askew. Perhaps what was wrong with so many of those youth clubs was the architecture of their surroundings. A well-painted cosy living-room might have made a great difference in outlook. If this is snobbish, then I am an unrepentant snob, but I did enjoy the very different atmosphere in a reform school near Bristol where there was the feeling of a well-ordered home, noticed not only by myself but by two visitors, old boys who had come for the week-end.

I suffered greatly, too, from councillors, aldermen and mayors. One of them said how pleased they were to welcome 'The notorious Arnold Haskell.' I believe that Sybil Thorndike can go one better with a mayor who introduced her as 'a distinguished member of the oldest profession in the world.'

Apart from my heavy schedule of lectures on Australia, sometimes twenty in a week, I would often be recognized and dragged off unofficially to talk about ballet. These lectures were always popular with every type of audience. Finally, they were made 'official' and I lectured for a number of bodies to soldiers, sailors, airmen, schoolchildren and others, explaining an art that was constantly growing in popularity. They were always packed and in Mansfield where the energetic librarian, Mr. Cronshaw, had built up an enormous lecture public, the doors were forced and I had to promise to pay a return visit. I lectured at Mansfield seven times in all, on the ballet that Mansfield had never seen.

III

As a result of these tours I know practically every provincial city in England. I always had plenty of time to explore between lectures. Superficially there is one provincial city that seems to have been hastily assembled from ready-made sections. It is made up of Boots, W. H. Smith, The Odeon, Woolworths, a Station Hotel, a more pretentious County Hotel, and as you pass the inner circumference, row upon row of little villas with miniature rockery gardens. There is a terrace or two of large crumbling stucco-faced mansions that belonged to the merchants of yesterday and that are now, at their best, guest houses. The musty last-week-mince smell in the hotel lounge is the same, the food is uniformly bad. Regional cooking is non-existent. Naturally the war was given as an excuse. I did once hear a grey-beard say to the manager, 'You make the war an excuse for everything. I ate rats in the siege of Paris and, believe me, they tasted better than your savoury mince.' It was the same before, it is the same today. A hotel with a bedside reading-lamp struck me as a luxury. I always carried my own attachment by way of precaution. A theatre is an exception, and if there is one it is usually playing a pier-end show with some such suggestive name as *Girls and Giggles*. A resident will always tell you that the repertory theatre has just folded up through lack of support or will have to do so at the end of the season. The town's historic monuments, often of great beauty, are completely dwarfed by the bad modern buildings so that there is scarcely a view or prospect of beauty or dignity. Even some of the great cathedrals are menaced by their surroundings.

Yet in spite of the drab similarity between town and town, once one came to know them with repeated visits there was a strong individual flavour. Audiences in particular varied so greatly within a small area that it was always necessary to give a fresh angle to a lecture. A favourite joke that was good for a laugh in Nottingham might be received in deadly silence in Lancashire. In general the farther north one went the more lively and stimulating the audience. There, where the maid or the newspaper women called one 'dear,' 'duck' or 'dearie' one could be certain of a warming welcome.

But with increasing speed, mediocrity, as deadening as the mousetrap or silver-papered cheeses that Dr. Summerskill assured us are what we deserve, will make every town into The English Town, type A, B or C. The cinema, the multiple stores, the national press and the B.B.C. in spite of its well-meaning regional policy, have made that inevitable. Is it to be wondered at that people want to travel and that the short ban left one with an intolerable feeling of claustrophobia?

The one bright spot in those war years was my election in 1943 to the Savile Club. My proposer was Doctor Wood, Australia's well-loved 'Cobber,' and I found a strong supporter in Edmond Segrave, a reward, he says, for my having taught him to drink. It was wonderful in those drab days to come into a civilized atmosphere, to listen to fine conversation and to ignore even for an hour or two what was going on outside. There I completely forgot my fear of bombs in spite of some nasty raids.

An English club, like a college common room, gives one an extraordinary feeling of security. It is almost unthinkable that the ugly and comfortable smoking-room chairs, the long table with its rows of newspapers and magazines, the billiard-room and the bar could ever be reduced to a meaningless heap of rubble. Ever since the Savile has been a home to me and a refuge where I can escape from the charming women of from eight years old and upwards that are the concern of my working life. I pray that there will never be any nonsense about a ladies' day and that the hall porter will continue to allow women callers to penetrate no farther than a yard or so from the front door where they are made to sit in a discouraging draught. He does that grudgingly, and I write of it grudgingly. One's club is a very private matter, somewhere where one can glory in being indiscreet; the only place, it seems to me, where the schoolmaster that I have become can allow himself the indiscretion of a glass or two too much without running into a parent.

IV

And so I passed my war, talkative and unheroic. There were interludes when the Sadler's Wells Ballet at the New Theatre brought a vivid pleasure that I thought I should never feel again. With the 'little blitz' I broke down completely, quite unable to sleep as I analysed every sound and waited. Our district came in for a bad time and the shut-in feeling of the London streets gave me a sensation of panic that I had never known in Bournemouth. An A.R.P. practice based on an undertaker's establishment, followed by a genuine raid, was the very last straw. Shortly afterwards I left to lecture in Edinburgh. After six sleepless weeks my actions became purely automatic. I could hear myself lecture without realizing that I was producing the words. I could only cross the road with difficulty. My friend and guide, Marjory Middleton, filled me with rum and took me round to a doctor. I was promptly packed off to a nursing-home where I stayed for some weeks learning to sleep. The incident has left me highly nervous of loud noises, and, except in the heart of the country, a very fitful sleeper. It had all begun on that morning in 1915 when I had been so rudely shaken by that first bomb.

After my recovery the doctor sent me into the country with firm orders to remain there; not that I needed to be ordered. I chose the Forest of Dean; first at a guest house and then at a neighbouring farm where I wrote, prepared lectures and did various odd jobs.

The guest house, where we began our stay in the country, was set in delightful surroundings and was made tolerable by the genial charm of our host and hostess. It was always in-

teresting to study the guests, especially as they revealed themselves at the Sunday concerts. I must have heard *Trees*, *I'll Walk
Beside You* and other ballads over a score of times, and also the
recitation of *Boots*, *The Green Eye of the Little Yellow God* and
Gunga Din. I was meeting people with whom I had nothing
in common and I found that I liked them and could talk to
them and join in their amusements. Every trace of my early
intolerance had vanished. The village children were a delight
and I went for long country walks with my own children and
got to know them far better than in town. I finished a long
novel, a *roman à clef* about the ballet. It remains in a drawer.
Some day I may revise it, but I feel that I have few creative
gifts. I have treated some of the incidents in this book. I also
coached two boys for a public school scholarship; they were
successful. I found that I enjoyed teaching and had the requisite
patience. I longed more than ever for the start of Sadler's Wells
School but it seemed an impossibility then.

So far I have scarcely mentioned my own children and I will
only do so briefly; children are easily embarrassed. From the
first my wife and I had, through our own experience, gone on
the principle that there is an inevitable period of antagonism
between parents and adolescents, and that when the moment
for such antagonism arises the parent must be patient and repeat
the refrain, 'Patience—patience—patience . . . the child may
well be right.' By that I do not mean spoiling the child or
giving way to every whim, but merely not holding the conviction that, just because of the relationship and their extra
age, father and mother always know best. They do not. We
received our warning when, after some abstract argument with
my eldest son, Francis—I think I must have been somewhat
pompous in manner—he informed us that we could not understand him because we belonged to a dying generation. He was
sixteen at the time and we both felt very young. After that
I was particularly careful not to pontificate or to contradict
as a parent when he began a sentence with 'I violently disagree.'

Also, I was fully prepared to be found as *vieux jeu* as I had found my own father. He soon grew out of his aggressive adolescence and, as we have so many tastes in common, we have struck up a friendship that I value. If this sounds patronizing I do not mean it in that way. The same has been the case with my second son, Stephen. He was never quite so aggressive, but he did go through a phase when he wanted to be a saint and that, too, had its difficulties. Both boys won Eton and Cambridge scholarships, the second winning the Newcastle medal and the Newcastle scholarship. But then, they never have had the chance of becoming dilettanti. My daughter, Helen, is still a schoolgirl with a refreshingly Victorian attitude to life. As my great ambition was to have a daughter, I am satisfied. Like the boys she is an admirable companion; and thank heaven she has no desire to dance except in the ball-room. I had an amusing insight into the complications that a dancing daughter might have brought into my life, when my daughter came to one of our school parties. I was sitting with Ninette de Valois, watching them play games, when Ninette nudged me, pointed to Helen and said, 'We must get rid of that child at once. Her legs are the wrong shape for ballet.'

All four of us love giving parties and agree on the guests to be invited. Our friends mix well. My wife tolerates even the unexpected parties and, after some grumbling, turns up trumps. We have become so expert that each one knows which piece of furniture to move. The arrival of any ballet company provides an excuse for a party. And what memories in common these parties have already given us; the picture of Muriel Smith, loved by us all, sitting on the ground, supper in her lap, singing with no preparation or accompaniment. Her complete simplicity and her radiance charm us as much as her voice. The memory of G. B. Wilson with a car-load of young people, his sixth that night. 'Surbiton? No that won't be out of my way. Hop in.' There is nothing I like more than to see the house full of young people. I should have had a Victorian family.

I think that, just because there is no physical manifestation, few people realize puberty is often more difficult in boys than girls. Both as father and schoolmaster I have realized that vividly. But enough about my own children; they must live their own lives and write their own memoirs.

It was in Gloucestershire that I learnt that my house had been knocked out by a V-bomb and my collection of pictures destroyed. I did not worry about the pictures in my joy at our escape. So my dreams of the ceiling caving in, the rubble and the gaping walls, dreams that I had had even in the days of Locarno, had come true.

On V.E. day the village celebrated with bonfires and dancing. And as the last flickers died down with the false dawn I felt secure again for the first time for many years.

PART II

CHAPTER TWELVE

That 'Whooping-Cough Summer'

I

FROM now on it is impossible to continue this story tidily and in chronological order. More's the pity. I love a tidy book beginning with *aetat* 1 in the top left-hand corner and ending at page 350 with *aetat* 75, *retirement at Cheltenham*.

This escape from strict chronology is a symptom: single events are no more of such time-measuring import, the pattern is decided, the middle-aged spread has set in, young men begin to call one 'Sir.' It is very unpleasant at first. Then one notices that there are no longer any babies in the house, no child to leap into one's bed in the morning just as one is enjoying the drowsy relaxation and feels the least disposed to answer brightly to the charge, '. . . you've gone to sleep again, Daddy,' in an indignant voice. Once Stephen bawled the Marseillaise into my ear at 6 a.m. and countered my fury by a hurt and surprised, 'but I thought you loved France.' How I miss those wild intrusions!

One finds, too, that a whole year has disappeared without a trace. 'What have we done the last ten summers?' We go over the list and there always seems to be a summer missing that can only be traced after a hard search from such clues as '. . . then there was that whooping-cough summer at Birchington, when it never stopped raining and Lady Godiva wore a macintosh at the fête.'

When this state of mind is reached one begins to think in topics: travel, friends, incidents at work, collecting, feelings, impressions and ideas. The beauty of middle age is that one can pause just a little to look back and to think. When exactly was it that I met those bachelor friends who drop in unexpectedly for a meal and who can be received by a host unshaven and in a dressing-gown?

There is Charles Lakin, Tasmanian merchant seaman and *balletomane*. I believe I met him over a drink in the foyer at Covent Garden, but how our friendship ripened I cannot recollect. I sailed with him for seven weeks on the *Ulysses* when he was captain and I felt that he was my host during a long country house week-end. He stayed with us in Bournemouth at the outbreak of war, and then went off to sail the *Charon* in dangerous waters. I heard from him continually, though sometimes by the time the censor had finished with his letters nothing but 'Dear Arnold' and a signature remained. Throughout the war he sent generous contributions to the Ballet Benevolent Fund—today he is on the committee—and numerous gifts to be distributed to the dancers. Now in retirement he is the godfather of every dancer, and a wonderful friend to those from the Dominions.

Then there is G. B. Wilson, Cambridge graduate, gasworks manager and *balletomane*, and also keen photographer of so many of the scenes that illustrate the book. I first met him during the war in Beryl Grey's dressing-room at the New. We had both invited her to tea, and, as she had accepted both invitations, she took the best way out by insisting that we come as her guests; a very fair solution for a fifteen-year-old. I cannot remember what happened or the how and why of our further meetings except that G. B. was always there with his car at critical moments, eager to give someone a lift. Since then I have seen him weekly, relished his witty and gossipy letters, to which I have never under any circumstances replied and, as he is highly susceptible ('she really is the sweetest girl') listened to his confidences. He is the nearest approach to a Maryinsky *balletomane*, a collector of books, prints and anecdotes. Even his car is littered with old programmes, framed prints and books, while some star's ballet shoe may foul the gears. He has an encyclopaedic knowledge, a Notes and Queries mind, and many a time he has identified a melody I have hummed over the phone.

The fact is that Lakin and G. B. turn up and if we do not see them for ten days, they are missed. They are taken for granted which, in a large family, is a compliment, but I cannot remember just how it all happened. Decidedly every family needs its bachelor friends, if only for 'baby-watching,' and Charles Lakin has been made to do his share of that.

II

I think it was during that 'whooping-cough summer' that I made my first great contribution to the art of the cinema. The event itself is unforgettable though I have forgotten the name of the company or of the proposed film.

I was rung up one day to ask if I would act as technical adviser to what I will call U. J. Sands Inc. (Union Jack Stars and Stripes) for a film dealing with Russian Ballet life. The sum mentioned was highly satisfactory and I accepted. For the following three months I received a weekly cheque but heard not a single word about the film, nor did I receive a copy of the script. Then I was suddenly rung up and asked if I would go to an important conference to be held in an hour's time: 'Drop everything, it's action at last.' My informant said that, of course, they would send a car for me.

I was shown into a luxuriously panelled room in which a Board Meeting appeared to be in progress, some twenty men round a table and a bevy of shorthand-typists hanging on their words. I was introduced to the producer who waved me to a seat and pushed a box of cigarettes in my direction. (Someone had fallen down on the script—cigars were so clearly indicated.) He then began: 'Mr. Haskell, this is a story conference and we require the benefit of your experience so that we don't put a foot wrong at the start. Now will you please tell us if, to your certain knowledge, it is possible for a Russian girl of good, even noble, birth to be called "Mary." '

After having given the obvious answer, which was recorded by at least three of the secretaries, I was bowed out and then taken home by the waiting car. That is all that I have heard of this super film of life in the Russian Ballet, though it is rumoured that the script was sold to another firm and turned into a Broadway backstage musical, or maybe it dealt with the mounties.

When a year or two later I received a similar request from another company I knew exactly what to expect, and I was not disappointed. This time I was asked to go to Paris to see a well-known film star and report on whether she could be appropriately cast as a ballet dancer. A very pleasant consignment though, since I knew her well, I could have told them then and there over the 'phone. The answer was 'Yes.' This film also never materialized.

Since then I have been interested in the film prospects of my friend, Dallas Bower, an idealist who may frighten the industry, but who managed to make *Henry V* work and pay.

With William Walton, Dick Kenderdine and others I was for a time on the board of Dallas Bower Productions Ltd. I am still unable to understand the elaborate game that goes on, complicated by currency problems that seem to make it necessary for an English-cast film with an Italian theme to be shot in Spain or something equally fantastic. However, I am fascinated by Bower and his ideas, and his extraordinary knowledge of the arts. I believe him to be more practical than the commercial boys. After working in the Wells organization, I am not scared by idealistic ventures. My rôle was confined to listening to Bower unfold his plans and reacting when called upon.

The only time we have been on the floor was in the test for an interesting project to film Berlioz' *Damnation de Faust* with a cast of unseen singers and danced and acted by a specially selected group of actors who could mime. Dallas, with Malcolm Baker Smith as his art director and with Michael Ayrton as artist, shot a short sequence and the result was extraordinarily interesting. It showed that the complicated method could be made to work. The choreography, and it was essentially a question of choreography, had been devised by Massine who was superb in the rôle of Mephistopheles; and Marguerite was Moira Shearer's first contact with the films. The rôle suited her even though the monochrome did not reveal her magnificent colouring. However, when the big boys saw the test they were not convinced; it was a bit much to expect them to swallow Berlioz when all along they knew that it was Gounod who had really composed *Faust*. The episode cost Dallas a great deal of money, and Shearer went on to act in the highly successful *Red Shoes*.

I saw some of the shooting of this film and was very impressed with the team Michael Powell had gathered round him, and with the serious manner in which the whole idea had been approached. I was bitterly disappointed in the result which struck me as meretricious in the extreme and sorry that Massine should have been associated with something that was such a travesty of the glorious life he had known. I can only think of this film as the Red peril. Its false glamour is the very thing ballet must avoid if it is to survive as a serious art.

I was, however, delighted with Moira Shearer's whole attitude. She had many valuable constructive criticisms to make, and she was never taken in for a moment by the publicity that built her into a star overnight. Her ambition was to be a ballerina and nothing must be allowed to interfere with that. She had no illusions about her ability as a dramatic actress, disliked the endless hanging about and the constant demand to provide a climax to a non-existent scene. She saw quite clearly that the director was the true creative artist. She made no secret about her feelings, and when she met with success turned down numberless tempting offers of rôles she felt that it was ridiculous for her to attempt.

It was all in keeping with an earlier event that I remembered when she was in the *corps de ballet* and would receive invitations to parties with the principals. She invariably refused. 'I'm not going because people say "that redhead might be amusing." I will go when I am invited for myself.' A proper ambition and a sense of proportion.

The most amusing scene of all in the bedlam that a film studio presents to the visitor was the methodical professionalism of Massine. There he was in a corner of what looked like Waterloo station on a bank holiday, hanging on to a lamp and calmly doing his *barre*, resolved that whatever happened he would still retain his astonishing form.

III

My association with television has been more fruitful. Though I have always loathed and mistrusted mechanical inventions, I have seen in television a medium that would benefit ballet and solve many of its financial problems, so long as it was kept in the right hands. My first contact with it was in the very earliest pre-Alexandra Palace days under the old Baird system. It was in November 1933 that I induced Colonel de Basil, always keen on novelty, to have an act of *Petrouchka* and some scenes from *Jeux d'Enfants* televised. Later with that pioneer D. H. Munro I took part as adviser and commentator for many Wells and de Basil productions. With great difficulty I secured Fokine's consent to a performance of *Carnaval*. We watched together at Selfridges, Fokine's only concern being with the detail of his ballet. That evening I had to give his comments in front of the camera.

It was after the war that the most exciting productions took place. The West End managers had made it difficult for English dancers to appear. I drew up an elaborate scheme for a series

166

With Jean Babilée on *Le Jeune Homme et la Mort* set

With Madeleine Lafond, *première danseuse de l'Opéra*
AT ALEXANDRA PALACE

of performances by French companies, including two by the Opéra who had not yet performed in this country. I sent my scheme to Philip Bate who was easily able to persuade his imaginative chief, Cecil McGivern. The planning of these programmes was enormous fun, and brought me into close contact with Imlay Newbiggin-Watts who has become a real friend. Imlay is bilingual and as at home in Paris as in London. He is efficient, but with an efficiency that is never dramatized. He has the great gift of putting the nervous artist completely at ease and of giving him the impression that he is talking to a dear friend who has all the time at his disposal. As a result of this meeting I am today godfather to Dagmar, daughter of Imlay and his beautiful French wife, Francine. This is a digression, but one that comes naturally in the friendly team spirit atmosphere of Alexandra Palace. It made possible the gigantic venture of bringing over three French companies of delightful but not always easy people. My Paris–Monte Carlo friend of the old days, Georges Reymond, whom I brought into the picture, Dagmar's other godfather, smoothed over countless difficulties by his tact and his Monégasque refusal to be hurried or harassed.

Philip Bate produced and I acted as artistic adviser, working easily with my old friends. Technically speaking it was a marvel that the ballets were ever seen. Eric Robinson was given a mass of complicated scores, usually in manuscript, and there were never more than four hours of rehearsal time for an hour's programme. It need not be wondered at that there were some failures, never musical ones, but on the whole the success was very great and *Suite en Blanc*, *Passion*, *Entre deux Rondes* and *La Mort du Cygne*, all by Lifar, set a very high standard. The series has done much for Anglo-French friendship, and the informal evenings at the Tony Mayers' flat will be remembered by all.

The medium is in its infancy and I must confess that my greatest pleasure was in the privilege of watching these magnificent performances on the floor, once the rehearsal was over.

There are two schools of thought about televized ballet; the one is to reproduce the choreographer's idea with tact and fidelity, the other to make as many interesting pictures as possible. There is no doubt that when dealing with an already composed work only the first is admissible. Even so, the producer can give variety by an occasional shift of viewpoint when music and grouping permit. Ballet is designed to be seen from the front, but it can be seen at stalls, dress circle or balcony level. In time we shall have another type of ballet specially devised for television and then the producer, working with the choreographer, can play all the tricks his cameras allow. Christian Simpson has worked on such ballets and has given some fine compositions, but the initial material was not to be compared with the already established ballets. However, the medium has come to stay and ballet will be an important feature in its programmes. D. H. Munro, Dallas Bower, Philip Bate and Christian Simpson are names to remember as pioneers.

IV

It was at Alexandra Palace during a visit of Lifar and a group from the Opéra that I saw Nijinsky for the last time. It was an experience that I would have given a great deal to avoid. Three days afterwards he was dead and that will fix the image for me. He was a portly man who looked somewhere around sixty. To glance at him one could not have told that he was not as other men. With his fur-collared coat he might have been a prosperous business man. It was only when sitting with him for some time that his intense silence became evident. It was not the silence of someone wrapped up in his own thoughts, a silence that will be broken when those thoughts have been resolved. It was something dead, like the awful silence of a building that has crashed into ruins. His expression was calm, his gestures automatic. If one held out one's hand in greeting, he grasped and shook it. He sat and watched the dancing, he sat and held a teacup; Petrouchka before his brief period of animation. His wife sat by him. She had married 'le dieu de la danse' under particularly romantic circumstances, and with great fortitude had protected and kept alive all that remained. She could interpret his needs, form some link between him and the world from which he had escaped these last thirty years. If I have not always agreed with what she has written, I have never ceased to wonder at and to admire her great devotion.

I saw Nijinsky as a child and I can remember in particular the impression made by Le Dieu Bleu. If I attempted to describe his dance it would be just so much dishonest writing. I cannot tell if he was the greatest dancer of all time or attempt to say how he would compare with the great dancers that followed him; with Lifar in Giselle, for instance, or with some thrilling moments of Jean Babilée who somewhat resembled him in build. Admirers tell us that he leapt high into the air and remained hovering like a hawk before he found the boards again. Science tells us that it is impossible thus to defy the laws of gravity. Science is wrong, of course, and the Nijinsky legend is true. There are such things as theatrical miracles; in our lifetime they have been performed by Bernhardt, Caruso, Chaliapin, Pavlova, Karsavina. The impression is magnified by time just because of the miracle-performing quality of the artist. The impression made by the merely talented soon fades.

Nijinsky shone for less than eight years; the legend began when he floated out of the window in Le Spectre de la Rose in Le Théâtre du Châtelet in 1912—before and not after his tragedy. Yet Nijinsky was not the immediate success of the first season. It was Adolf Bolm and his Polovtsian archers who made the immediate conquest of Western Europe. Diaghileff at the height of his powers as a creator willed the success of

Nijinsky. *'On dirait que Nijinsky est peint au plafond!'* The phrase caught on. Then Nijinsky, a classical, aerial artist, turned towards character and created the earthbound Petrouchka and his own Faun, showing an extraordinary versatility. 'The amazing thing about Nijinsky,' Alexandre Sakharoff told me, 'was his intense concentration, greater than I have seen in any artist. He shut out everything and became the character he portrayed.'

Perhaps it was the very intensity of his concentration that later caused him to shut out a world that had become too complex and to retire into one of his own creation. If Diaghileff assisted in the building of the legend, and there is no doubt that he did, he could not have done it without the extraordinary quality that was Nijinsky's, the quality to transform himself from what many have described as a very ordinary rather dull young man into a creature from another world.

And the legend has been a fruitful one. It finally liberated the male dancer from the ban imposed by *La Sylphide* of 1832, and from the scathing strictures of Gautier, apostle of romanticism. It extended the frontiers of choreography, banishing the buxom, strutting wench *en travesti*. No one could have served the dance more completely than Vaslav Nijinsky.

CHAPTER THIRTEEN

Travel

I

IT is difficult to write about travel without falling into those facile generalizations usually summed up in slick anecdotes about Englishmen, Frenchmen, Poles and elephants. Such generalizations invariably made round the dinner table give one immense satisfaction, but look rather sorry in print. I doubt, however, in spite of all my resolutions, whether I shall have the strength to avoid them altogether in this chapter.

Ballet has provided the reason for my many travels, has taken me into the homes of people of all classes and given me a vast correspondence with acquaintances all over the world. It is only in the home that one can learn to understand a people. The Ritz is the nearest approach to the international super-state that mankind has yet devised. I would no longer enjoy travel as a tourist, it is travel with work that has given me real pleasure and, I hope, some profit.

I have already written a great deal about France, but since I can think in French, I have never looked on France as 'abroad.' And in France it is Provence that I love with a special love, and it is there that I dream of retiring some day to a small *mas*, the Provence of Mireille, Tartarin and le Boulanger. I can see myself ambling up and down the Alyscamps at Arles, straying into some café for my *pastis*, or sitting in the Arena, having taken care to provide myself with a cushion—watching the lads gaining their *primes* for removing the *cocarde* from some '*redoutable et terrible taureau.*'

I remember well one such occasion: it was a night gala and

as no famous bulls were advertised the sport was not too thrilling to distract the attention from the beauty of the scene or from the Pagnol characters that surrounded us. Monsieur le Maire was gracing the occasion with his presence, a well-fed figure whose tricolour scarf accented his rotundity: Charpin would have filled the rôle. The *razeteurs* that night were past their prime and needed considerable inducement to go into action.

'*Monsieur Costecalde, chirurgien-dentiste ajoute cent francs à la cocarde. . . . Monsieur Besuquet, propriétaire du Garage Rex-Mondial, ajoute deux cent francs à la cocarde. . . .*' and so on, punctuated by great applause and an occasional sarcastic remark.

Then came the *clou* of the evening, a special attraction for the children, and there were masses of them, from nurslings at the breast to toddlers, sprawling all over the arena. The sooner the lads accustomed themselves to bulls, the more worthy of Provence would they become. Excitement became intense as some attendants brought two large tubs into the centre of the arena, right under the glare of the arc lamps. They were full of large live wriggling eels. The game was to withdraw them bare-handed from the tubs in the presence of a large ill-tempered bull. Because the contestants were lads, some not much older than ten, the bull's horns were padded. Even so I felt safer on my hard stone seat some yards from the scene. The kids *en masse* formed a great circle around the barrier; the bull charged in full pelt like a taxi going down the Champs Elysées. The cautious vaulted or tumbled over the barrier to cat-calls and hoots of laughter. The bolder spirits held their ground. After his initial charge the bull completely lost interest in the proceedings, walking gently round the arena as far away as possible from the tubs, which were soon swarming with lads; even the most fearsome had tumbled into the arena again. And then the air became alive with eels, most of them flying in the direction of Monsieur le Maire. They landed with a thud, they wriggled on the stone seats only to be hurled back into the arena. Ferdinand alone was bored and refused to be drawn into the battle. Then came a voice through the loud-speaker—surely it was Raimu's, rich, polite, but with just a hint of menace:

'*On est prié de ne plus jeter d'anguilles.*'

Only the advent of a second and more sporting bull put an end to the memorable Battle of the Eels.

My longest journeys have been to America and Australia; I have fully covered my Australian experiences in four books, *Dancing Round the World*, *Waltzing Matilda*, *The Australians*, and *Australia*. The Australian experience still lives with me not only in memory—I cannot smell wattle (mimosa) without being out there once again—but also in the many warm friendships that have been maintained. The vast surrealist landscapes of Australia taught me something about myself, gave me a proper perspective and the chance to listen. It is only in unfamiliar surroundings that one can truly assess what one has and what one is. In the pre-war Australian scene I suddenly became aware of Europe and, looking up at Europe, I gained a far wider political sense than I had had before. I heard people ask where was Czecho-Slovakia and why should they be involved in a bloody war about a place they could not even point out on the map, though, of course, if Great Britain were involved it was a different matter. I suddenly felt that, as a European, Czecho-Slovakia was tremendously important to me and that there was such a thing as a good European that included being a good Englishman. The temptation of chucking the whole thing, giving it up as a bad job, and settling in Australia was there from time to time—possibly it would have been the practical thing to do; but on reflection it always proved emotionally impossible. To spread a faith or a civilization may prove a powerful incentive to emigration, but not to escape from one, unless driven out by persecution.

I have visited forty of the American states and I have scarcely ever met an American I did not like or find easy to contact. Everyone has written of American hospitality and largeness of heart, most English writers have rediscovered America and most of their accounts make good reading. Yet I can think of few countries where I would enjoy living less or feel less at home. American films, and those excellent magazines *Time* and *Life*, depict a mode of living and a point of view that I find more alien and remote than in any corner of Western Europe. The naïveté, the glorification of the teen-age, the belief in success and its particular definition, the bustle and all the drama of efficiency, the tendency to put knowledge into digests and to over-simplification and the particular brand of sentimentality—one is always intolerant about the sentimentality of others—frankly disagrees with me, and it is not a question of approval or disapproval but of personal feeling. Yet I find the architecture magnificently impressive, and the literature, so often a revolt against existing standards, stimulating in the extreme. My greatest grouse against Americanism is the rapidity with which it spreads as Europe feverishly seeks the dollar; the ubiquitous coca-cola, symbol of American conquests, standing on the bistro zinc and the café table alongside the healthy product of the vine, product of hundreds of years of culture. The coke and the jazz band, American make-up and hair styling, the Hollywood movie, the comic strip and the pulp magazine are everywhere destroying things that are valuable because they belong to the personality of a people. I admire many American artists, but the European artist, tainted by American success, soon loses all personality. The dollar colonization of Italy is already well on the way. What a dilemma if the only means of avoiding the degradation of Soviet materialism is to fall a victim to the gentler sway of American materialism. And because we in England speak very much the same language we may well be the last to succumb, accepting the dollars with gratitude, loving our American friends, and retaining our way of living, uncomfortable though it may be.

II

To me, one of the great joys of travel has been to come across changes in ideals of feminine beauty and also to meet with a fresh cuisine. The cinema, alas, has almost killed the first. Even the Italian is coming to believe the incredible proposition that Grable is more beautiful than Magnani. The superior beauty of the typical American girl is a pure myth of the same manufactured kind as that coca-cola is something more than just another very ordinary soft drink. Paris, Madrid or Rome can produce a greater variety of beauty than New York or Hollywood, and certainly more charm. The cover-girl and the pin-up are deadly bores. I find it exceedingly difficult to distinguish one film star from another. The beauty of Paris fashions consists in the fact that they are devised by strong individualists for individuals and not for mass production. The couturier and the beauty specialist will get hold of the apparently ugly woman, study her with care, and then launch her as a *belle laide*—and thank heaven for *la belle laide*. There must obviously be far more plain women in a country where there is a single ideal of beauty based on photographs of slim women with just enough bust to wear a sweater alluringly or to look attractive on the beach. The more clothes a woman wears, the more feminine she becomes. In all my travels I have never seen more beauty than on a Sunday morning in Madrid when the women in the modest black dresses and lace mantillas are on their way to Mass, in the sari-clad young women of India or in the laughing Tyroleans with their crown-plaited hair.

In spite of mass-produced tinned food, regional cooking is still an obstinate survival. Only in America is the average meal, looking like those ghastly luridly coloured food advertisements in the magazines, without distinctive taste. But in any case, after a mouthful of iced water and a cigarette, the palate would not be in a very receptive state. Yet I have had memorable meals in America, in New Orleans. The best of all is not the chef's cooking in the smart French restaurant, but the simple dish provided in the ordinary bourgeois home. What pleasure I have found in doing the household shopping in France. The dealer does not just shove meat or vegetables over the counter, he is interested in what is going to happen to his goods; 'This will make a good *ragôut*, that an excellent *rôti*,' and so on. The wine merchants will then recommend the very thing for your particular meal.

Our home food in England has greatly improved, in spite of restrictions, since the housewife has done her own cooking. It is only in restaurants, even the smart ones, that every dish tastes the same in spite of its elaborate French name. Food in canteens is a disaster, and the canteen habit has come to stay. Gastronomy here is too often associated with a special type of snobbery, and the wine and food snob can, in fact, be a dreadful bore. I have always attached a tremendous importance to what I eat and drink and to that wonderful feeling of well-being after a tasty and well-served meal. My ideal is not too out of the way and should not be unattainable, it is merely that of the average French concierge.

Another of my travel pleasures lies in acquiring comfortable and outlandish articles of dress. I have worn a beret since 1919, when that most sensible headdress was only known in France and Spain, and the Tyrol has furnished me with a cloak, a jacket and a jaunty hat. I have not yet had the courage to wear the question-mark plume that goes with it; it would droop sadly in our climate.

Yet it is only when I travel that I really lose my temper and that the family handles me with a certain amount of caution. The particular bee in my bonnet is the farce that takes place at frontiers, tedious, fatiguing and, in spite of all arguments to the contrary, illogical. At times it seems almost blasphemous. One of these times is at the Brenner, notorious for the meetings of Hitler and Mussolini. Here the setting is among the most beautiful in Europe, of such a grandeur that the tin huts and sheds and the numberless *guichets* look even more sordid than usual and we, the travellers, and the unshaven officials who plague us still more insignificant. On both sides of the frontier the people look the same, speak the same German, and the quaint Tyrolese architecture is unvaried. Both worship the same God in the same manner, as the picturesque wayside shrines testify. Yet from the image of one gentle madonna to the other, a few hundred yards of sublime scenery, there is the barrage of an Austrian passport officer, an Austrian passport official, a French military control official, an Italian passport officer, an Italian customs official; five inquisitive men concerned with the birthplace of Tom's father and mother, with the money in Dick's pocket and with Harry's luggage. And such concern, though usually politely expressed, is always organized in such a way as to cause the maximum of queueing and discomfort. Of course it puts me out of humour; no wonder *The Consul* found in me an ardent admirer.

III

Italy has never failed to delight me, second only to France; but of recent years it is Spain that has interested me the most and, were I young enough for adventure and the learning of a new language, it is Spain I would study.

I came very near to learning Spanish at Westminster. I was deeply interested, and it would have been difficult not to be interested by the dapper little spade-bearded man who was our master. Rumour had it that he was a grandee. Whether it was true or not, he might have stepped straight out of a Velazquez. He was, unfortunately as it proved, a great *aficionado* and, living in the wilds of West Kensington, he was obviously starved of his favourite spectacle. Somehow or other he always succeeded in turning every lesson into a disquisition on bullfighting. He was a superb actor, able to convey all the thrills of the arena and the mannerisms of his special favourites. On the unfortunate day that I shall never forget he had drawn a bull on the blackboard and, after a brilliant display of cape-work with an M.A. gown, he was showing us how to plant the *banderillas*, his *banderilla* being a blackboard compass. He had missed several times and we were behaving in the characteristic manner of the arena, shouting insults, throwing chalk and books, and bellowing, when in walked the head-master. Our grandee left and I never learnt Spanish, but he did give me a lasting love of the *corrida*.

To know Spain would take a lifetime of study, for no country reveals itself more grudgingly, is more completely self-contained or more completely indifferent to strangers. I cannot call it xenophobia, because the stranger is treated with a greater courtesy than in any other country; but he is made to feel that he has nothing to give that Spain really wants. Cross the frontier from French Hendaye to Spanish Irun and there is scarcely a soul that speaks or understands anything but Spanish. Even in hotels the servants have not the usual gift of tongues. Only the aristocracy is fluent in French or English. Once across the frontier one is faced with something complete and something apart, something belonging to another period of history. There is Europe and there is Spain. I can feel it, I wish I could understand and explain. Perhaps no foreigner can really understand, and it is the attempted simplification of the Spanish political scene before, during and after the Civil War that has caused so much unnecessary suffering.

Let me set down some plain facts. There was no clear-cut issue in the Civil War that can be stated as Democracy versus Dictatorship, Red versus White, Atheist versus Catholic, or any variants of that kind. The powerful propaganda of the International Brigade, which still dominates so much so-called democratic thought, is deliberately misleading. Those unfortunate men of many countries who were killed in Spain died for an ideal, it is certain; an ideal that they then thought was evident but that becomes more difficult to justify with every day that passes. Had their side won, their ideal would have prompted them to fight again for the liberation of Spain from a far worse fate. The War Office was greatly abused during the World War, when it was chary of giving responsibilities to those with experience in the International Brigade; yet there was great wisdom in its attitude. The Spanish Civil War was not—as it was and is so easily called—just the first round of the greater conflict, even though the Germans did use it for a dress rehearsal.

There were in fact a number of civil wars going on at the same time, as well as an international war between Fascism and Communism, in which the democracies could play no useful or honest rôle except to adopt the much abused non-intervention policy. The Spanish war itself was much more complex; there were the weak and well-meaning 'Kerenskys,' certain to lose whatever happened, the anarchists, communists, Trotsky communists, the Basque separatists and the Catalan separatists who, by sheer accident, found themselves on one side. On the other side there were some genuine fascists, some royalists, some militarists, who wished for a stable order, some business men with an eye to profit, a strong Jesuit influence, and the Church out to defend itself. Even that is far too simple to explain happenings in a country where regional loyalty and mystique is so very strong. On the so-called Government side there were a number of minor civil wars being fought, with the Basques the greatest victims, and even the Basques were divided between those who felt that they were Spaniards first of all and the out-and-out separatists. Both sides accepted foreign aid and at the same time despised the foreigner and resented the intrusion. When a Franco-Spaniard was told by a German 'We have routed the enemy and put him to ignominious flight,' he retorted indignantly, 'The division you refer to is a Spanish one and Spaniards do not flee, though they may have retreated under pressure from vastly superior forces.'

It was in the Basque country that I heard of the worst suffering on both sides, stories of courage, idealism and brutality that only a civil war, and a civil war in Spain, can produce, though we saw something of the kind in Ireland. I met one young man whose family of seven brothers and sisters had been murdered with their old English governess, machine-gunned in cold blood in Bilbao. I heard of brothers engaged in aerial combat, who had first dipped their planes in salute and had then fought. The wounds are healing, the bitterness is fading, and I saw more than one reconciliation take place under the neutral roof of the British Institute in Bilbao.

What of Spain today? No one is in a better position to give an impartial and objective view than a visitor on an artistic or scientific mission. It is easy to speak to those whose interests are the same. Spain is a dictatorship, but again this is an over-simplification. Were it left to a free vote, the vast majority would, I feel, back Franco. They would do so without any fanaticism, 'surtout pas trop de zèle' is the motto, but they would do so because they never want another civil war, because he has given them stability, because even those who fought against him are appalled by what is taking place in the so-called 'people's democracies,' and by the power of the communists in France and Italy. They are frightened, most of all, of their own anarchists, a powerful and irresponsible faction of fanatical criminals who would stop at nothing. They see Franco as a temporary ruler who may one day give way to a more democratic monarchy, and they are willing to surrender some initiative for a long period of calm. They have shown more enthusiasm, though enthusiasm is too strong a word, for the régime since foreign nations have tried to bring pressure on them. And their instinct, product of intense chauvinism, has been right, for to remove Franco would mean, without a doubt, a resumption of bloodshed. There is no resemblance between the Franco régime and Mussolini's Fascism, just as there is no resemblance between the Spanish and Italian peoples. People talk quite openly in front of their servants and in restaurants, and voice their criticisms. They meet foreign visitors freely and talk with them. There is, however, a very strong censorship of the written word. The newspapers give a false sense of national well-being and order, just as when the person who is untidy by nature sweeps the dust under the bed. This censorship is exercised both on moral and political grounds. There is, of course, a strong political police, but it is kept for actual subversive movements, to save banks against the type of armed robbery that Stalin committed at Tiflis, and against anarchist bomb-throwers. These, when caught, are treated without a doubt in the same inhumane manner as they themselves would treat their victims if they had the chance. The Spanish political police is even less gentle than the French gendarme or the American copper as shown in their films. The artist and the intellectual are left alone, always provided that they are content to dwell in their ivory towers. For instance, a fine drawing presented by Picasso to the Republican Government hangs in a prominent position in the Barcelona museum; an impossibility in Nazi Germany or Fascist Italy. Picasso is admired as an artistic genius, admired for his Catalan skill as a business man who can sell anything and everything, but is not taken seriously as a political thinker.

I have been shocked by much of the propaganda I have seen which reduces the whole of Spain to a series of Falangist processions. True there are Falangist processions but that is only a very small part of Spanish life, and I never chanced on one. Where the average Spaniard is shocked is in errors of taste. He does not like to see streets named after the Generalissimo and invariably calls them by their original names. He deplores the fact that the Generalissimo does not wear mufti more often, and he is embarrassed by bad paintings of the little man that find their way into museums; and he says so. When in Spain I saw, in an American left-wing paper, a picture of Spanish workmen shot down by Franco's police. They were, in fact, the workers having their daily siesta on the perpetual building stones in Madrid. There is undoubtedly a great deal of graft in high quarters. I met also with many party men who were intellectuals and idealists. There are, as there have always been, great extremes of wealth and poverty; the simple expedient of beating up the wealthy and sharing out their money, while it might give considerable satisfaction to some, would not go anywhere near to solving the problem of poverty. American aid to Spain might, though there would always be poverty in the south, where the philosophy of the benefit of work finds little sympathy as against the apathy induced by fatalism. The régime could and should improve things: the Church has said so on occasions, notably the Bishop of Barcelona recently, where luxury flats are going up rapidly while the poor live in shacks worse than any I saw in Africa. But the régime is not responsible for the original poverty. The Italian peasant, under a democracy, is in an equally bad way. I find it difficult to believe that the standard of living in the people's democracies is so much better.

What the Spaniard cannot understand, and no honest person can answer him, is the United Nations' hypocrisy, and the callousness of the democracies. 'You have an ambassador in Hungary and other countries where your English passport would not protect you and where I would have been shot for speaking so frankly to you,' said a schoolmaster to me on the train; 'yet you treat us as if we were unclean.' I felt ashamed and promptly changed the subject.

The blackest U.N.O. marks against Franco are on account of the speeches he made in favour of Germany during the war. Remember the Germans were at Irun yet they did not pass the frontier though it might have given them victory. While they did not pass, countless refugees did. As usual it is Churchill who has understood.

It is an extraordinary thing how many well-meaning sentimental democrats wish to give Spain, Portugal, Turkey

Greece and even African tribesmen a type of democracy that history shows us they cannot use, and that would lead them to disaster.

IV

I admire what I understand of the Spanish character immensely: its vast charity, its mysticism and its ability 'de concevoir les choses en grand.' I believe that the corrida would explain many points if one really understood it. During my first visit to Spain I became a rabid aficionado and wrote a series of articles for Orage's New English Weekly on the corrida as a spectacle. They followed much the same line as Death in the Afternoon which had not yet been published, but without Hemingway's great expertise and naturally without his skill as a writer. They resulted in several dozen bloodthirsty letters from animal lovers, revelling in details of gored matadors and wishing a similar fate to the writer, and were, to my great satisfaction, reprinted in some Spanish and South American papers. The letters I received from Spain wished me a better fate.

The corrida is thought of as an art and in no sense a sport; the clumsy matador a butcher, the great matador the equal of poets and painters. It is my greatest regret that I never saw Manolete. I heard him discussed at great length as a tragic poet.

Here is the supreme ballet of life and death, a ritual dance in which the aim is not to kill the bull as quickly as possible without getting hurt, but to sacrifice him according to the ritual in as perfect a manner as possible, with beauty and infinite respect for the courage of this king of beasts. To kill him unfairly is not a foul or a clever move, if you can get away with it, but a lack of manners and especially a lack of artistry that the public finds inexcusable. The aficionado may be bloodthirsty, so is the boxing fan for that matter, but he is essentially a connoisseur able to appreciate the beauty of perfect cape-work for its own sake as well as for the skill and cunning of its rôle in the sacrifice. It is necessary to see a whole series of corridas in order to find one or two that have a real meaning, and it is essential to understand its aim as a spectacle and to watch out for the finer points. One should visit one's first *corrida* in the company of an expert.

I have not yet mentioned the question of cruelty. I will not attempt to gloss it over. Every country has its own brand of cruelty—no one today can afford to point the finger at his neighbour's cruelty whether it be fox-hunting, stag-hunting, the circus ring, pigeon shooting, the punch-drunk boxer, the boiling of lobsters alive or the degrading spectacle of all-in-wrestling. The Spanish belabour their hard-working and pathetic little '*burros*,' but they are genuinely appalled at our many cases of cruelty to children that necessitate a large national society for their prevention. They are also bewildered, strange people, at the tiny sentences of a fine or at most few months given by the law for such inhumanity and by the fact that petrol and currency offences are so much more severely punished. I love animals in moderation—I have always had a dog—but the 'professional' animal lover I regard as intolerant, bloodthirsty—so long as it is human blood, of course—and entirely lacking in any sense of proportion.

From the immense bloodstained spectacle of this great dramatic pageant one comes to the scenes in the street and the café, to the family groups and the children, masses of them, running in and out, to the promenaders passing the time of day or night, to the gnarled old man holding the hand of his three-year-old grandchild. This old man and the toddler are as typical of Spain as the matador and his richly dressed retinue. The Spanish love children and their children live with them and share their lives. They are not spoilt just because they are taken so very naturally and not petted for a special rare treat. A friend of mine, a Scotsman with four delightful children, took them and his wife to the best restaurant in Madrid for a birthday celebration. The maître d'hotel rushed up to them and showed them to the very best table, because, he told my friend, they would enjoy and remember the scene. When he brought the menu he said that, as the food was too rich for the children, he was having a special meal prepared. And when the bill came the children were charged half-price. That is an everyday occurrence. In Spain it is easier to get a flat or a house when you have children. In England it is far more difficult, children are a handicap as I know from bitter experience. In Spain family life is a happy one. The Church may be oppressive and politically over-powerful, but it does give the immense benefit of Catholic family life, something I have felt in a concrete manner in every home I entered. Remove the influence of religion and Spain would be lost, with every individual seeking his own way of salvation in anarchy.

What colour in names: Carmen, not an opera or novel heroine but a commonplace, shouted across every market-square; the graceful Rosario and the dedicated Nativitad, Concepçion, Maria-Montserrat, Marie-Lourdes. Sometimes they can be embarrassing to the foreigner. The chauffeur of a British consul-general was called Jesus. When the consul was on leave in England he sent a telegram to Spain, worded 'Please send Jesus to meet me at the station.' The postmistress not only flatly refused to send the cable but threatened him with a prosecution for blasphemy.

What increases the enigma of Spain, making it the least obvious of countries, the very reverse of cosy Switzerland, is its regionalism; its sudden changes as one travels, not only oi character, art and architecture, but of periods in time from the Middle Ages of Avila or Segovia to the perpetual nineteenth century of Madrid. South and North coexist at separate periods of history. Even geography conspires to confuse one with the semi-deserts and the barren rocks of one province to the bright green and fast-flowing rivers of another. Physical types change with the scenery until one feels that one has not seen one country but a vast continent. No, Spain cannot be reduced to a formula and neatly labelled.

V

The British Council is doing magnificent work in Spain and Walter Starkie is a name to conjure with; an Irishman upholding the British point of view, yet at the same time a lover of Spain, who knows more of its background, literature and traditions than most Spaniards. His rôle in Spain during the difficult war years cannot be overrated and has been inadequately rewarded. No ambassador could have succeeded without his guidance, his contacts and the high respect in which he was held. In every part of Spain with rich and poor the name 'Starki' acted as a passport, even with a difficult railway official, and it was the only word of English (Irish?) that he understood. Starkie has gathered round him a fine group of men who understand and appreciate the Spanish point of view and remain British. The quality of their work was especially noticeable in the difficult separatist provinces of the Basque countries and Catalunia where R. A. C. Duvivier is director in Bilbao and Hardy in Barcelona. There on the neutral ground of the British Institute—and it was in every way non-political—people of greatly differing views who would never meet outside came together to discuss some aspect of British life and thought and, even wider, European art in general. Thousands were learning the English language, but the word British 'propaganda,' in its modern crude sense, would certainly not apply. The atmosphere was academic and not commercial or political. The work of the Council in Spain has greatly compensated for much political blundering. It would be folly to curtail it.

VI

Quite obviously I went in search of dancing on every possible occasion. Théophile Gautier remarked that the Spanish dance was a Parisian invention. There was a great deal of truth in that. Paris undoubtedly sees the very best of one branch of Spanish dancing, the theatrical as apart from the folklore. But

Spain has contributed enormously to ballet from the time of Fanny Elssler to the present day. Diaghileff gave us *Le Tricorne* and *Las Meninas*, René Blum *Don Juan*, Ninette de Valois *Don Quixote*, Roland Petit *Los Caprichos* and *Carmen*; these are but a few. It is in painting that Spain's contribution has been the greatest with the Catalans, Sert, Picasso, Pruna, Miró, Andreu, Dali and the astonishing newcomer Clavé; seven outstanding decorative artists from one small corner of Spain. And Barcelona explains Picasso, brought up to look at the Catalan primitives and the fantastic architecture of Gaudi, just as Gaudi and Bosch in the Prado explain the vision of Dali. Spain has thrown out individuals of genius, but it is France who has used and organized them in the teamwork that is ballet.

It was Antonia Mercé, the unforgettable Argentina, who in our time brought Spanish dancing to the European stage, translating it and using its idiom to express herself. She made of it a universal language and yet still retained its authenticity. That is the problem of the Spanish dance. The Spanish dancer is essentially an individualist who must express himself in a solo. There is no Spanish school in the Russian sense of the word. I went to see the best-known teacher in Madrid, a woman with a vast repertoire of steps. She sat in a chair, her hands by her sides clicking out the rhythm with her castanets. She roughly indicated a step, rarely made a correction and paid not the slightest attention to the arms. Each pupil was given a half-hour session and bought a certain amount of information but no artistic guidance. It remained for the pupil to use the information artistically, and it was often supplemented by ballet lessons in Paris. I went also to visit the great gypsy dancer Estampio, now well over seventy and an artist to his finger-tips. He had been with La Maccarena and others, one of Diaghileff's *Cuadro Flamenco* at the Prince's Theatre in 1921. The trip, his only one abroad, had neither pleased nor interested him. He commented on the 'society women' in 'Spanish combs, wearing their shawls and mantillas as if they had dropped from the ceiling.' 'And we danced in a set by Picasso a completely ridiculous affair quite out of the picture, whatever anyone may have said.' He stood in the middle of his tiny studio—garret would be more correct—rolling a cigarette and glancing every now and then in evident disapproval at his pupil, a young Peruvian girl. Her freedom of movement was restricted by a charcoal brazier that was heating the room, and a dog and a cat that romped round the floor at will. But the little man's body was quivering to the sound of the guitar and one felt that even at his advanced age he could give a thrilling performance. If the Spanish dance in its more classical sense is in some danger of extinction, the Flamenco dance will always produce a few performers of instinctive genius who, even when corpulent and old and seated like the divine Pastoria Imperio, can transport one by the movement of their arms or the flick of their wrists. Years ago in Barcelona Chaliapine went down on his knees to her and kissed the hem of her dress in homage. But it is not in the caves or in the tourist centres that one will see much dancing today. Many of the caves are luxurious dwellings with electric light and modern plumbing. One must search for it deliberately and it is expensive. A connoisseur will tell one of such and such a dancer who is really superb. He will then try and track her down; she may have gone south or as far afield as South America. Then she and her guitarist and usual retinue of grandparents, parents, aunts, uncles and cousins must be invited to some tavern and a price agreed upon. The hunt may take several months, but no one except the tourist whose pesetas are fast melting is in any hurry.

Some gypsy Flamenco dancers such as Carmen Amaya have become world-famed and deservedly, though their art suffers a little in the cold and less intimate atmosphere of the theatre. The disordered flying hair, the falling rose and other external signs of internal fire are unwelcome in the right setting in Spain where the full subtlety of the dance is understood.

Although the Flamenco dancer is more fully clad than any other, her dance is the most sensual in existence. The impresario who lures them away from Spain must be a bold and understanding man who fully realizes that wherever he takes them they will carry with them their little corner of Spain, cooking their traditional dishes on the elegant pile carpet of a Paris luxury hotel because 'the food there is so bad.'

The Duca di san Lucar la Mayor, Spain's genial and learned representative in London, and a born artist, realized the form during Amaya's sensational visit to the Prince's Theatre in 1948. When he invited her and her brother to a dinner party he was neither surprised nor perturbed when she turned up with eleven members of her family including Papa with his hat pulled down over his ears to protect him from the draught. Neither was His Excellency at a loss when Carmen came to him one morning and announced that one of the girls in her company was expecting a baby.

'Is she married?'

'Yes, of course.'

'Well then, there are no complications. People have babies in London every day.'

'But Your Excellency, we are living in a London boarding-house.'

'No matter, I can arrange for an excellent clinic where every care will be taken.'

'But that is not the point; don't you understand Your Excellency—this baby must be born on Spanish soil.'

The Duke fully understood the great necessity of this and, regardless of the consequences, offered the mother-to-be a State bedroom in the Embassy. 'What is more,' he said, 'I will ask the Cardinal to perform the christening.'

Unfortunately the London season ended sooner than was expected and the babe was born in France—much to the regret, I feel sure, of the bachelor diplomat.

The non-Spaniard is inclined to believe that all Spanish dancing is Flamenco dancing, thus making yet another of those over-simplifications so very dangerous when it comes to politics. Spanish dancing is exceptionally rich and varied, as that magnificent artist, Mariemma, Argentina's successor, has shown us. An unusually gifted musician, partly trained in ballet in France but Spanish to the finger-tips, Mariemma was born in a village near Valladolid. The commune of her birth-place has named a street after her and presented her with a property. (Why not a Fonteyn street or a de Valois terrace?) Like Argentina before her, she has made a systematic study of the dances of Spain and has stylized them for the stage. I shall always remember a scene in my house where I gave a party in her honour. I had proposed a toast and she replied by saying that she would answer it by her castanets. The guests grouped round her, Enrique Luzuriaga, a magnificent pianist, began to play and Mariemma took us to Spain for an hour, making those small wooden discs into a sensitive musical instrument; dancing with her arms and wrists as the castanets sang and sobbed, whispered, mocked and laughed.

The people's dance can be seen in every town and village to mark religious occasions, family rejoicings or just for its own sake. I saw the dances of Segovia in the grandiose setting of the Alcazar at a mediaeval banquet in which lambs and sucking-pigs were roasted whole and skins bulged with the fine wine of the country. I saw the stately but intricate Sardana in a Barcelona palais de danse and on Sunday mornings in the city parks and squares. Not in costume, as had been the dances of Segovia, but in the ordinary prosaic clothes of soldiers and civilians. I passed one whole unforgettable day with Olaetta and his Basque dancers in Guernica where we sat down together round a table varying the meal with the dances and songs of his people. His lovely daughter, Maria-Lourdes, wishing to pay me a compliment, said demurely, *'Je connais une chanson folk-lorique anglaise—Est-ce que vous voulez que je vous la chante?*

Ça s'appelle Jingle Bells.' With her Basque accent and her small sweet voice it certainly sounded '*folk-lorique.*'

If anyone in these days can make a travel programme, and my travels depend on work or chance, it will be to revisit Spain many times, to savour its essential difference in a world that is too rapidly becoming fixed in shape.

CHAPTER FOURTEEN

Collecting

I

I AM, as I have shown, one of those fortunate people whose work has been his hobby and the work itself includes literature, music, painting, sculpture, folk-lore, sociology and the interplay of human relationships. My publishing and my art gallery experiences, my travels and my reading have all been a part both of my pleasure and my work.

From my earliest years I have been an inveterate collector, a frequenter of junk shops, galleries and sales rooms. I cannot lay claim to a single spectacular find. I like to believe that I have had some bargains. I know that I have enjoyed myself. My successive collections form a diary of my tastes and emotions.

I started in my Paris days by collecting contemporary paintings, especially by those artists in the ballet entourage. Today not a single picture of my original collection survives. The majority was wiped out by a V 1 on July 4, 1945; the remainder I sold at a considerable profit that allowed me to begin collecting all over again. I had, because I collected unwisely no doubt, in truth grown very tired of my 'moderns'; I found them restless and out of tune with my mood. Even had the secret weapon not dispersed my collection I would have started all over again. The novelty of the 1920's had become more dated than I could have believed possible when in feverish excitement I unwrapped it, knocked another nail in my sadly scarred walls and stood back to enjoy it. My more conservative friends would be startled and I was young enough to relish the feeling of superiority that their shocked horror engendered. The great thing was to be *dans le mouvement*. When I took my bride to our new home she says, as I have already related, that she was amazed to find the walls full of pictures and not a single chair. This may be an exaggeration. She soon grew to like the 'one-breasted woman' and the others, though she was dubious about the effect of them on the children. These, however, took them for granted. Unfortunately I never went in for the pretty doodles of Paul Klee, though I had the opportunity. I write 'unfortunately' since I could have realized handsomely on them and collected more Greek or Egyptian antiquities.

At no other period has contemporary painting ever had such skilled and extensive publicity or so many dealers with a large financial interest in the launching of the latest 'star.' And at no time have the critics been guilty of such treason, petrified as they are of being considered old-fashioned. The famous Cambridge hoax of the bogus modernist exhibition was a milestone. There are times when either reason or sincerity must be suspect. The most popular argument to encourage buyers has been: 'At no period is the artist recognized in his lifetime, look at the impressionists for instance—once you could buy a Renoir for a few shillings.'

The argument, with very few exceptions, happens to be both untrue and irrelevant. Those very impressionists who lived a full span met with complete recognition as did the majority of old masters. For that matter the moderns, from Picasso downwards, enjoy an even more complete lifetime success, entering the museums far earlier than did their pre-decessors. Time alone will do the necessary sorting out, and time has rightly condemned the majority of the Chantrey paintings, highly priced sensations in their day. But precisely the same sifting process will go on with the works that the Tate Gallery, who seemed to have the best of the argument, have adopted as their standard and about whose enduring merit

they are as cocksure as were the Chantrey purchasers. In literature, too, who knows—even Eliot may go the way of Tupper!
This, however, may be *lèse-majesté*. Many contemporaries I
greatly admire; would that I could afford a Braque or a
Rouault, a Derain, a Matisse or a Picasso, when it is not a
laboratory work. I love him for his genius and hate him for
his betrayal of it. He destroys everything including himself.
Primitive art I have always loved, carefully distinguishing it
from savage art, but the highly conscious modern primitive
is an abomination and even the *peintre de dimanche* is sadly
overrated since the well-deserved recognition of the Douanier,
of Vivin and Bauchant.

I have never regarded pictures as stocks and shares and have
collected to satisfy my mood of the moment, fully conscious
that every purchase was not a masterpiece and not even necessarily a friend, but an agreeable acquaintance with whom to
pass the time of day.

I wrote a book on drawing, *Black on White*, that attracted
a fair amount of attention. It had in it a dialogue with Henry
Moore, an artist I have admired profoundly from the start. The
book's main point was a plea for the collection of original
drawings instead of those Van Gogh sunflowers and other
mechanical reproductions so badly shown up when we saw
the exhibition of Van Gogh originals. The original drawing
was and still is at times cheaper to buy, more stimulating and
will play a far greater rôle in the collector's artistic education.
He can say to himself, 'I have something unique, I made a
deliberate choice, I chose this because. . . .'

My next picture collection swung me back to the early
Victorian romantics, admittedly minor masters, but very agreeable living companions. My long lecture tours gave me ample
free time to visit the provincial museums and picture dealers.
I started with a small Frith, a delightful narrative painting by
Leslie, and Landseer's *Highland Shepherd's Home*, painted in
1842 before he had become popular at court.

Repeated visits to Edinburgh made me acquainted with the Scottish school, almost unknown across the border, and so much closer to Holland and France than our own painters. The early work of that charming domestic painter, Hugh Cameron, some sketches by MacTaggart, a true and, outside of Scotland, a still unrecognized master, and paintings by Chalmers, Hornel and others all continue to give me the greatest pleasure. Lately some early drawings by Rossetti have given me an awakened interest in the Pre-Raphaelites who, though they started as rebels against the Victorian aesthetic, are still looked upon by many as typical of their age.

I have also collected books but have never been bitten by the first edition craze; few who have been closely connected with publishing are. After my first Australian tour I started a collection of Australiana, which was of exceptional human interest in showing the rapid development of the Common-wealth from the convict to the present day. I read all the books, pamphlets and manuscripts in my collection and used the information as a background for my books on Australia. When the search became fruitless and I had exhausted all the sources in England, leaving only those items inaccessible in price, I sold the collection advantageously. It had first gone through a narrow escape, the items being picked out of the debris of my house one by one and recovered intact through the friendly skill of Frank Maggs. Any but an expert would certainly have taken some of the old papers and penny pamphlets to be rubbish.

Another small collection that has amused me has been of books and pamphlets dealing with Walter Scott. At the out-break of war I wanted to read something that would carry me as far away from actuality as possible. I had struggled with *Ivanhoe* and *The Talisman* at school but had not got very far. This time I started with *The Antiquary* and *The Bride of Lammer-moor* and so enjoyed them that I have read all the Scottish novels several times, though I fared little better with *Ivanhoe* and *The Talisman*. Scott's journals gave me an intense admiration for the man himself which Lockhart's *Life* increased. I have always made a habit of reading systematically rather than dipping here and there and Scott and his friends occupied me for many years and became my friends. It was during my many Edinburgh visits that I browsed in the finest bookshops of any city and picked up contemporary items that brought Scott nearer, including some manuscript letters and a pencil sketch by Watson Gordon. Scott has been damaged as being looked on as a writer for boys, who were, at any rate in my time, forced to read him in school. He is essentially for the middle-aged person who enjoys leisurely reading and who has given up the illusion that it is possible to keep in touch with all that is published. Anyone starting with that humane and heroic book, *The Journals*, will want to get closer to its writer.

But my true passion as a collector has been for Greek antiquities, mainly of terra-cotta with a few Hellenistic marbles by way of luxury. I cannot remember when it started, possibly years ago in Pompeii. I went for a moonlight walk up Vesuvius and, coming down on the Pompeii side, I clambered over the turnstile. It was easy to square the night watchman and I passed three wonderful hours alone in the city, which gave the impression of being asleep like the many villages I had passed through on the way, but soon to waken into busy life. What moved me most of all were the wheel-ruts on the pavements and the rubbed steps with their imprints of feet. As usual I set out to read everything I could get hold of on the subject of classical archaeology. I had seen Greek figurines in the British Museum and the Louvre and had studied Greek vase painting as a subject very close to ballet, so close in fact that I have always had an intense dislike for what is today called the Greek dance. The sight of a monster demonstration of Greek-clad business girls prancing round the Albert Hall found me struggling between hysterical laughter and indignation. I had never realized that it was possible for a small collector to own such works and that they would cost far less than the scribble of some publicized contemporary painter. Chance led me to a well-known dealer and I began to fill a shelf with the delicate works of the inspired toy-makers, votive offerings, scent bottles, dolls.

'Zeus caused a russet cloud to draw nigh to them and rained on them abundant gold, while grey-eyed Athene herself bestowed upon them every art, so that they surpassed all mortal men by their deftness of hand, and along the roads rose works of art like unto beings that lived and moved; and great was their fame.'

Most of my pieces came from well-known collections and had been exhibited in museums so that I came to have the feel for the genuine, something unmistakable, though it cannot always be justified in words. The faker nearly always overdoes things. If, as every collector, I have a few fakes, no matter, they are still imbued with the Greek spirit. My Greek shelves give me a perpetual ballet and I spend many restful hours playing with these enchanting toys. Apart from their intrinsic beauty there is the sentimental attraction that is relevant to all collections from first editions upwards—or downwards. An Attic baby grasped this cicada-shaped rattle 2,500 years ago, a Rhodian girl played with this jointed doll, a Macedonian laughed at the snub-nosed dwarf warrior, a Cretan placed the image of this goddess in a shrine, a Boeotian schoolboy is depicted in the small squatting figure with its conical yellow headdress, the bronze lamp with its masks of comedy and tragedy served to light a theatre of the Roman Empire.

In teaching classical history I have shown some of these objects to my children and believe that it has given them the same direct contact that it has given me, the feeling that these were people like ourselves, actuated by the same motives of pain and pleasure but with a far keener artistic perception. The rattle and the doll are living history, objects that can give even to dates, rulers and battles, a new meaning.

Apart from the work of the choroplasts, I have a few model figures of serene and subtle beauty that quiver into life in the candlelight by which classical marble is best enjoyed. One, a faun, bears an extraordinary resemblance to Nijinsky. They are at home with my Maillol, my Dalous, my Epsteins, and my most treasured modern possession, a Carpeaux study in bronze for *La Danse* on the façade of the Paris Opéra. The only item that I have in my house directly associated with the dance is also a strong sentimental link with the earliest of all the ballet academies and with the modern Athens.

Not only can periods of art be mixed, they should be mixed if the home is to be personal and not a museum. Lately I have been collecting Egyptian antiquities with enormous zest. They are complementary to the Greek and satisfy another mood.

The pre-dynastic alabaster or diorite bowls and vases explain another modern artistic slogan, one of those easy clever half-truths of so much contemporary criticism. 'The nature of the material dictates the form of the sculpture.' That is true beyond a doubt, but it is now carried so far as to become an absurdity when a chunk of stone is worked on just sufficiently to give it the appearance of a chunk of stone, another chunk of stone. At its best this complete subservience to the material may give an interesting contrast of surfaces and present a pleasing shape, but then so may the pebble on the beach carved by the action of the wind and the waves. The Egyptian stone-worker with the simplest tools fashioned his diorite, alabaster or breccia into vases of admirable shape making full use of the veining to produce designs of great beauty. These pots are a joy to handle. But they were made to hold oil or other toilet requisites and so well were they made that they can still serve the same purpose after six or seven thousand years. The point is that they were very properly rated as a craft. While great sculptors in every age respect their material, no great sculptor allows it to dominate him.

The danger with the teaching of art appreciation these days

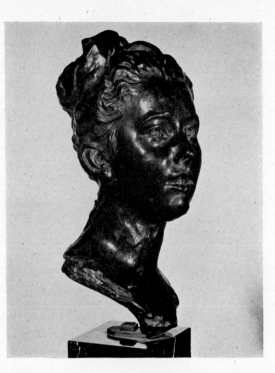

Candeur, by Jules Dalou

Some Egyptian Pots
COLLECTING

is that it starts with Van Gogh instead of reaching back into antiquity. The Van Gogh Exhibition drew a queue that Metro-Goldwyn-Mayer must have envied while the much more important exhibition of French landscape painting could be seen in comfort.

This is not the diversion from collecting that it may appear to be. One of the great joys of collecting is that one's objects are so magnificently alive. One small bronze may prove so disturbing that it makes one attempt to reassess a period, causing one to tramp the British Museum and to read dozens of volumes. My objects have made me turn to the classics with fervour and also with a deep regret of wasted Westminster periods when a sound grounding was mine for the asking. They have given me a definite point of view as a teacher of young children and the desire, if not the ability, to bring a remote period to life.

And what fun it is; the hours spent with my friend R. E. A. Wilson, the best kind of dealer, he collects himself, the swaps and bargains over a good glass of wine. Since I wrote the above he has turned me in a gothic direction.

I have never collected for sentiment alone. The ballet *maquettes*, photographs, prints, programmes and play-bills that I have acquired over the years are filed away for reference. Such things as letters and relics I have given to dancers for whom they have a special meaning, and to whom they can be a direct inspiration as they never could be to me. I have kept, however, in a special drawer the manuscripts of Karsavina's *Theatre Street* and de Valois' *Invitation to the Ballet*, the most important books on ballet of our time. These are gifts I value.

Collecting has been a joy and in spite of my wife's vague hostility to my 'cluttering up the house,' I shall remain an impenitent collector. I rejoice that my sons share my passion and my taste.

CHAPTER FIFTEEN

Four Dancers: A Record of Friendship

I

I HAVE lived constantly among dancers, first travelling as a colleague in a company and then as a friend, teacher and adviser. In spite of my criticism I have never had a major quarrel with any of them. With a few I have enjoyed an uninterrupted friendship of many years' duration. I have, also, never fallen in love with a dancer or even had a narrow escape; for which blessing I am grateful. I have already written of my friendship with the 'seniors' who gave me my education in ballet and who shaped the art as we know it today. Here I want to write of four friendships that I value. On looking through my press-cutting books I find that I have been particularly outspoken about these four dancers, commenting on occasions on the 'frigidity' of Markova, the 'lack of simplicity' of Toumanova, the 'over-eager clumsiness' of Skorik, and the 'unmusicality' of Lifar. This has never altered our relationship. To quote Lifar, '*Quand on est ami on peut s'engueler. Viens boire un coup.*'

Obviously had I not respected and admired their work as a whole there could have been no basis for our friendship. The very qualities one admires in the artist one likes in the friend; artist and private person are one in so direct an art as the classic dance.

I have written in *Balletomania* of my early friendship with Alicia Marks, Markova-to-be, which led directly to my close association with the world of ballet. I have always looked upon Alicia as of the family and she and her three sisters are very dear to me; moreover we have too many memories in common ever to drift apart. I can see Alicia now, sitting at lunch at Queen's Gate, trying to choose a *nom de theatre* and insisting that whatever happened it must begin with an M, so that she could use a little dressing-bag she had just been given with the letters A. M. I can see her dancing the *Sylvia* pizzicato at my twenty-first birthday party, or walking along the backs at Cambridge. I can see her at the children's parties I gave for the four sisters, always choosing the least conspicuous part in any game or charade. No one could have been less of a theatre child. Each one of these 'little women' had a clearly defined character. They were and have remained devoted to one another. The sisters admired Alicia intensely, but they did not flatter her or defer to her because she was going to be a star. They do not now, when she is the most popular ballerina of the day. This happy family atmosphere they owe to their mother, one of those exceptionally rare dancers' mothers who made it her duty to provide a calm and restful background, and who never under any circumstances interfered in the theatre life. She was left a widow while still a very young woman and in difficult circumstances with four little girls to keep. In a surprisingly short time each girl was contributing to the home; Alicia in the ballet, Doris at the Windmill Theatre, Vivienne in the Civil Service and Bunny first at Sadler's Wells and later in revue. The whole story of the four Marks girls might well read like a rather sentimental late Victorian novel, but however it may appear from a literary point of view the reality is inspiring.

I saw Alicia frequently in the Diaghileff days, in London, Paris and Monte Carlo. It was during her second season that she was left stranded, a truly pathetic figure. Diaghileff had not wanted the responsibility of the care of a child and she had been placed in charge of the devoted governess of the more prosperous days who had refused to leave the family in the lurch. This governess was suddenly taken ill and died. Alicia, who had never travelled alone and who was not used to coping with practical problems, was left in Monte Carlo while the company went on for the Paris season. Then a telegram came from Diaghileff that if she wanted to retain her place in the company she must join them at once. My mother put her on to the Paris express for a journey that she still remembers with horror. She grew up overnight from a timid little girl who only really awoke on the stage to a young woman, naïf it is true, but practical. It happened just in time to allow the artist to develop.

The first rôle created for her was Balanchine's *Le Chant du Rossignol* and later she excelled in *La Chatte*. Balanchine has always had an extraordinary flair for developing young talent. It is funny today, when young dancers especially in the *ballet russe* are so sophisticated, to remember how Alicia reacted to the backstage gossip and happenings, how she accepted a new world of strange ideas without really knowing what it was all about, without either being shocked or particularly interested. Diaghileff was often surprised at her attitude, wondering when 'his little English girl' would begin to react and to show her emotions.

When Diaghileff died Alicia began a new and very difficult career. Ballet was by no means popular and there was no place awaiting her. She danced in variety houses for a good fee and in her beloved ballet for a pittance; for the Camargo Society, the Ballet Club and at Sadler's Wells. She played a very large rôle in shaping our ballet, making the classical revivals possible and assisting our young choreographers by her experience as a dancer. She succeeded so well in her new career that after six years she headed her own company, touring all over England. To thousands in the provinces ballet meant the Markova-Dolin company.

Naturally I was pleased at this success, pleased yet puzzled. This star was not the Markova that Diaghileff had expected. She was light, and to the great public lightness is everything, she was precise, but she was totally lacking in the ability to

'The Little Women' when I first met them
Alicia—Doris—Vivienne—Bunny

And today—New Year 1949–50
Vivienne—Doris—Alicia—Bunny

MARKOVA AND HER SISTERS

portray the emotions and also in the really grand manner. To me she was lost somewhere between the artless child and the consciously artistic woman. They acclaimed her as a great ballerina. I could not agree, nor could I conceal my feelings from someone so close to me. It made no difference in her attitude or in that of her family, but it did embarrass me. I wanted so very much to applaud with the crowd.

There was one particular occasion when I had been the only critic to give her a poor notice as Columbine in *Carnaval*, and the fans outside the theatre booed and made half-hearted attempts to throw things. The tension was relieved by a superb cockney voice yelling out, 'Leave the poor b—— alone. 'E can't 'elp it. 'E's in love with Lilian Baylis.' Baylis was delighted with the story when I told it at a public dinner given in her honour.

In 1939 with the ending of her own company Alicia began a third career, her first contact with the post-Diaghileff *ballet russe*. Here she had to compete on equal terms with such dancers as Danilova, Toumanova and Slavenska, to fight for the limelight in a way that she had not known before. I only saw the beginning of this career. She left for America and the war separated us. I heard of her American triumphs and took them with a grain of salt. The Markova they were describing was so very different from the one I knew.

She returned to Covent Garden as guest artist and danced with a new maturity, but it was in 1949 when she danced with Dolin in that great barn of a place, the Empress Hall, in surroundings quite unsuited to a subtle and delicate art, that I received my great surprise. I entered to the hoarse cry of 'Programme,' the cry of vendors used to a noisy sporting crowd, and it echoed round the hall. A garden had been planted over the ice of the vast stadium, an oh-so-green lawn with flower beds, pergolas and rustic benches straight from a banker's Weybridge home. In the middle there was a tiny wooden stage, flush with the ground. In fact it was not tiny at all, it was about the size of Covent Garden stage, only measurements have no meaning at all in such surroundings. After an overture unevenly relayed, some pupils performed under glaring lights, confirming my worst fears for the evening. And then Markova appeared, and brought about that rare thing, a 'theatrical miracle.' The phrase is Benois' and he used it to describe Pavlova's transmutation of base material into pure gold. This was no longer a synthetic garden covering an ice rink, but a vast setting for a superb artist who could dominate the scene and make it disappear into a misty background. This is not, thank God, a volume of criticism, but a book of reminiscences where the writer can glory in being personal and subjective. For me the pleasure that evening was threefold; I was watching a superb artist, I could go to her dressing-room for the first time since Monte Carlo and say 'thank you' and tell her how moved I had been, and, more than anything else, Alicia had at last kept faith with Diaghileff, his 'little English girl' had grown up, the dancer had become an artist. I am glad that her mother was still alive to hear my enthusiasm. She understood so well exactly what I was feeling. What a wonderful mother she was!

The triumphs she has enjoyed have not altered Alicia in the slightest degree. She is still a trifle shy and reserved, still conscientious and precise, thoughtful of others and at her happiest when she can relax with her sisters and her old friends. She is practical and travels round the world by air with none of the fears that marked that first memorable journey from Monte Carlo to Paris. Glamour and temperament are reserved for the stage and I know of no other artist of comparable fame, save Margot Fonteyn, who has such dignity. In her long and difficult career there has never been a single backstage incident.

II

When I think of those early days in Astafieva's studio I am amazed that none of us ever doubted that Alicia Marks and Pat

Kay were potentially great dancers with a glorious career ahead
of them. We had absolutely no grounds to go upon since ballet
was not the spectacular career it is today and English dancers
had scarcely ever risen to the heights. But we all took it for
granted that Pat and little Alicia would become world-famed.
They danced together even in those studio days and he was
always perfectly charming with her, a critical elder brother:
'That child should have been in bed hours ago.'

Pat also has altered but little from the evening he first took
the name Anton Dolin, the hectic evening of the optimistic
Astafieva's pupil show, held at the Albert Hall of all places.
There have always been two Pats; the first a highly critical
artist of great intelligence and charm, the second a popular
music hall artist also of great intelligence and charm. Each is
well worth knowing so long as they do not meet together on
the stage but keep *ménage apart*. Anton Dolin, the critical, has
an altogether extraordinary appreciation and understanding
of the art of the ballerina whom he handles as no one else. I
am convinced that without him Alicia would never have
reached her present position. He was a very considerable
dancer, he remains a partner of genius and that is a rôle that
requires a sensitivity that seems altogether impossible when one
watches him bring the house down with *Bolero* or *Hymn to the
Sun*; not that these are not, in their own grim way, tremendously effective pieces of theatre. I believe that while he is
dancing them he is entirely sincere. He gives the public what
it evokes from him; Dolin at Covent Garden and the Empress
Hall were two different people; only Dolin the partner
remained the same.

One may at times disapprove violently of Pat: it is very
difficult not to like him. He has in the first place a delightful
sense of humour and then he is no hypocrite. After a performance of *Bolero* in which he brought the house down:
'Well, Arnold, it's unfortunate, but after all the years you've
spent educating the public they still like it. What can we do

about it? I give them up as hopeless.' Much as you dislike *Bolero*, you cannot help liking the man who can greet you in that way.

Where Pat has a genius is in turning on his very Irish charm. He is able to give the impression, whenever he runs into you, that you are the very person in the whole world he most wishes to meet. And it is probably sincere, at any rate for the ten minutes or so that it lasts. I have so many happy memories of our early days and so keen an appreciation of his intelligence that, whatever his feelings, I never meet him without pleasure; even so I wish he would not dance *Bolero*. I do not like to be embarrassed by an old friend, the memories of whose Blue Bird and *Beau Gosse* I treasure.

III

Another of my closest friendships has been with a dancer I first met as a little girl, Tamara Toumanova. It was Trefilova who first turned my thoughts to the serious study of ballet, Markova who brought me into close contact with Diaghileff and the ballet world, and Toumanova who, as I have already related in my chapter on de Basil, turned me from criticism to practical work with a company.

I first saw her at the Trocadéro, Paris, in 1925 when, as a pupil of Preobrajenska's, she took part in a performance with Pavlova. I cannot claim to have discovered the talent in this five-year-old, but I remember the occasion in detail because she was handed over the footlights and given a box of choco- lates that was almost her own size. My attitude, judging from what I would feel at the present day, was most certainly one of irritation at the sentimentality that had prompted the inci- dent. I had come to see Pavlova dance and anything else that happened was, as always, an unwelcome intrusion. I would have been prepared, probably, to take on a bet with anyone that the pretty child with the big bow would never be heard of again.

I first saw Tamara as an apprentice artist at the Savoy Theatre in *Les Ballets 1933*, a short time before de Basil came to the Alhambra. In Balanchine's creations, *Songes* and *Mozartiana*, she moved me more deeply than any dancer since Karsavina, Trefilova or Pavlova. I had taken it for granted that Russian Ballet had died with Diaghileff and, though I was very active and in a practical manner with our English effort, I was too blind and had, as yet, little real faith in its future. Here was a beautiful, though a very plump, fourteen-year-old who had already inherited the traditions of the Russian school, traditions that were fast dying even before the death of the inspired *animateur* himself. Her appearance foreshadowed the brief and brilliant renaissance, the St. Martin's summer of *ballet russe*. In London, May 1933, Toumanova was the Russian Ballet, the forerunner of its final glorious phase. Today she is one of its sole survivors; a *prima ballerina assoluta*, but without the ballet or the artistic direction. Before the applause had died down on the *première* at the Savoy I ran backstage to meet this child who had given me such pleasure and such hope. And after that I saw her daily, both in the theatre and the squalid 'digs' that she was then able to afford. Often she came to our house and found refuge in the nursery from the problems of a ballerina's life. At five o'clock she would be playing with a doll's house or a toy train, at nine o'clock bowing to an enthusiastic public after a ballet in which she had impersonated a child. She was equally at home in both rôles. I was interested to learn the other day that when I took her to visit a great physician, an intimate friend of mine, he had written on her case sheet 'An admirably balanced person.' He had summed her up to perfection, if being balanced means following a career with a blind devotion and excluding anything that might interfere.

The *Ballets 1933* soon ceased its efforts after an exciting start, and when de Basil came to the Alhambra on July 4th of that year and began Russian Ballet's brief renaissance it was without

Tamara. I received sad little letters from her in Paris. She never had the slightest doubt that I could and would arrange things. My immediate task, therefore, was to convince de Basil and everyone else that his company was incomplete without Tamara. I succeeded: it was too obvious to be difficult. And so began my close association with a company that took me on three long voyages.

This active association with the de Basil company had, in time, the effect of withdrawing me a little from Tamara though it could not alter my affection for her. There were many others, especially the enchanting Baronova, the most versatile and naturally talented dancer I have seen, and who only lacked the intense concentration needed to last the pace. In many of the rôles which she shared with Tamara she excelled her and I did not hesitate to say so. Irina and I have always been the greatest of friends. They were rivals who respected one another, watched one another closely, but had little in common. I had to choose whether to remain so closely identified with Tamara's career that I would become *malgré moi* a ballet parent and so lose not only all my influence, but eventually my self-respect and my love for ballet itself. Also—and this is important—knowing her as I did, I always expected more from her than from anyone else—I still do; and I criticized her severely at times. Such a friendship could only be based on a completely honest attitude. In truth, nothing could ever have separated me from Tamara and she always knew it. I was closely associated with the beginnings of her career, she with mine. We brought one another luck.

Her friendship is infinitely precious to me. I love her as one loves a member of one's own family. I felt really happy the day that I met her husband and knew beyond a doubt that he was the right man and that my friendship could be extended to him. I feel proud when she does something brilliant, though it is in no sense my doing; sad when she does not excel. If she stopped dancing tomorrow—provided she were happy—it

In Paris when I first knew her

In her Hollywood home with Mama

TAMARA TOUMANOVA

would not pain me. The person is more important than the artist. I coined the phrase, 'the black pearl of the Russian Ballet,' that was so much used when she made her American début, but it is not her glamour that attracts me. By now I am glamour-proof. It is herself, the real Tamara I know so well in every mood from wild indignation at a slight only sometimes real, generally imagined, to a bout of schoolgirl giggling. And I know from experience that whatever I said to her or wrote about her it would always be the same. However far apart, and we are both bad correspondents, there is this tremendous bond that is a part of ourselves.

But to know Tamara it is first of all necessary to know her inseparable companion 'Mama,' a great character and a great woman. 'Mama' Toumanova has the good nature of both Cheeryble brothers, far-fetched though those characters may seem, but she can be transformed into a tigress and a man-eater at that if she imagines that anyone is ill-disposed towards Tamara, and she has a vivid imagination. She is of a dramatic disposition so that even the most ordinary conversation is apt to sound like a violently explosive quarrel to anyone not knowing the language or the form. She is apt, too, at times to see a slight where there is merely indifference, and then her imagination is worthy of a Dumas and unsettling to Tamara. She has accompanied Tamara to the theatre every day of her life save once for a fortnight in 1934 when she was seriously ill. Then Tamara was committed to my care and had to be brought daily to her mother's bedside to have her hair done. This was always a dramatic occasion as Tamara yelled 'Mama, you hurt, you've got it in a tangle,' and mother retorted 'Nonsense,' and went on combing. 'Mama' might very easily have become the most dangerous of all stage mothers, were it not for the fact that in her way she is as great an artist as Tamara. Tamara and her mother are one; as she dances on the stage Mama follows anxiously from the wings, noticing every detail and criticizing where necessary. And however loud

the trumpet may blow in public—and it can blow embarrassingly loudly—in the privacy of the dressing-room her detailed
criticism is of the greatest value and is not blinded by her love.

Mama's doings were always the talk of the company—they
always will be. During the first American tour she developed
a formidable reputation as a poker player. The boys, especially
the Poles, used to gamble half the night in the ladies' dressing-
room. One night they could not make up a game so they asked
Mama to play. 'I can't play poker; I've never played before.'
'That doesn't matter,' they told her, 'it's quite easy, we'll soon
teach you.' Tamara, with visions of being stranded, made a
dramatic protest but Mama went. She returned early next
morning with all the boys' salaries in her pocket and, at the
next stop, Tamara received a new summer outfit. 'Beginner's
luck. You must give us our revenge.' Next pay-day came along
and again Mama won all their salaries. For their next session
they were careful to wait until she was safely in bed, and only
then did they creep out one by one. 'What, are you so mean
as to play poker without me? I'm coming, I just feel like a
game.' This time she won all their available money and some
I.O.U.s as well. They were desperate. How on earth could
they keep her out of the game? By now Tamara had a smart
fur cape. Then one of them hit on a bright idea. 'It's very hot,'
he told Mama, 'and we're all going to play naked, with no
clothes on. Do you understand? So that it wouldn't be proper
for you to come.' 'Not at all,' replied Mama, 'I shall put on
dark glasses,' and she followed them into the washroom.

The result of this close association with her mother is that
Tamara has remained completely childlike. Successful, wealthy
and happily married to someone who understands her to perfection, she has not altered in essentials from the small girl I
met in the dressing-room at the Savoy. Living in Hollywood,
courted and flattered, she has not gone 'Hollywood,' on the
the contrary she has reacted strongly against it.

And, if she is childlike, she is in no sense childish. She has courage, determination and a mind of her own. When Serge Lifar made his return to America in 1948 and so many dancers picketed the theatre, mainly from motives of jealousy thinly disguised as political idealism, it was the normally aloof Toumanova who, at considerable risk to her career, constituted herself his champion. Although she had come across him but little in her career she respected the artist and knew the man himself incapable of baseness. He has told me what this moral support meant to him at the time.

I have not yet mentioned Tamara's father, a scholarly and singularly retiring man. He has, however, played a great rôle in her career. It is obvious that with dancing as a major pre-occupation from the age of eight, Tamara's general education was bound to suffer neglect. Apart from the difficulties of keeping alive, and the sacrifices involved, it was her father's chief worry that he would have an illiterate daughter. As soon as she had earned sufficient money he called a halt for a year, resisting every offer, and Tamara was provided with tutors and made to work as hard at her lessons as she had ever done at the *barre*. I believe that this saved her career in the dangerous period when the instinct of a child prodigy must be replaced by the reason of the adult artist.

Tamara has come at the wrong period in ballet for the full development of her extraordinary gifts. She started with an admirable repertoire based on her personality: *Mozartiana, Songes, Cotillon, Concurrence.* Balanchine, her real discoverer, made the most not only of her technique but of her fine sensibility. Rôle and dancer met completely. Then she took over works from the standard repertoire, both the classics and the Diaghileff ballets. Her performances were curiously uneven, sometimes outstanding but often marred by intense unrestrained eagerness for self-expression, by over-dramatization. Also, at this period of transition into womanhood she was always handicapped by quick changes from excessive weight to slimness and a lack of strength. Nor did she always find the right make-up for her great beauty, over-dramatizing herself in front of the mirror as she did on the stage. The end of the renaissance of *ballet russe* was not propitious to an artist of such extreme sensibility who needed the careful guidance of a *maître de ballet*. Yet if one followed her throughout a season, one performance in five brought complete perfection. For this reason it was rare that amateurs discussed the same Toumanova. She has but rarely tried out tricks for effects of showmanship; everything has usually come from within. The mannerisms of 1938–39 were all due to a lack of restraint through an excess of temperament. She is a baroque artist.

I feared that a long residence in America would accentuate those mannerisms and would give the metallic brilliance of the American school. Not at all. It has given her the dazzling virtuoso technique so appreciated by American audiences, but also, when she wishes, the dignity that is her heritage as a Russian ballerina. She can make the *Don Quixote pas de deux* not merely tolerable but exciting, because the technique has style and complete finish and because she uses it to express a mood. Only in *Giselle* is she given the opportunity today to show herself complete and, to me, from the moment that she is conscious of Albrecht's betrayal, her Giselle sets a standard both in interpretation and technique. Only in the opening scene does it lack the simplicity that Giselle must have had to feel her betrayal so deeply. From the many Giselle's I have seen I am convinced that this first mood is the most difficult of all to convey; Fonteyn and Chauviré reveal it magnificently.

As I write, Tamara is at the Opéra and she will have a hard passage where family feeling is so strong. When she first came there immediately after the war she put a foot wrong by giving some nylons and silk tights to a young dancer who looked poverty-stricken. When Tamara left the building that evening she saw her poor young protégé very much bejewelled stepping into a very smart car.

In any case wherever Tamara is, there will inevitably be the scandals and intrigues of those early de Basil days. They had their rules and conventions, but today in other surroundings it may not proceed with so light a touch. I hope that her art will not suffer, but I have grave doubts. At any rate she has a home and a welcome awaiting her.

IV

Another more recent friendship has been with the Franco-Russian ballerina, Irène Skorik, one of the most interesting and complex personalities that I have met with on the stage, if only because she is so completely different from the usual ballerina. The use of a Christian name, a casual kiss, or a 'darling' do not enter into her mind. She is intensely shy, the French word *farouche* is more explicit, extremely sincere and with an honesty that is so uncompromising that even the ordinary civilities are at times beyond her. When the usual throng of *balletomanes* came round after a performance with the usual run of more or less sincere compliments, Irène was accustomed to lock her door and no amount of banging would make her open it until she had washed and dressed; by which time, of course, the corridor was empty. I write in the past tense because I have finally been able to persuade her that this is impolitic.

It was an accident that led to our friendship and that made it a firm one from the start. Without that accident I could never have penetrated her reserve. I had greatly admired her dancing since I saw the magnificent interpretation of Leda in Petit's *Les Amours de Jupiter* during the first season of *Les Ballets des Champs Elysées*. I was, however, bitterly disappointed when, on the first night of the second season, I saw her dance *La Sylphide*. She appeared completely earthbound; her enchanting half-smile had given place to a frown. After the performance I heard that she had been taken mysteriously ill—at least ten dread maladies were listed, in a company even more given to rumours than the average—and removed to hospital. She was shifted from surgical to medical ward as the doctors shifted their diagnosis. The terrifying thing, for a dancer of all people, was the paralysis that affected almost her whole body. I knew that, with a company in active rehearsal, she might be lonely and I rang up the hospital for permission to visit her. Strangely enough I had diagnosed her illness, botulism, from the very start, having seen a case many years ago when Alicia Markova's sister, Vivienne, was similarly affected. I told one of the doctors on the day that it was officially diagnosed. I wish that I had not been so diffident and had spoken earlier.

I found Irène in a pathetic state, with a deep almost ventri-loquial voice and staring eyes. Fortunately she did not realize the gravity of her state and was only relieved to learn that she was not going to have an operation. She was reading the poems of Victor Hugo, held with great difficulty at arm's length. She croaked a series of questions about the performances, and who was doing her rôles. I visited her at intervals, noting at each visit a great improvement, and she soon came off the danger list. Her one wish now was to dance again, and even the sub-stantial damages that she won from the restaurant that had served the tinned macaroni cheese, that killed the customer who had shared it, was no consolation for her enforced rest.

She shares with Toumanova and Jeanmaire the distinction of being the hardest worker in this hard-working profession. Under no circumstances will she miss a class and, with her, the class is prolonged until it almost merges into the per-formance.

Skorik is perfectly formed as a classical ballerina with the most beautiful legs in ballet. She belongs to the *terre à terre* school rather than to the aerial dancers. She has the strong and very positive personality that goes with such dancing and intense concentration. Some people find her cold. With this I cannot agree. She is never obvious and her strong temperament is kept under firm control. As with Toumanova, when that control is removed she overplays, always a tendency with the

Slav dancer. While a powerful and complete technique allows her to perform the virtuoso fireworks of the *Black Swan* and to do so better than most, it hides the essentially romantic-dramatic side of her nature, leading at times to an over-emphasis that stops the flow of her line. She is, however, essentially musical in a manner rare in the ballerina; emotion and knowledge are combined. Especially attractive is her smile, which that subtle critic, Gautier, realized was so very much a part of the dance. At times Skorik seems to smile because of the sheer physical pleasure of movement. It is not your stagecraft semi-grin tossed to the audience in hopes of repayment, but the smile of someone who has just had a pleasing thought of a memory or a project, and who is unconscious that she is being overlooked. It hovers round her eyes and lips and is gone. Sometimes, as in *La Sylphide* and *La Nuit*, it is a sad smile as if at the memory of something that has vanished. Then one can feel that she is close to tears, the tears of the romantic Keepsake lady that moisten and brighten the eyes, then drop like pearls, but that never under any circumstances redden the nose. Skorik is essentially a romantic closely identifying herself with her romantic heroines, the Devil's bride and others. It is not mere chance that she chose to read Hugo when so desperately ill. But where I admire her especially is from a purely subjective point of view. When she is dancing I never feel bored, my attention never wanders however well I may know the work. Here let me make the point once again; it is not because I like a dancer off-stage that I admire her work, but because I admire her work that I like the dancer and, indeed, in this case as in every other it was my reason for getting to know her. To the watcher of experience no longer dazzled by novelty or technique, the character of the dancer lies revealed in her dancing so long as this is classical and not concealed under the mask of a very positive dramatic rôle. One can learn more of character in the two or three minutes of a variation and *adage* than in many months of close friendship. That is not the least of the fascinations of classical ballet. And for that reason, granted that the dancer has the amount of technique needful, criticism of dancing as apart from the rest of ballet can only be subjective and the words 'the best' have no universal meaning.

One of the most interesting series of performances I have seen were those of *La Sylphide* at the Prince's Theatre in September 1949. The principal rôle was danced at *à tour de rôle* by Irène Skorik and Nina Wyroubova. The critic of the *Observer*, Richard Buckle, a writer of great taste, head and shoulders above the rest of the new school of critics both in knowledge and sensibility, summed up by stating that Skorik was good but Wyroubova great. A very positive statement and one easy to defend, but unfortunately there was no space for amplification. Wyroubova, a magnificent dancer, was lighter and more ethereal, a very strong point in a sylph ballet. Her resemblance to the Taglioni lithographs was amazing and gave this romantic period an extraordinary feeling of nostalgia. Certainly a great and memorable performance by any standard. It gave her a London reputation overnight. Skorik was more *terre à terre* though equally fluid, and certainly the line of her arms and wrists was more perfect. Where she excelled, however, was in bringing home the tragedy of the being who could not live and love as a mortal. Her mime was superb and well within the romantic classical framework. Never did the Skorik smile serve to finer purpose.

That, too, was a great performance by any standard. It happened to move me far more deeply and its detail remains more vividly in my memory. I have always felt that Elssler, *ce volcan adouci*, rather than Taglioni would have been my dancer.

One day some choreographer may bring out what there is in Irène and I think the result will be astonishing. Meanwhile I am grateful for the many hours of pleasure I have had in watching her and for the friendship of someone who gives it with such difficulty.

V

'*Lifar*. He is larger than life; the complete artist though some-times without judgment or taste, a discoverer and inspirer of talent without an equal, generous and expansive as only a Russian can be, vain as Vestris, yet able to recognize the fact and on occasion to laugh at it, does not bear a grudge even to his worst enemy and is the least malicious of people. Certain, because of the self-dramatization in his character, to be the centre of distressing incidents. Is the hardest worker I have met, forgets to eat, shave, sleep when there is a job on hand, but is in no sense an ascetic since he has the Parisian's love of good wine and good cooking. Quite impossible to know him really well and not to like him really well, apart from any feeling of approval or disapproval.'

I leave these notes as I find them in my diary. I will elaborate them, and with a greater sense of freedom than in writing of any other contemporary, since Serge, partly through his colossal self-confidence, partly through a happy-go-lucky attitude that does not dwell on criticism or nurse imagined slights, could not resent the frank estimate of an old friend. I find the subject an interesting one and the record worth the making. Only those who do not know Lifar have spread malicious stories about him, many of which have stuck. Those who know him really well cannot fail, even while recognizing his faults and his overwhelming egoism, to like him really well.

In a sense we learnt our *métier* together, always a strong link. I have followed him through all the periods of his extra-ordinary career; first as raw material in the hands of Diaghileff, next as the idol of Paris, enjoying a popularity that even Nijinsky did not know; then through the downfall caused by jealousy, hatred and his own indiscretions that not only nearly brought about the end of his career, but that might have cost him his life; and back again, in an amazingly short time, to his old popularity through the full realization of his artistic worth by a highly sophisticated society that is notoriously fickle and critical of its artists. Thirty years of fame with a touch of notoriety by way of spice, thirty years of creation, some of it truly inspired.

I first saw Lifar at Astafieva's studio, The Pheasantry, in King's Road. It was at the memorable party given to celebrate little Alicia's joining the company, all of whom had been invited. Diaghileff was fond of 'Sima' who had been a member of the company for many years. There were few strangers present and the atmosphere was the congenial one of a children's party, so often the case with a large group of Russians, however sophisticated. Alicia danced for her frightening audience, Pat Dolin, I remember, did some amazing acrobatic feats of the type that made him famous in *Le Train Bleu*; he was in evening dress and retained a completely unruffled appearance throughout. Then someone, it may have been Grigorieff, drew my attention to a small group of boys laughing and ragging in a corner of the room. 'You see that very young, very slim dark boy, *cette petite panthère noire*? He's recently joined us from Russia. He's raw but what wonderful material and what talent.' 'His name?' 'Serge Lifar.' I had already noticed him and was interested. In the Diaghileff Ballet people did not talk of discoveries *à la légère*. We were some way off the period of stars and seasonal prodigies.

A few months later I was in Monte Carlo for the début of Alicia. Anton Dolin was the undisputed *premier danseur*, dancing superbly both in the creations and *l'Oiseau Bleu*. It was he who next drew my attention to Serge Lifar. Pat has always had a generous and extremely objective attitude in assessing a dancer. Lifar was now being groomed for his first important creation and the grooming was intensive. Dancers are used to long hours, but I have never seen the equal of this. Classes, long private lessons with Cecchetti, rehearsals, and performances. As usual with Diaghileff the mental training was not neglected. Lifar made his first contacts with Picasso,

Braque, Matisse, Benois, Stravinsky and the various writers and poets surrounding Maecenas. It was a hot-house atmosphere that would have destroyed nine out of ten. There was a close parallel between the eighteen-year-old Serge and those heroes of the romantic ballet he loves so well, whom the *wilis* made dance to their doom.

His first rôle of note was as the shopkeeper's assistant in *La Boutique Fantasque*, with Cecchetti as the shopkeeper; superb casting. Diaghileff was a happy man that season, with the makings of a brilliant company after the lean years of his enforced separation from Russia. Alice Nikitina and Alexandra Danilova were beginning to emerge as *solistes*. Nikitina had the most extraordinary angular charm and an elegance that made her particularly suited to the modern Parisian-inspired ballets. With the serenely classical Danilova and Lifar they formed a perfect *pas de trois*, a choreographer's inspiration.

Serge's first creation was to be *Zéphyre et Flore* with music by Vladimir Dukelsky, later famous as Vernon Dukes; *décor* by Braque and choreography by Massine who had rejoined the company. I followed all the rehearsals closely and there could be no doubt about the hit that Lifar would make in what was not a very interesting ballet. The whole rôle had been built to show him to maximum advantage. It was a personal ballet, an act of faith on Diaghileff's part.

Then came the eagerly awaited dress rehearsal, a long drawn out affair in which Lifar did not spare himself; he always worked full out. The accident itself was unspectacular. One moment he was dancing, a second later he lay crumpled on the floor in agony. Confusion, hustle and curtain-fall.

He himself has described the suffering of the next few weeks, the doubts and anxieties, the dreadful possibility that this might mean the end of a career scarcely begun. The accident was ultimately to his benefit. It gave him time to reflect and digest all the experiences he had undergone since the lean and hungry boy had left his native Russia, and turned up as an unwanted and unexpected fifth member of the party of new dancers with the two Hoyers, Efimoff and Unger.

When I next saw Lifar one could no more speak of raw material. Both on and off the stage the impulsive, almost aggressive eagerness had been replaced by ease and self-confidence. *Zéphyre et Flore* was a failure but Lifar emerged triumphantly in *Les Matelots*, *The Triumph of Neptune*, *Apollon Musagète* and finally *Le Fils Prodigue*. He was beginning to excel in the classics. I remember one remarkable performance in *Swan Lake*, not merely because of the mishap that occurred but because it was the first sight of the fine classical dancer that he was to become. It was at the Lyceum. He had been prac-tising leaps backstage and had hit his head on an iron staircase. He only noticed the effect when at curtain-fall he took repeated calls and the blood trickled from under his wig.

His own greatest memory of those days was dancing with La Karsavina, a legendary figure to him, in Constant Lambert's *Romeo and Juliet*. He often talks about it with all the old excitement. She saw the quality of the youth she called 'the little black cat,' and recognized that same singleness of purpose of the heroic days. She treated him as a fellow artist, gave him the accolade and he was completely happy. Once as a gesture of encouragement she sent him a bunch of red roses, and there was a memorable scene with Diaghileff. Lately I brought Lifar to see her after an interval of nineteen years and those days were lived again, and Serge was once more the unknown aspirant, so excited that he nearly fell up the stairs.

During these last Diaghileff seasons people began to like the man for his own sake, and in Paris especially he made a circle of devoted friends.

Diaghileff had just started him as a choreographer with the curious *Le Renard* when he died, and to many it seemed as if ballet had died with him. Lifar's grief was intense and to this day he pays a yearly pilgrimage to Diaghileff's tomb. He and Boris Kochno were present at Diaghileff's death-bed and were the heirs. It is a tragedy for ballet that they have been estranged and have played their great creative rôles apart.

Cochran brought the small group together in one of his revues, giving us a memory of what had been lost. Then, by the same type of good fortune that had first taken Serge to Western Europe, he was engaged by the Paris Opéra to dance and to mount a ballet, *Les Créatures de Promethée*, for which Balanchine had been originally engaged but had to forgo through illness.

The Opéra had been dormant for years, strangled by administrative red tape, and a sterile academism that made its always competent dancers faintly ridiculous to anyone brought up on the Diaghileff formula. It was both dowdy and provincial, reactionary in attitude and inclined to chauvinism. Lifar immediately brought the smart public with him, gathered round him the Diaghileff entourage and made his first sensational success. The impact of his first ballet was tremendous, 'like a wolf in the sheepfold,' to quote Levinson. His future was now assured. The significant thing is that, at the most ancient of all academies, he turned from the last phase of Diaghileff modernism to a living classicism, carrying with him both the Opéra academics and '*les snobs*,' eager for any novelty. That is the key to Lifar's work in France. The first signs of it were his revival of *Divertissement* (*Aurora's Wedding*), his dancing with Spessivtseva in *Giselle* in which the rôle of Albrecht became of equal importance with that of Giselle, his *Spectre de la Rose* and *Chopiniana*.

I am not concerned with criticism in this chapter, only with the character and development of the man himself. It is certain, however, that after the Diaghileff era no one outside Paris has ever seen him dance even nearly at his best, nor have they seen his works adequately presented. In England he has always danced with a flamboyant ostentation as if he were trying to impose his personality in a violent hurry, which probably was the case. In Paris he felt that he was loved and knew himself to be surrounded by dancers whom he was forming, and to whom his very word was law. When he danced the Blue Bird at the Savoy Theatre in London in 1933 it was difficult for me to recognize the very great dancer I had seen in Paris the month before. Nearly all the Opéra dancers suffer a similar eclipse when they leave the most flattering of all settings.

I visited Paris frequently at that time and never failed to spend a day with Serge, talking, watching him at work and seeing his many *premières*. It would be difficult to describe his popularity since there are no real comparisons. To mention the usual film star would make a totally false impression. He was certainly a household word with the masses, as no dancer since Nijinsky and Pavlova, but it was especially with the smart public and the intellectuals that he shone. Within five years Serge had become an institution. He might well have made the remark attributed to Vestris when a lady trod on his toe: 'Madame, never mind about the hurt to me, but Paris will be in mourning for a fortnight.' Indeed, I can hear him make a remark of this kind. He was petted, flattered and considered above criticism. The finest writer on ballet since Gautier, André Levinson, a man singularly independent, who almost alone had attacked the last manifestations of Diaghileff, devoted his last volume to an appreciation of Lifar and hailed him as a genius.

I always found him eager to welcome a friend of the old days with open arms. He was exuberant and enthusiastic about himself, his work, his dancers. Conceit would be the wrong word about anything so fundamental. He was not boosting himself because he felt insecure or because he wanted to impress me. It was not in any sense an act; or more correctly it was a permanent self-dramatization. Yet he had a sense of humour and he was really humble in his attitude towards the art itself, and the ancient academy over which he presided. With Kchesinska, glory of the old régime in Russia, he behaved quite naturally like an admiring schoolboy though she, equally naturally, treated him as a distinguished colleague. One of my most treasured memories is when they danced a mazurka for me, making the small studio into a courtly ballroom. He lived quietly and spent most of his money on others, namely members of the emigré colony. This was done without the slightest ostentation and he never so much as hinted at it. He was always highly conscious of being a Russian and never adopted French ways.

As he talked I could have wished that he had left me something nice to say about his impressive achievement. He never did. 'When I was going to Brazil,' he said, 'I was standing on deck when we entered Rio and I saw that everyone on the quayside was kneeling. I was deeply moved at the appreciation these far off people had for art and was actually a little embarrassed. Then I happened to turn round and I saw Cardinal Verdier, my fellow traveller, with his hand raised in a blessing.' A malicious story, but he told it himself with relish. On that same voyage the great Cardinal made friends with Lifar, whom he had naturally never seen in the theatre, and asked him to put on a special performance. The result was an enduring friendship and a photograph 'from a Prince of the Church to a Prince of the Dance.'

It was during these years when Russian Ballet, under de Basil, was enjoying its brief renewal of popularity that Lifar, at the Opéra, did his greatest work, discovering and encouraging young dancers and finding a way of circumventing the civil service hierarchy that reigned. He may have been the most popular figure the dance had known in France, but he still had a hard fight with a tradition that gave to so many of the dancers a powerful protector who would want to know why they had been overlooked in the casting of an important rôle. He was ably seconded by that great director, Rouché, but he possessed a suppleness and a patience that only those who knew him well can credit.

His popularity inevitably led to incidents reported with relish by the press. He had a great gift for the dramatic and many jealousies were aroused.

VI

During the war I naturally lost touch with him, but I continued to hear of his doings in the most lurid fashion. At the time of the liberation even the B.B.C. informed us that the traitor, Lifar, had been or was about to be shot. As soon as communications with Paris were restored I began to receive a considerable number of letters, none from dancers, accusing him of every known type of collaboration. He was in hiding and certainly in considerable danger. I found it impossible to believe in any conscious guilt—I knew his complete political naïveté too well—but I had no particular reason to doubt the facts, and I greatly feared where his vanity might have led him. Also, he loved the old Russia and detested the Bolsheviks with all the hatred of someone who had suffered as a child. In any case it was quite impossible, from any of the accounts, to understand the facts of collaboration where an artist was concerned. He had to dance or sing, to play, paint, or act during the long years of occupation and the more in vogue the more difficult his position. It was easy for the nonentity to pat himself on the back for his position as a resistant. He was lucky that no one asked him to collaborate. True, there were heroes who braved everything for their principles, but how few. I, at any rate, am quite certain that my extreme physical timidity would not have found me amongst them. Today we realize that many of those who resisted the Germans with the greatest courage would have been the despised collaborators had the Russians marched in, and this thought should sober the witch hunters, if they still exist. Only those who denounced and whose very profession should have led them to resist are odious; and yet sometimes how greatly to be pitied.

IRÈNE SKORIK. *La Sylphide*

AT ALEXANDRA PALACE
A. L. H., Irina Baronova, and Serge Lifar

In 1946 *Les Nouveaux Ballets de Monte Carlo* came to the Cambridge Theatre and, after some story about a delayed passport, Serge Lifar came with them. He had been tried and suspended for a year from the Opéra stage. The thing that I wanted the most in the world was not to meet him. I felt that it would be impossible to resume where we had left off, and I was also frightened of being dragged into a limelight that might have jeopardized the work that I was doing. The very first person I met in the Cambridge foyer was Serge Lifar. *'Arnold, après tant d'années. Qu'est ce que tu es devenu?'* He held out his hand, I hesitated and took it. I then retreated as quickly as I could.

He found me in the next interval and drew me aside. 'I saw you were not very eager to greet me and that you had heard all the dreadful things. You have known me from the beginning and all I ask is that you listen to my side of the story and make up your own mind; then you will do what you think fit.'

I arranged with Jay Pomeroy to meet Serge in his office the next morning.

If there is anything I really dislike it is sitting in judgment on anyone, especially a friend of the old days. After a sleepless night I went. He told his story in great detail, calmly on the whole, though it was quite obvious under what a strain he was suffering. When he had finished I told him there were many things I wished otherwise but that I believed him because I knew him so well. I doubted whether others would. The stories that were going the rounds had had so long a start.

'Why should I bother to contradict them?' he said. 'I have my work and the dancers all believe in me.' He went on to tell me that almost the only London friend who had greeted him publicly was Emerald Cunard, and I felt a little ashamed of my own hesitation.

It took a long struggle to convince him that, without an effort on his part to clear himself, his work would prove impossible. I asked him for a number of documents confirming what he said, some from resistance leaders of undoubted integrity and also for an official transcript of the trial.

These were all produced a few days later and, on my advice, some photostats were made and circulated to the press. The visit as a whole was not a success and the works were badly produced, but the atmosphere had been cleared.

Later for my own satisfaction I tracked down a mass of evidence in Paris. Much of it that he had refrained from mentioning was not merely negative but proved that he had actively saved many Jews and others from deportation and had, as usual, helped those out of luck. He had made the greatest effort of all to save René Blum, but had been defeated by Blum's own valiant but short-sighted determination to remain.

I am not going into the whole story here; it is a mass of petty intrigue and the lapse of time has seen the complete rehabilitation of Lifar everywhere save in America where, for some unknown reason, people like Walter Winchell, instead of being ridiculed when they write 'Widows get out your weeds, Lifar is in America,' or similar twaddle, are able to bear influence on the unintelligent. I will at present merely summarize my findings.

Lifar was undoubtedly indiscreet and sensitive to praise from the Germans. He believed that they would save Russia, and he said so. He also believed that they would give him great artistic scope. He met many Germans and 'collaborated' closely with one, a conductor and composer of great merit. All of which is regrettable. Negatively he never showed Hitler round the Opéra, or flew in a German aeroplane to his native Kieff, two of the most persistent stories that circulated. I also tracked down another calumny about some missing funds, the disposal of which he himself could not remember. They were handed over secretly to a lady, a Jewess as it happens, for distribution to prisoners of war, and when she heard I was making this investigation she cleared him with great indignation of the calumny. Positively there is this great fact, that more than anything the Germans wished the Opéra Ballet to visit Berlin and that Lifar could have brought it about. There was no such visit, though many other French companies did go, and this was solely due to Lifar and the tactics that he adopted.

The trial sentenced him for his indiscretions to one year's suspension from the stage. He was guilty of not being a hero and of excessive self-interest.

If anyone, either in Europe or America, is prepared to swear that under the same circumstances he would have acted better or even as well, I shall be greatly surprised and possibly I shall not believe him. The pickets outside the Metropolitan Opera House in 1948 most certainly could not have been relied upon to behave equally well. I can see them not only collaborating with the commissar in charge of American affairs, but denouncing everyone who does not follow the party line, or who has succeeded in his profession better than they have.

Since that interview in Pomeroy's office I have seen Lifar frequently both in London and Paris and our cordial acquaintanceship has ripened into friendship.

He has altered but little through the experience. He is a trifle mellower, a little less excitable and bears no grudge. 'He wanted to have me shot, after the liberation, but he's a very nice chap really,' is a typical comment.

His reinstatement at the Opéra was due to the extreme courage of Monsieur Hirsch, its new director, whose war record shows a similar courage and the highest integrity throughout the occupation. By the unanimous wish of the dancers he reinstated Lifar at the Opéra after the year's interval. The Communist-inspired stage-hands threatened to strike if he were allowed on, the dancers if he were not. Hirsch found a compromise by which Lifar might resume work as *maître de ballet* but not appear on the stage. The result was that whenever he appeared in the auditorium he received an ovation.

Out of curiosity I talked to various of the stage-hands; he had completely won them over and they had a high regard for him, realizing that without him their very jobs would have been insecure. This compromise lasted until February 2, 1949, when he made a reappearance as *premier danseur étoile*. The scene was a moving one. First came the *défilé du corps de ballet* with the vast stage deepened by the opening up of *le foyer de la danse*. Then the *défilé du corps de ballet*, the procession of dancers starting with the smallest *rat*, the *corps de ballet* following in order of seniority. Right at the back stood Serge Lifar, a slight pause and then a run across the stage to take up his position to salute a public that had remained so faithful. Magnificent stagecraft and deep sincerity as the whole episode came to a close with the acclamation of repeated curtain calls.

VII

My most recent memory of Lifar was in Venice, August 19, 1949, where we went together for a small ceremony to commemorate the twentieth anniversary of Diaghileff's death.

On the morning of our arrival we went in search of the Greek priest who had officiated at the funeral. He was still alive and remembered Serge as the young man who had been so deeply distressed. He said, 'I often wondered what had become of you.' Sir Kenneth Clark was staying in Venice and found us at the cemetery; so that by chance Covent Garden and Sadler's Wells, as well as the Opéra and the Teatro Fenice, were represented. A wreath from Karsavina was placed on the tomb itself and others were laid on the ground around it. The ceremony was simple and moving but in no way sad. Diaghileff's work had flourished and, had he been alive, he would have been an old man. That was unthinkable.

In the evening there was a lecture and a demonstration by Lifar and two of his dancers, Emile Audran and the beautiful

Ludmila Tcherina. They gave excerpts from the Diaghileff ballets. The elegant theatre, perhaps the most charming in existence, made a magnificent setting, but there was the large cold stage with no scenery and only three dancers. The event might easily have been a fiasco, had not Serge, deeply moved, risen to the occasion. '*Ce type apporte son décor avec lui,*' said a stage-hand. Lifar had not regained his figure or his technique but the artistry was magnificent, and then nature took a hand. As, trailing his purple robe, he was advancing to lay the lilies on Giselle's grave, three bats flew down the beam of light and fluttered round his head. The scene was set for the appearance of the *wilis,* creatures of the night.

VIII

It was through Serge Lifar that I came to know the Paris Opéra Ballet well and, though it is the doyen of companies, *balletomanes* outside Paris know little of its history, traditions or present artistic position. For some unknown reason it has never appeared at Covent Garden. Only television at Alexandra Palace has presented it, of course in a greatly reduced manner. Its disciplined dancers have proved ideal for television and many of Philip Bate's productions have been masterly. The Opéra Ballet has an atmosphere unlike that of any other company. Its dancers are well aware of its great traditions and consider themselves the aristocrats of the dance. They are gently patronizing to the dancing stars of visiting companies. '*Je suis de l'Opéra*' is the equivalent of being in the Guards after Eton. Also, they are very much a civil service organization gaining their grades by a series of technical examinations up to the rank of *première danseuse.* The *étoiles* are nominated from the ranks of the *premières danseuses* and salaries are graded according to promotion. This means that the public and the impresario have little influence over the dancers they see. The critics may rave about some particular young dancer but, great artist though she may be, if she has not the tough brilliance required for her examination she does not reach the top. Recently such talented dancers as Liane Daydé and Josette Clavier have jumped several ranks so that the young dancer is at last being given a fair chance. Once at the top however much an *étoile* may bore her audience she is difficult to remove. Hence the Opéra has its days to avoid.

Then there is *le foyer de la danse*, that gold-barley-sugar colonnaded steeply raked rehearsal-room-green-room where, during the intervals, the privileged can mingle with the dancers, a picturesque corner in which the age of Dr. Véron and Degas still lives. There, as in the days of Madame Cardinal's daughters, the man about town can survey the scene and the dancer can, if she wishes, gain a powerful protector; or, when that faithful habitué, the picturesque but cautious Viscomte de N. is around, a chocolate. This business of protection is still in evidence and when the protector is a political personage it is apt to complicate casting. Recently a French friend of mine astonished me when he asked me, during a talk about the casting of our ballets, 'But XX must be well in with the Labour Party, like our YY who is in with Monsieur Z, since she gets so many rôles?'* It took me some time to seize the point, and when I thought of the churchwarden respectability of our ministers and, I hasten to add, of the dancer in question, I was delighted. But although protection still exists, its importance is rapidly fading and talent has a far better chance of success than ever before. Indeed the most luxuriously 'protected' usually neglect their work and drop out of the picture. It does, however, cause an endless topic of conversation in the wings and, according to most of the talkers, it is never plain talent and hard work that has given their rivals a lead. In taking Toumanova and Wyroubova on as *étoiles* from outside,

* I have through English reticence hidden the names of the minister and the dancer, not because either would mind; he especially is extremely proud of a liaison which, by doing credit to his taste, enhances his position.

the venerable institution has received such a shaking that only good can result. I fear, however, that it will be a long time before the old system vanishes and the French dancer of talent has the same honest opportunity as her English sister.

PART III

CHAPTER SIXTEEN

The Dance Profession and the Child

I

TO many this may seem a dull chapter as it deals with a very unglamorous though important aspect of ballet. It is worth a little trouble, however, since its details affect many thousands and are not realized by the majority. To me it is a most exciting chapter as it combines my love of the dance with my interest in education. It also marks a definite period in my life, when the free-lance and the critic began to work through committees and organizations and tried to turn criticism into action. I have found committees trying and tiring on occasions, but generally I have enjoyed their 'drama,' the unexpected alignments, the sudden displays of irritation, the humour and even the pages filled with doodles during a lapse of interest. The rebel inside an organization goes farther than the skirmisher from outside.

It was a long time before I discovered that there was a flourishing dance industry as distinct from the ballet that I knew so well. The teachers with whom I was familiar were all enjoying a second career after having made great reputations as dancers. Some, such as Preobrajenska, had a genuine teaching vocation while others succeeded if only because the beauty of their movements was a constant inspiration. The pupils that they trained went straight into ballet, knowing nothing of examinations or competitions. The best of them were bespoken by managers and their choreographers from the tenderest age, and discussed when plans were made like pedigree yearlings for their future classics. When Markova asked Diaghileff whether she should go in for examinations he replied dryly, 'You can't take your certificate on to the stage with you.' All that I knew of this vast hidden industry came from the photographs in the early issues of the *Dancing Times*: Madame Smudge—ten letters after her name—and her successful pupils. Madame Smudge, a fat woman with a smirk, was shown dressed in pseudo-Greek draperies with a bandeau around her forehead and the pupils were draped around her bulky form in winsome elfin poses. On a table were exhibited the cups, shields, medals and other trophies annexed by Madame's winsome elves. The whole thing was a source of the greatest amusement to me. I used to cut them out and gloat. What an anthology they would make, what gems for the *découpages* of a more than usually morbid surrealist. I never dreamed of any possibility of contact with this strange world.

I have called it a hidden industry because the average *balletomane* knows so little about it. No mention of it is ever found in the growing number of ballet books, no novelist has ever taken it as a background, perhaps because it has no trace of glamour. I recommend it to the novelist. It has, if treated with equal thoroughness, all the romance of Arnold Bennett's *Imperial Palace*. It is of absorbing sociological interest, of great educational importance and ultimately of strong influence to the future of ballet. It is indeed the submerged four-fifths of the iceberg, and this picture of a period would be incomplete without a sounding. The former ballerina may have some hundred pupils, Madame Smudge fifteen hundred or more, to say nothing of two score of students or apprentices. Here are some figures that I still feel are staggering, though today I am so familiar with the scene:

Number of entries for major examinations: 1947—2,084, 1948—2,523, 1949—2,452; number of entries for children's examinations (ballet in education) from 1946 to last season of 1950, 102,738.

If we take into account the non-Academy pupils and members of other bodies, this means that there are some 50,000 children learning dancing in Great Britain. But in ballet proper there are probably not more than twenty *corps de ballet* vacancies a year. There is more chance of being run over or of winning a pool than of becoming a soloist, let alone a *prima ballerina*.

II

Some years before the war I was induced to become a member of the executive of the Royal Academy of Dancing, by Adeline Genée. I did not want to join; I was somewhat hostile. I believed it to be a worthy but thoroughly stuffy body that placed small girls on a swiftly moving conveyor belt, turning out at the end anonymous white-tunicked figures clutching a scroll of paper, their advanced certificates. But Madame Genée, now Dame Adeline (the title suits her to perfection), is not a person to whom one can refuse anything with ease. She has the glorious carriage of the dancer of her period, enormous driving power and a dignity that I can only describe as regal. Added to that there is a quick brain and an amazing eye for detail. She can completely paralyse a nervous person, not in any sense because she deliberately sets out to do so, but because I believe that she herself is reserved, possibly even shy. She was born with every natural gift, brought up from childhood in the great ballet tradition by an uncle, Alexandre Genée, whose firm intention it was to make her into a star and with all the hard work and exercise of will power that that involved. She became a star at the earliest possible date but then, more than ever, she was under the control of her uncle who like all ballet masters of his time and reputation, must have been something of a martinet. Isolated by her work, exceptional talent and early success, she must have missed much of the fun of childhood.

I accepted in the first place partly maybe because I was over-awed, but mainly because Madame Genée is one of the most gracious hostesses. After the charming luncheon at her house it would have seemed churlish to refuse, moreover her arguments were convincing. Ninette de Valois capitulated at the same meal. Now that I know Madame Genée better, the feeling of awe has given way to one of admiration and affection, even when she receives my suggestions with ill-concealed distaste. She can on occasions be distinctly acid with some committee member who has said the wrong thing from her point of view and she does not relish too much independence.

It is possible that when the Academy was started under its more humble title of the Association of Operatic Dancing, some of its prime movers, knowing only the charming dancer of Swanilda or La Camargo, may have imagined that this great and universally respected ballerina would make an admirably decorative figurehead. They may not have noticed, as did Arnold Bennett, the commanding presence and the strength behind the Dresden shepherdess. Adeline Genée has governed the Academy ever since, with the regal dignity of a Hapsburg, but, unlike that conservative dynasty, she has, as I will relate, usually been behind every progressive move the Academy has made.

The very name Royal Academy of Dancing is a mystery to the dance lover who knows that l'Académie Nationale de Musique et de Danse is in fact the Paris Opéra Ballet. It has something to show on the biggest stage in Europe, it is the parent academy, the very cradle of ballet. The Royal Academy at Burlington House produces pictures and controversies, the French Academy a dictionary and an impressive *habit vert*. What then does the Royal Academy of Dancing do? Where are its coryphées? Who is its *première danseuse étoile*?

Up till recently the Royal Academy of Dancing has scarcely taught at all yet its influence has been felt in thousands of homes all over Great Britain and the Commonwealth. It was started mainly as an examining body. Ballet had gained enormously in popularity, teachers were springing up like mushrooms—most of them like toad-stools—and it was the aim of the association to work out a common system and, by examining first the teachers and then their pupils, to see that the system was being properly taught. It could not enforce its will or banish the incompetent teacher but, by gaining prestige with teachers and parents, it could reduce the amount of dangerous teaching and secure a minimum level of competence.

This bare minimum it has partially secured, and that is a considerable advance but it does not go far enough. Most of the teaching of dancing in this country bears no relationship whatsoever to the art of dancing; much of it is incompetent and, from a physical point of view, some of it is positively dangerous. The Academy has not failed, because as I shall show it has found another long-term solution. As an association of teachers it has had to be too lenient to teachers, and has had to bring in its reforms with extreme caution lest they affect the pockets of members, so many of whom are running a business and do not have the vocation of teachers. Some of its influential members are diehards, but in a peculiarly dense interpretation of this already damning word. They cannot be defenders of a tradition because they know nothing of ballet tradition. They refuse to see the necessity of the reforms that will set our Academy in line with the great tradition. At least one of these Ballet Blimps has not seen a performance of ballet for the past twenty years, admits it, and yet voices strong and influential opinions on a technique that can only be of value when it serves a living art. Fortunately the progressives are just beginning to have the upper hand, but much time is wasted by the necessity of long and involved negotiations at meetings, a pastime that wearies and tends to wear out the active and progressive more than it does the Blimps who find salvation in the rigid placing of a little finger, and in the multiplication of examinations, so many of which have no true *raison d'être* and are educationally unsound.

I have called myself a rebel within the organization because it is this exam-mindedness that I am trying to fight. Many believe that there is nothing that a good exam will not cure. Quite apart from the great harm done to children by a number of exams and those at an early age, nothing could damage teaching more effectively than to keep the teacher's nose buried in an exam syllabus. This only covers up the bad teacher and prevents the inspired one from getting on with her job. The most pathetic remark I ever heard, made by someone advocating yet another exam, was: 'How are we going to keep the children's interest between their nine-year-old and thirteen-year-old exams?'

I shall write more about these examinations later on. I feel strongly that an Academy should discard old-fashioned methods even if it means hitting hard at a certain class of teacher.

III

My first realization of the picture as a whole was when, at the end of the war, I made a long lecture tour for the Academy covering most of the country. Miss Gordon, director of the Academy, wisest and most diplomatic guide such a body could have, provided me with a list of teachers, their qualifications and her private opinion of them. It read like the synopsis of a psychological novel set during a rainy winter in a commercial hotel in a provincial manufacturing city. I was most careful to memorize and then to burn it. It proved invaluable. I was determined to make this a study tour, to watch classes and to discuss problems both general and local with dance teachers, schoolmistresses and local education authorities.

I soon realized that in most provincial centres the dance, apart from the professional ballet, had a bad name with school teachers. I also realized, and I am more than ever convinced of it now, that the school teacher, especially the woman teacher, is the cream of any community, the leading spirit in art clubs, music clubs and dramatic societies. I met a score of head-mistresses who, for intelligence, width of interest, humour, zest and charm, would be ornaments of any society. The typical 'schoolmarm' of farce may possibly exist. I did, it is true, on one occasion see a sinewy games-mistress running about brandishing a hockey-stick and hear her shout, 'Play the game, girls, play the game,' but she was a museum piece, valuable through her very rarity, and through serving as a model for Joyce Grenfell's satire. May God preserve her; she made my afternoon.

The schoolmistresses' grievance against ballet was a simple one. As taught locally it had no educational value and wasted much time when pupils were begged off for examinations or, worst still, competitions. If the child did win a competition and earn a mention or a photo in the local press, she usually became unbearable; her mother certainly did.

I could sympathize with the headmistress over these com-petitions. Even when they serve the most deserving of all charitable causes I find the whole idea abhorrent. Both from the point of view of the art and from the view of general character training they give an entirely false set of values. No child dancer is, as a general rule, fit to entertain the public as a soloist. It is for the highly experienced ballet mistress to decide when one of an ensemble has something worth showing to the public, something that merits applause. The child who has won a medal, and especially her parents and teacher, gain an altogether false opinion of her merits. This is not prejudice, but daily experience. The typical stage child, poor little beggar, is a complete pest. Exceptional talent and temperament need retarding. They require rest and a normal disciplined back-ground. The defence generally used is that the judges are chosen from experienced and conscientious teachers and there-fore raise the whole standard in a neighbourhood. It is true, if unfortunate, that experienced dancers often judge these com-petitions, but the argument does not hold. It is still damaging to the children involved, to the winners especially, but also to the losers whose parents are nearly always persuaded that there has been a miscarriage of justice. Ballet is bad enough, but the 'tap,' musical comedy and acrobatic sections are truly horrible in the knowing precocity that they encourage. Eleven-year-old Master Preston in topper and tails ogling ten-year-old Maureen Tonypandy.

Recently I gave evidence before a commission called to study the subject of the employment of children on the stage. My point was a simple one. '*The interests of the child, physical, mental and moral, are identical with the interests of the art itself.*' The child under sixteen has nothing to contribute to ballet. There might be isolated exceptions—the foreign child matures more quickly than do our own—but from what I saw in my Russian Ballet experience I was convinced that the damage to the child and potential artist was too great a price to pay, even when she succeeded in giving something positive to her audience.

Examinations are another matter. If properly understood, they are of great value though they have little connection with the art. Unfortunately the tendency in the profession has been to teach for examinations alone and to see success in statistics. This will be very difficult to eradicate. The only possible means is by 'legislation,' to make the dates of entry at as late an age as possible, after school certificate, so that pupils can take examinations in their stride and really profit by them. I have no patience with people who say that examinations, whether school certificate or dancing, are of no real value. The argument runs that the examination does not discover the best workers, that there are many who may not have the right temperament to do themselves justice. That is all very well, and is true as far as it goes, but examinations do not serve only to reveal knowledge, they also serve to reveal temperament and personality, to show how the candidate might behave when called upon to act rationally in an emergency.

During this long lecture tour from Edinburgh to Exeter I made copious notes of every conversation I held. School teachers all realized the value of dancing in education. They mostly enjoyed ballet as an art when it visited their districts and took parties of pupils, but they were terrified, and I think with justice, of the term 'ballet' as applied to dancing in education. For the most part, when dancing was taught in their schools it was some form of expressionist dancing imported from Central Europe and taught by a gymnast who had taken a course for a few months. The gymnast was always a well-educated woman highly trained in her speciality, and usually was by no means satisfied with the dancing she was teaching, or with her ability to teach it. The justification for this Central European cavorting was that it acted as a release. It was carefully justified on psychological grounds and looked impressive on paper. I doubt the value of such a Pandora release and even find it dangerous. The local ballet teacher could not begin to speak the same language. The Royal Academy of Dancing's children's syllabus, as it then existed, had nothing to give the 'once a week child' and precious little to give to the intending professional. I discussed this problem from the dancing side with the very few dance teachers who, by their education and ability, had succeeded in gaining an *entrée* to educational schools. I found them in complete agreement with one another and with me. On my return to London I submitted my report to Madame Genée and within twenty-four hours she acted on it, asking me to set up an education committee to study the problem. The executive committee afterwards ratified her action.

My work as chairman of the committee was to state the problem, to postulate what I felt were the needs of the dance in general education, and to let the technical experts get on with the job. At the many sessions, enlivened by our members dancing round the board-room table to illustrate a point, I adopted a Rosa Dartle attitude.

My first point was to make it quite clear that there was a strong dividing line between the 'once a week child' in a big class, and the would-be ballerina with more time, a greater aptitude and a greater concentration. That dividing line could not be ignored yet it must not be so absolute that the exceptionally talented 'once a weeker' could not step across it and change her status.

The requisite for the dance in education was a disciplined framework from within which the child could express herself. That is, the minimum of basically correct technique and the maximum of joy in movement. It must, of course, be physically sound, avoiding the use of the *pointes*, undesirable in a mass class of that type. The dance must be closely related to music and not merely accomplished by dull thumps of the notes or the beats of a stick. The dance has much to learn from Dalcroze eurythmics, a magnificent system of applied musical education. It must include acted scenes that give a chance for individuality as well as a basis of the technique of mime to direct that individuality. It must also include simple national dances that could be linked up with history, geography and costume design. The teacher must not conceive of the dance as something totally divorced from everyday life and from the other school subjects. It should be a part of the general education.

My terms of reference were rather narrowed by the fact that this new curriculum had to serve both the would-be professional and the 'once a week' child. This in itself did no harm as the curriculum was a sound pre-ballet education for the professional. What has been more damaging is the name, 'Ballet in Education.' Had it been entitled 'The Dance in Education,' success would be achieved very much more quickly. The work itself answers its purpose and, if in the educational school the teacher prunes the technique just a little and does not worry about putting pupils through an early examination, it should prove ideal.

v

But even the ideal syllabus drawn up by a committee of muses with Terpsichore in the chair is worthless without the constructive teacher. The majority of our teachers look upon a printed syllabus as holy writ. They wear their pencils to the stub in taking notes at any demonstration; even the rare jokes find their way into the notebook. There are, within the profession, endless violent and futile discussions about the respective merits of the R.A.D. syllabus and the Cecchetti Society syllabus. I call these discussions futile because everything depends on the individual teacher who interprets the syllabus. Cecchetti, whom I so often saw at work, taught according to the strict rule and daily programme of the very valuable material that has been assembled by my friend, Cyril Beaumont, and called the Cecchetti method. But he was a teacher of genius, which makes all the difference. The present-day teacher must be familiar with the French, Italian and Russian schools and, if she is an artist and a craftsman, she will so combine them as to get the best results. She cannot have a common method since every one of her pupils will vary in physique and temperament.

In 1939 Madame Genée and certain members of her committee realized that, if the level of teaching was to be raised so that the dance teacher had the same status as the physical training teacher, it was necessary for the Academy to start its own teachers' training course and to grant its diploma to those who had qualified. Educationists were consulted, in particular Miss Gwatkin and Miss Charlesworth, and a course of study drawn up that included not only dancing but anatomy, physiology, the theory and practice of teaching, music, French, costume design, elocution and literature; a hard three years of study. The war interrupted this plan, but in 1946 it was implemented and Professor Winifred Cullis and I were asked to be its joint directors.

The Academy acquired a large house, Fairfield Lodge in Addison Road, as hostel and headquarters. The minimum requirement for entry is School Certificate and the Royal Academy Elementary, and candidates are selected by interview. This selection is of the greatest importance, since we aim at teachers by vocation and not at failed dancers. Our first problem in selection lies with physique. The girl with the perfect dancer's figure usually tries to find her way into ballet. As example is so important in a branch of education where children copy so easily, can a girl be a good teacher when, because of her build, she cannot perform all the movements correctly? The answer must be a compromise. To train intending artists it is important for the teacher herself to move as an artist. Otherwise so long as the teacher fully realizes her own physical shortcomings, and that is important, she can do all that is required of her within her terms of reference.

My work with the course, apart from the actual organization, has been to give a weekly tutorial to the students, so that I can sum up each individual. I have enjoyed this immensely. We have discussed, during the past years, a vast variety of subjects, roaming far from ballet. My main aim has been to teach these girls to argue and discuss, not to be frightened of ideas and especially not to take things for granted, one of the greatest faults at the present day when there is so much regimentation and spoon-feeding, and individualism must fight for its life. The 'first years' are usually shy; I have to do most of the talking and it is hard going. The 'second years' can give and take in discussion, while the 'third years' are so keen that it takes all my time and ingenuity to keep up with them. Some of them have, as a part of their training, lectured at the demonstrations arranged by the Academy and have coped with questions like old hands. They know their subject, have been taught by such experts as Tamara Karsavina, Ninette de Valois, Catherine

Devillier and Phyllis Bedells. Frederick Ranalow has taught them how to speak up and has eliminated a too pronounced Birmingham or Kensington accent. These girls have a vocation and the same fine outlook as other members of the teaching profession. They have moved a long way from our Aunt Sally, Madame Smudge. (She has served her purpose; let us not be too hard on her.) They are the pioneers of the dance in education and they are aware of their responsibility. Our first three groups have passed out and found good situations teaching in schools both at home and abroad. Audrey Knight, the first to complete her course, has had the exciting task of assisting Joy Newton in forming the first ballet school in Turkey according to the scheme laid down by Ninette de Valois. There is room for these girls throughout the Dominions and the Colonies as well as nearer home. They can both create and then supply the demand.

I have been fortunate to be chosen for this work and to have so experienced and charming an associate as Winifred Cullis, who has been such a pioneer in the higher education of women. She wears her immense knowledge with ease, is a keen practical psychologist, human and humane. When she looks at a candidate through her monocle she puts that candidate at her ease, but she has soon summed her up. 'A silly little thing,' or 'fine material, just what we need, but we must give her more self-confidence.' She has what I have come to regard as the greatest quality in a teacher, an immense sympathy for her pupils without a trace of the sentimentality that destroys judgment and that always leads to favouritism and injustice. I love children from the cradle up, but I hope I have never been sentimental about them. Since I have been a teacher I have found that while one cannot help having preferences, it is almost impossible not to like and be interested in all, always so long as one really knows them and looks behind the surface of an angelic smile or a ready answer.

VI

I have over the years come to look upon my Academy work both as intensely irritating and highly important. I feel that it is more constructive to be something of a firebrand inside rather than outside the Academy and that the Academy has done invaluable work and is becoming more necessary every day.

However, one must face the fact that the standard of ballet teaching in this country is still dangerously low, that scores of children are being damaged physically and mentally and that hundreds of parents are wasting hundreds of pounds. Much of this is outside the control of the Academy. Sixteen-year-olds are giving dancing lessons at anything from sixpence to one-and-sixpence a time with no possibility of any outside control. That is the dance racket as apart from the dance industry. But the time has come when the Academy must resolve certain problems logically and fearlessly. It must recognize a definite dividing line between dancing as a theatre art and dancing as a part of education. That line will grow wider as time goes on. It must boycott the bad teacher, instead of merely disapproving and hoping for the best. It must have a strong independent examining board trained by itself, and none of the examiners must have any interest in an existing school. Moreover, the examiners must be properly briefed. Are they examining potential company members, potential teachers or children who learn dancing as they do history or geography? Examiners of the first category must have stage experience and a knowledge of contemporary ballet needs; examiners of the second two categories must understand educational methods. Also the Academy must ask itself a series of pertinent questions about examinations in general. There are, as I have said, far too many examinations with no *raison d'être*. Many schoolchildren are overtaxed by dancing examinations taken at far too early an age. We may know that certain of these examinations are of no importance, the children do not. Dancing for the nonprofessional is meaningless if it is not a pleasurable activity. *Ballet is a vocation for the very few, dancing is the privilege of every child.* It is for the educationist to guide us here. I strongly disapprove of early vocational training, but for physical reasons it is inevitable in ballet. It should, therefore, be strictly limited to the very few whom experts decide are fitted for it. Hence the great importance of not giving a vocational slant to the dance training of the average child by stressing the examination side before the age of fifteen. The work of teachers could be checked by an inspection of children in general rather than by an assessment of the individual child. This may sound out of place in a book of memoirs but, apart from the fact that it has been one of my greatest interests over a number of years, there are thousands of parents and teachers all over England whose intimate concern it is.

I cannot leave the subject of the Academy without mention of the remarkable work it has done through its Dominions' scholarships in bringing talented dancers to London, and once they are in London in looking after them and giving them a 'home.' They have found in Miss Gordon a wise and generous friend. The training course and the Dominions' scholarships alone thoroughly justify the existence of the Academy that has received too little notice in books on the ballet. If I criticize it, I do so with affection.

CHAPTER SEVENTEEN

Sadler's Wells as a National Ballet
Lilian Baylis: Ninette de Valois

I

MY work on committees, especially those connected with the dance from an educational point of view, was bringing me closer and closer to what I regard as my life's work. Some autobiographers are fortunate in being able to divide their lives into neat compartments of sevens, octaves or decades. As I have already written mine has been an untidy life. I planned nothing, things just happened to me: meeting a child at a Christmas party, thinking of a book in my bath, lunching with a friend at a restaurant, talking to a brilliant woman in a Birmingham street. But, if there is any discernible pattern in my life, it is this, a period of unconscious preparation in which everything was leading me to the *job*, followed by the *job* itself. At the same time everything that was happening in ballet in England was leading to the creation of the *job*. But before I write of Sadler's Wells School it is necessary to take a brief look at ballet in England immediately after the war that it had so splendidly survived.

My war-time contacts with ballet were confined to a few welcome interludes at the New Theatre and to the occasional strokes of luck that found me lecturing in the same town where the ballet was on tour. This long rest from what had been a continuous contact with ballet gave me an opportunity to assess the great change that had taken place. First of all ballet was no longer the diversion of a smart London clique; it was popular all over England. I shall not easily forget a visit to Coventry after the bombardment and the enthusiasm shown for this gentle art by a series of packed houses. The Coventry people were naturally very sensitive to their much-publicized suffering. Ballet and music brought them repose. This new popularity may have been partly due to what is sneeringly called escapism, but that very word properly understood need not be so damning. Not to escape at times leads to ulcers or insanity. It is the type and quality of escape that matters and also its duration. 'Escapism is all wrong,' says the pompous man puffing at his own brand of escape. What I saw there in Coventry convinced me that these people welcomed art as a restorative, a very different thing. The launching of C.E.M.A. during the war showed what a value was attached to such *re*-creation. Once or twice I witnessed the impact of ballet at a camp where the atmosphere was the frankly hostile one of 'this sissy stuff is not for us.' The sudden spontaneous burst of enthusiasm was revealing. It was the classical ballet that proved the most popular, while what seemed a 'natural' like *Façade* often passed them by. On reflection, this should have been obvious since such works appeal to the experience and not to the emotions. The same thing happened in the case of opera with the troops who had come across it in Italy. Theatre managers have always systematically underrated the public's taste.

The next big change that I noticed was that ballet was accepted as an indigenous English art form without the slightest need of a Russian disguise. This had taken place with far greater speed than in Russia where the Italian dancer held sway for so long. The third important change was that Sadler's Wells had come to be regarded as the national ballet even before it had found its home at Covent Garden. I was the first to call it so in my book, *The National Ballet*, a manifesto that traced its development and showed how it satisfied the conditions. The pattern of post-war ballet development had been laid down before the war itself was over.

Marie Rambert and her company were doing pioneer work

in factories and hostels and a new company, the International, was constantly touring the big provincial centres. This International Company, which has been seen by hundreds of thousands, has for a number of reasons received unduly harsh treatment from the press. It was originally started for a young dancer of considerable talent, Mona Inglesby. She had been trained by Rambert and a number of the Paris ballerinas. By good fortune she was able to start her own company, and by ill fortune to become its *prima ballerina*, director and choreographer. Obviously these functions cannot be combined, however intelligent the person, and Mona Inglesby is intelligent. The result of having a *prima ballerina* director in a company is to kill the ambition of all the other dancers, even if they are fairly treated. This can only end in monotonous performances. Moreover, to be able to carry on, the International has for the most part had to restrict itself to *Coppélia*, *The Sleeping Beauty*, *Giselle* and *Swan Lake*. The provinces will flock to these and stay away from triple-bill programmes, especially those that contain novelties. The International has miraculously paid its way, brought ballet to a new public but at great sacrifice. The contemporary dancer is only kept alert by the opportunity of learning new works by a number of choreographers. The dancer also requires the stimulus of a successful London season, but this company is not geared to the West End. I can see no way out, yet I like and admire Mona Inglesby, respect her sincerity and feel that she is filling a necessary place in contemporary ballet. It should be possible for ballet critics to speak the truth without the special bitterness that they seem to reserve for the International, but perhaps an embarrassingly fulsome book about Mona Inglesby has made her some enemies.

A promising company, the Metropolitan, failed to survive through lack of support. It went in for novelties which were just not quite good enough, and it introduced some admirable dancers, among them Colette Marchand, Serge Perrault and Svetlana Beriosova. It was probably that idiotic entertainment, the modern version of the Christmas pantomime, that sealed its fate by immobilizing theatres all over England for some three months of the year. I believe that Birmingham, already theatre-starved, can endure four months of this unpleasant rubbish. I know that sleepy elegant Bath with its fine traditions uses its theatre for several weeks of pantomime and then leaves but a short interval before its summer show, which I find indistinguishable from the pantomime.

Ballet today in England, in spite of its popularity, cannot exist without subsidies which is very much the position of the intelligent theatre outside London. If pantomime were really designed for children instead of for the childish adult, I would not write in this way. Robert Donat's *Glass Slipper* was a joy for the children and Clinton Baddeley's pantomimes are splendid fun for the true adult.

II

Ballet must have its home and it was Lilian Baylis, that incredible woman, who gave our ballet its solid foundation. I never knew Lilian Baylis really well, but her story has always fascinated me intensely and I am certain that she has left behind her an atmosphere of practical idealism that looks on nothing worth while as being impossible. I can feel that in all my work; the dreams that turn into realities. I am pleased that, the very last time I saw her at the end of a season, she included me in her offering of a sprig of flowers—it was rosemary on that occasion —with the words, 'I look upon you as one of us.'

Although I have been a member of the Wells organization for years, it has taken a considerable amount of research to understand its ramifications. I will repeat the story in some detail as all that happened since Emma Cons' temperance drive in the Waterloo Road guided the theatrical destinies of this country and gave me my great opportunity to serve. To a non-Englishman this illogical but essentially smooth-working compromise between private enterprise and state-aid may well prove incomprehensible. It is essentially a romance, but then we are very romantic.

The Old Vic, home of the most polished British acting; the Young Vic, a junior theatre; the Old Vic School; the Bristol Old Vic; the Bristol Old Vic School; the Sadler's Wells Opera, the Sadler's Wells Theatre Ballet; the Sadler's Wells Ballet, now resident at the Royal Opera House, Covent Garden; and the Sadler's Wells School. Nine large enterprises all stem from a common source, the passion for temperance in an energetic South London social worker, Emma Cons.

Emma Cons, who was a pioneer in housing, tracked down much of the drunkenness in her South London district to a music hall in the Waterloo Road, where drink was sold in the auditorium and was indeed the main feature of the entertainment. In order to put a stop to this she and her friends raised enough money to take over the music hall, and it was opened as a Temperance Music Hall on Boxing Day, 1880. Its name was the Royal Victoria Hall, but affectionately it was always called 'The Old Vic.' The somewhat uninspiring entertainment in the now respectable 'Vic' included lectures and high class variety programmes, washed down by cups of tea and lemonade, and half the theatre was used as a working-men's college.

In 1889 the freehold of the building was bought by public subscription and the title deeds were vested in the Official Trustee of Charity Lands. Under the terms of the contract the Old Vic could not be used for any purpose that was political, denominational or sectarian, and naturally no intoxicating liquors could be sold on the premises. The primary purpose of the scheme was the production of high class drama, opera, music, lectures, and other entertainments and a certain number of seats were to be 'at such prices as will make them available for artisans and labourers.' The Charity was run by a board of governors.

It might all have ended there with a few hundred Londoners saved from the 'demon rum' and given evenings of uplifting entertainment, had not Emma Cons' niece, Lilian, then appeared upon the scene. Lilian Baylis was a practical, idealistic, God-fearing and ruthless woman, who might best be described in the words of Napoleon about the great Catherine: 'She was a master woman, worthy to wear a beard upon her chin.' That she was lovable as well is testified to by the anecdotes without number that are always recounted whenever her name is mentioned. One cannot help loving someone who cooked sausages on a spirit stove in her Vic Theatre box or who prayed God to 'give her good actors, cheap.' Lilian Baylis had been a teacher of music and dancing in South Africa and had come to England to recuperate after an illness. Finding her aunt over-worked, she took over the management of the Old Vic and from 1898 until her death in 1937 the 'Vic' and later the 'Wells' became her life-work.

She started by giving concerts and popular excerpts from the well-known operas, but in 1914, and against all expert advice, she started giving the plays of Shakespeare and from that date onwards the Old Vic was almost entirely devoted to Shakespeare, classical drama and the opera. By 1923 every one of Shakespeare's plays had been performed at the Vic. So great was the prestige of this theatre that, in spite of the small salaries that she was able to pay, the very finest actors were proud to have their names on the bills. Many started their careers with her. Among those closely associated with the Vic were Sybil Thorndike and Lewis Casson, John Gielgud, Peggy Ashcroft, Charles Laughton, Edith Evans, and later Laurence Olivier and Ralph Richardson. The list reads like a 'Who's Who' of the serious theatre.

Not content, however, with these triumphs and like that other master woman, St. Teresa of Avila, Lilian Baylis set out not on a mule but in her baby Austin to found yet another new centre. In 1925 a public fund was started to raise money to purchase and rebuild the historic Sadler's Wells Theatre on the site where, in 1683, a Mr. Sadler built a Musik House, and rediscovered the holy well which was accredited in pre-Reformation days with miraculous healing powers. The well, a chalybeate spring with medicinal properties, is preserved to this day under the auditorium of the theatre, though its waters are no longer used or usable.

It was with the purchase of Sadler's Wells that ballet enters on to the scene. The theatre was opened on Twelfth Night, 1931, under a similar charity scheme to that of the Old Vic, except that the prohibition on intoxicating liquor was no longer considered necessary owing to the general decrease in drunkenness. The idea was to alternate opera and Shakespeare between the two theatres, so that a wide popular public could benefit from both.

The idea of a ballet company on its present scale was not originally in the intentions of Miss Baylis. The popular operas in the repertoire needed a few dancers, and that was the extent of the original scheme. However, Lilian Baylis was never one to do things by halves. Not herself a woman of great artistic knowledge, she had an uncanny instinct for surrounding herself by experts and also the ability to handle those experts—either by a pat on the back, or by deflating them with a word or two whenever she found it necessary. No, Lilian Baylis was by no means an artist. I remember that on one occasion before the war, when Bruce Ottley had the magnificent idea of bringing Covent Garden under Lilian Baylis' control, I shared a box with her during a performance of *Le Coq d'Or*. She watched, entranced, for some time and then gave me a nudge. 'Beautiful, my dear, beautiful and so typically Spanish.' She once told me that the secret of success was always to go to the very best people when you wanted anything done, 'because they would understand,' she said, 'and,' she added, 'they would usually do it for far less.' This was characteristic, as there was never a penny to spare in any of her organizations. For her ballet she went

APPLAUSE

Frederick Ashton and Ninette de Valois on the stage at Covent Garden, 1950

straight to the one person who could help and understand—
Ninette de Valois.

III

I first met Ninette de Valois at Monte Carlo at one of those
Hôtel de Paris luncheons given by Lord Rothermere. The
meeting did not make any particular impression on me at the
time. I admired her dancing, especially in *Aurora's Wedding*
where her technique and attack stood out even among the
Russian dancers, who at that time seemed so much more
interesting to me. I liked what I knew about her because she
was so kindly protective to the little Alicia whom she took
under her wing when Alicia's governess was suddenly taken
ill and died. I was also amused by the many tales of her absent-
mindedness. On one occasion, Alicia told me, she was surprised
to see Ninette's alarm clock outside the hotel bedroom door.
This was explained by the fact that her shoes were resting on
her bed-table. I saw but little of her and I do not know if
already, then, she was thinking along creative lines or if she
was merely suffering from the ache to express herself. Certainly
no one could have predicted that this very attractive young
grand sujet would be the only person to inherit, at any rate,
Diaghileff's authority. I lost sight of her when she left the
company and only met her much later in Camargo days. I did,
however, receive many rather violently expressed letters whenever I criticized any of her doings and was definitely set down
as hostile, which was far from being the case. I was merely
amicably indifferent and quite unaware that she had anything
more to express than the countless others who were making
frenzied choreographic experiments with studio groups. I was
especially interested in the work of Marie Rambert and her
brilliant group at the Ballet Club. It was in an idiom with
which I was familiar and its results were immediately evident.
My first realization of de Valois' creative gifts came from *Job*
at the Camargo Society, followed by *La Création du Monde*, a

masterpiece that deserves revival. I believe that Lilian Baylis found it slightly shocking. The early Wells left me sceptical. I was frankly disappointed in Markova from whom I expected so much, and I found the company colourless. By then, also, de Basil had come on the scene and the Russian renaissance was in full swing.

It was only in 1935 when Markova left and the products of the Wells school were given their first chance that I saw how firm were the foundations that had been laid. The work was on a modest scale, but it progressed from performance to performance while Rambert was hampered by lack of space and the Russians with all their resources were slipping back. From 1935 onwards I seldom missed a performance and it was only natural that I should come first to understand and then to work devotedly with Ninette de Valois. My first service was to arrange with Michael Fokine for his ballets, *Les Sylphides*, *Carnaval* and *Le Spectre de la Rose*, to be performed by Sadler's Wells. I was very friendly with Fokine at the time and was able to convince him that his work would be respected. It was characteristic of de Valois that she refused to put on these works which, through the difficulty of copyrighting ballet, had become common property, without paying a royalty to their creator. I believe that they are the only versions given anywhere today from which his estate benefits. Shortly after I was able to arrange to have Benois' original setting for *Les Sylphides*. My next service was the founding of the Ballet Benevolent Fund. This brought me into the closest contact both with Ninette de Valois and Lilian Baylis and so largely led to my present work at the school.

In spite of the obvious results of her work, and the extent can only be measured when one realizes that in 1939 'going to the ballet' meant to the Russian Ballet while in 1949 it means 'going to the Sadler's Wells Ballet,' in spite of the honours she has received, it is necessary to work with her to realize her many-sided brilliance. She is a masterly organizer, able to understand a balance sheet in all its intricate details, putting her finger on a weakness that has escaped others. She can handle people, whether in committee or singly. She will sit at some protracted meeting—I remember one at the R.A.D. that lasted seven hours —quietly doodling and apparently absent, then when the subject has been tossed to and fro she will wake up, ask a few pertinent questions and produce a plan so simple and logical that it finds its way into the minutes. This is often done on a cup of tea and a couple of aspirins since at times she suffers badly from migraine.

She is masterful but nowadays always impersonal, so that few people who have risen so high and in such a personal profession can have less enemies. There are two attitudes she dislikes in particular, sentimentality and 'dishonest' criticism. When she is roused by either of these she can be withering. Objective criticism, however hostile, she positively enjoys. It gives her an opportunity for argument and, like every good Irishwoman, she can argue with the best. She dislikes 'yes-men.' She is satisfying to work with because it is a joy to meet such creative intelligence. It is not always easy. She thinks with extraordinary rapidity but in jerks, so that it is never obvious in which way her mind is working. She will, for instance, completely forget an idea that she has just evolved because she has already discarded it, while her listener is still patiently developing it. She always arrives at the just and logical conclusion, but sometimes by a logic that it is impossible to follow unless one knows her really well. At a Critic's Circle luncheon a speaker referred to her as an Irishwoman with all the English virtues. That is an apt description but, to be absolutely accurate, he should have added—'and all the Irish virtues as well.'

So far I have only mentioned the administrator and it has rather overshadowed the artist. Of the choreographers I have seen at work she is, with the exception of Fokine and Massine, by far the most intellectual and professional. By that I do not necessarily mean the best. Choreographers are of two kinds, those who compose a complete work in their heads and then teach it to the company with no hesitation or alteration, and those who compose a ballet with and on the company, using the dancers' personalities and incorporating them into the work. De Valois belongs very definitely to the first and far rarer class. In her ballets every movement has a definite meaning that she could justify and explain. All her ballets can be repeated with complete changes of cast yet with identical results.

De Valois created our national ballet, I will not say single-handed because she has always inspired good friends and colleagues, yet without her there would have been no national ballet but a number of talented dancers without a real home or a clear objective, and the present writer still at a loose end. Today she *is* the national ballet and I can see no one capable of taking her place. The prospect is a terrifying one, for no committee can run such an enterprise. Even after these very few years we are apt to take our ballet for granted. It must at any rate be placed on a sound and permanent footing; first and second company and the school must be a financial whole and not merely connected through the strength and leadership of a genius. The opera must be left to work out its own destiny. Unless the machine is sound this wonderful achievement might one day crumble more rapidly than it has grown.

CHAPTER EIGHTEEN

Sadler's Wells School: I become a Schoolmaster

I

HAD I been asked to choose the ideal job I would have said that I wanted something that combined children and ballet. I have that job now and I am satisfied, though I have had to give up many things, notably extended travel.

Yes, I am more than satisfied, but at the same time I am terribly afraid of settling down to what could become routine and of feeling smugly that our ballet was the best in the world and that I was in charge of a valuable part of its mechanism. Anyone in what is virtually a state artistic enterprise runs that great risk. More than ever I try to keep in the closest touch with what others are doing in order to gain a clear objective picture of our merits and our shortcomings. As long as I retain that independence of outlook I will be doing my work properly. I am trying, also, to safeguard my pupils from the parochialism that threatens all academies and successful recognized organizations.

The germ of the school idea arose during the lifetime of Lilian Baylis. I mentioned to Ninette de Valois the possibility of a fund that could be used to enlarge the scope of the ballet school and in that way plant a permanent tradition. We all three met over lunch and the Fund was launched. Its exact purpose was not then very clearly defined and the money that came in as a result of our appeal was insufficient for a complex educational programme. We gave some dancers the opportunity to study in Paris during their vacation, paid some doctors' bills and purchased some sketches of costumes and *décors* that we felt should belong to the tradition of British ballet. During the war the Fund was able to make a loan to the theatre to replace the ballets lost in Holland. As we worked it became more and more clear that the main object of this Fund should be to give benefits to the dancers and, when circumstances permitted, a pension for long service. The Fund ultimately became the Sadler's Wells Ballet Benevolent Fund, so admirably run by its honorary secretary, Eveleigh Leith, and though pensions are still in the future, it has done very useful work in cases of sickness and hardship.

However, Ninette de Valois clung to her idea of an educational and ballet school combined. The need for it was obvious. The dancer must begin her ballet training around the age of nine, at a time when general education takes most of her time and energy. If she is in an ordinary boarding-school it is impossible to combine the two; if she is in a day school she can only attend her dancing lessons in the evening after a hard day's school-work and possibly a long journey across London. Education and ballet come into sharp conflict and both suffer. The only possible solution was to combine the two under one roof and to have the dancing as early in the morning as possible, when the pupil was fresh and could get the maximum of benefit from the exercise.

All this was, of course, a dream that it was pleasant to dwell upon, but that seemed, to anyone but de Valois, impossible of realization. I remember one war-night in Birmingham walking with her up and down the blacked-out streets discussing the dream school in the closest detail. The return to my hotel and a plate of surly spam could not dispel the excitement of that conversation.

When the war ended I started my present close association with Sadler's Wells by taking a Saturday morning discussion class with the members of the second company, and by mobilizing my friends to give talks on various artistic subjects. I enjoyed this teaching immensely and at any rate taught my pupils to ask questions. I found those from the Dominions more vital and inquisitive, partly no doubt through the food and sunshine, partly because they were a selected few who had found their way to this country through sheer force of character. They were excited by their discoveries and opportunities.

II

Then one day without the slightest warning word reached me that premises had been found, that the school was to be started as soon as possible and that I was to be its first director. The official intimation came in an extract from the Minutes of a Sadler's Wells Governors' meeting enclosed in a letter from George Chamberlain, Clerk to the Governors. The Minute also entrusted me with the engagement of a headmistress and staff.

At my first meeting with George Chamberlain our venture was sealed with a handshake and a letter by way of contract. Then we went to an A.B.C. in Islington with Mrs. Thellusson and Ursula Moreton and started to create a school on the tea-damp marble slab of the café. Depressing surroundings for the start of a great adventure, but as we juggled with figures and numbers we were anything but depressed, and judging by our animation the tepid tea might have been Veuve Clicquot. From that very moment I found George Chamberlain a friend and a pillar of strength. He dismissed nothing as impossible and was the living embodiment of Vic-Wells practical idealism. The school is but one small facet of his interests, all of which are complex, yet he is always ready with help, advice and with tact. No honour could be too great for such a man.

The very first problem was to find an office in the over-crowded Sadler's Wells Theatre. After some searching I was given the end of a corridor between the board-room and a fire escape, a small closet that contained a peg, a wash-basin and an enormous panel of Chinese embroidery that belonged to Tyrone Guthrie. I never discovered what it was doing there. Mrs. Doris Thellusson, secretary to the existing ballet school, was my only colleague and, with her *on-se-débrouillera* spirit she scrounged a desk, a chair and a long chest that had belonged to Charles Kingsley and had his name on a plate. It made a useful bench for visitors but I never found out from where it came. I grew to love my little office, from which I could hear snatches of opera, though, when a board meeting was in progress next door, I was virtually locked in unless I climbed to the top of the building and found my way through a maze of corridors, during which journey I would have to tiptoe through rehearsals of *Carmen* and *La Tosca*.

The first thing I did was to visit the school premises, formerly the Froebel Institute and at that time a furniture depository. It was stacked high with chairs, tables and bedsteads, its windows were shattered or covered in grime and there were large holes in the floors. The only thing that suggested a school was a photograph and memorial plaque over a fireplace to a former headmistress of the Froebel. The picture of that serene and dignified educationist was friendly and gave me courage. Vaguely we mapped out the rooms, noted the most urgent repairs and had a cup of sweet milky tea with the depository foreman. It was impossible to fix a date though the occupants were due to leave in three months' time. The thought of the permits required was terrifying in itself, especially as the wooden floors were laid on concrete and quite impossible for the teaching of dancing.

For the time being I postponed all thoughts of engaging a staff but continued to make plans on paper, and to try and master the endless forms that confronted me. Meanwhile much of my time was filled in looking after the educational requirements of the post-school ballet students who had their headquarters in a large church hall on Primrose Hill. These forty pupils, boys and girls, required a continuation programme of some two hours a day. They were of different ages from fifteen upwards, and as we only had one hall for lessons and dancing the organization of a time-table was highly complex. We concentrated on the English language, French and play-reading. I looked after the English myself as good practice for the school to come; apart from the experience in teaching it would tell me a great deal about the type of child involved.

Discipline could have been a difficult problem with such a large group in a restricted space. I found it easy and never had the slightest trouble, though I afterwards learnt that one teacher who overran the hour was sharply reminded by a battery of concealed alarm clocks. The worst trial of all was the hard winter of 1947 when we had to crowd round a small fire-place, wrapped in coats and mufflers, too cold and con-gested to do much writing. There was a wonderful *esprit de corps*, the feeling that, inadequate and inconvenient as this might be, it was the beginning of something really important. Occasionally to cheer both myself and my pupils I talked of the new building and the amenities that would be ours. But when?

On January 1, 1947, I visited the now deserted building again in company with Doris Thellusson and the Wells archi-tect. We scribbled the names of the various rooms on the doors with a piece of chalk. I was deeply moved when I wrote *Lilian Baylis Hall* on the largest room of all and thought of how she would have relished the realization of this plan made possible by all her work. Another room in the school whose name I scribbled in chalk that day is dedicated to the memory of a pioneer. It is the Pearl Argyle Memorial Library equipped for us by Curtis Bernhardt, her husband. And what a pioneer she was! I have never seen a more perfect human being, and it was not only the superb bone structure of her face but the serene character that was reflected in it.

III

I remember well the first time I saw her, in the autumn of 1929, on the *barre* in Marie Rambert's studio. I had met Marie Rambert at the exhibition I had organized in memory of Diaghileff. I had often seen her at Monte Carlo. We talked of classicism, of which I had become a staunch defender, and she invited me to her studio to see some of the great *adages* and variations then so little known, and also the work of a young man of great promise, Frederick Ashton. What a treat it was! There on the *barre* were Prudence Hyman who, if the commercial theatre had not claimed her, would have become an outstanding ballerina, swan-necked, elegant and brimming with vitality; Andrée Howard, attractive, intelligent and highly individual, already beginning to create and design; the tall Grecian Diana Gould—now Mrs. Yehudi Menuhin—how wonderful she looked in the red costume of the *Capriol Suite* pavane—and Pearl Argyle. It was not Pearl whom I noticed so much that first time. She was still the schoolgirl with a suggestion of schoolgirl plumpness and she did her exercises with a concentration that did not invite the gaze of a visitor.

A few months later it was Pearl who held one's attention. She was no longer a schoolgirl but a woman of extraordinary beauty and her movement was now the expression of a personality. She had less technique than her companions but from that early stage she was mature and complete. I count her performances I saw in class and on the Ballet Club stage as among the most moving and memorable in my whole career as a spectator. And how well Ashton understood her needs and brought her out! There was *The Lady of Shalott*, when Pearl danced it as perfect a translation of a poem as *Le Spectre de la Rose*, and such translation is rare; I can only call *Thamar* to mind, *Les Masques* in a more modern idiom, and *Mars and Venus* where for once Venus came to life. I took her one day to tea with Epstein and he immediately began her bust. I saw the clay after the first sitting and it was shaping well. Rehearsals prevented further sittings. What a missed opportunity!

It was not merely the beauty, but the use made of it that turned my attention to English Ballet, and not only mine. Balanchine saw her and she danced in his *Ballets 1933*. The chauvinistic Russian Ballet world began to talk of *la belle anglaise* who did not disguise herself under a Russian name. She danced in Cochran's *Helen of Troy*, looking radiant in Oliver Messel's costume; he excelled himself in this white *décor*. Her excursions into the films were less successful, perhaps because her heart was always in ballet. But it was through the films that she met her husband, Curtis Bernhardt, and knew the great joy of a perfect marriage.

She joined Sadler's Wells at a period when she could show herself to the greatest advantage and also be of the greatest help to the company. Markova had left, Fonteyn was yet to become the greatest ballerina of her day. In that period I remember her best in Ashton's *Le Baiser de la Fée* where her aloofness lent a rare quality to the character she was portraying. She stayed in the company just long enough. Although in the classics her lack of strength was evident, and it worried her, the interpretation was always admirable. She had that completeness that the younger and more technical dancers lacked at that moment.

The last time I saw Pearl Argyle before she went with her husband to Hollywood was as a mother, and how the rôle suited her! I do not think I have ever seen anyone look more radiantly happy. I did not hear from her till after the war, when I received a parcel and a note. I wrote her a long letter in reply. Then I heard that she had dropped dead suddenly, without pain or illness. Her husband wrote to me, sent me photographs and, saddest of all, a very long letter that she had not been given the time to finish. It spoke of her great happiness, of her life as a wife and the mother of two boys. Her death was a tragedy but her life had been magnificently complete.

Anyone who saw Pearl Argyle will remember her art, her beauty and the inspiration she brought when our ballet was still so young. Anyone who knew her will never cease to mourn such perfection.

The Pearl Argyle Memorial Library, given to us by her husband and endowed with books by Edward Astley, Charles Lakin and many others, plays an important rôle in the life of the school.

IV

In spite of the architect's pessimism, and no architect can be anything but pessimistic these days, I decided that we should open in September and I went back to my cubby-hole office to draft an advertisement for a headmistress in *The Times Educational Supplement*.

Fortunately I had considerable experience of schools and headmistresses from my countless visits as lecturer during the war. I had often spent a full day looking round and discussing various problems with the staff. I must have seen well over two hundred schools situated all over the country. Unconsciously I was preparing myself for this task.

Within a week we were flooded with replies, over two hundred of them that we managed to narrow down to sixty-eight. All were interested in the pioneer nature of the venture and willing to make a considerable sacrifice and to take a risk in working with a small group; some were *balletomanes*—I eliminated the more extreme—but the majority were interested in the educational opportunity. The letters of application made interesting reading. One lady with an impressive list of degrees wrote to say that, by way of a change, she had been a snake charmer in a circus, had played the banjo at Collins' music hall and had contributed to the *New Statesman*, so that she could not fail to be exactly what we required. I saw her out of sheer curiosity but she was disappointing and had left snakes and banjo at home, though she was well armed with copies of the *New Statesman*.

The interviewing was long and tedious. It was usually obvious from the very first moment when an applicant was not possible, but in order not to hurt her feelings I had to continue for at least ten minutes. Each time I had to explain the workings of a school that only existed in the imagination. Doris Thellusson was an admirable companion, possessing just the right sense of humour and usually able to hold her laughter till the applicant had left the room, when she exploded with the noise of a soda-water syphon as it nears the end. I had also to answer a puzzling series of questions about Burnham Scale, increments and allowances. I still do not know the answers, though I know now where to turn for advice. I have never yet met a school teacher that understood it or knew the salary to which she was entitled. In any case not one of the applicants I interviewed was really interested in the finances so long as she could do good work and keep going.

Finally the list was narrowed down to two, one of whom eliminated herself for a reason that I do not clearly know; either through a legitimate fear of such an adventure or through taking umbrage at one of our governors' criticisms of a Latin proverb that she had devised for the school. He said it was bad Latin; she differed. Whatever the reason, she resigned two days later. She was succeeded by Miss Frances Packe, who fortunately had no strong ideas about Latin proverbs and who did fine pioneer work. When Miss Packe left to take up training college work her place was taken by Miss McCutcheon who had been in the school from the start.

Shortly before the school actually opened the Governors of Sadler's Wells formed a separate governing board for our school. Among its members are four good friends of other days and activities: Bernard Mortlock, Shaw-Zambra, Doctor Cawadias and James Smith. Bruce Ottley's help at the two meetings he attended showed us what a loss we had sustained.

The chairman is the dynamic Mrs. L'Estrange Malone, whose vast and practical knowledge of the educational world has been invaluable. It has been a mystery to me how she finds the time for all her activities and for the zest that she finds in theatregoing and other pleasures.

The Governors' meetings, held once a term, are the only ones among the forty or fifty I attend annually that I thoroughly enjoy. This 'Wells atmosphere' is an extraordinary thing. Ninette de Valois has defined it, as far as the company is concerned, as putting art before self, which she herself has done. It is the same thing with a committee of busy people, all strong individuals, experts in various fields or creative artists. The only thing that matters is the school and nothing is impossible. 'Where are those building plans?' I am asked. 'I thought we could not afford it.' 'Of course we can't, but you must always be ready with plans.' It is the Lilian Baylis touch. No detail is too small, but also no scheme is too large for consideration. Already many 'impossibilities' have become facts.

I have been fortunate both in my governors and my colleagues. The principal of dancing is my old friend, Ailne Phillips, daughter of the Carl Rosa Phillips, and a worker with de Valois from the pioneer days. There could have been no better choice. Miss McCutcheon and Miss Phillips, like Miss de Valois, are Irish, which adds wit to life.

A spacious building, full of attractive new furniture purchased through the kind help of the chairman of our Governors, Mrs. Malone, and the L.C.C.; an active governing board, an enthusiastic director and a headmistress, sole survivor of sixty-eight candidates, do not make a school. It was necessary to have pupils and we were looking for pupils of a very special type, the finding of which will always be our main problem. The nucleus of the new school naturally came from those who were already learning in the ballet school. For the rest we had to hold a series of auditions, interviews would be a more accurate word, and from the moment that the school was announced we received hundreds more applications than we had vacancies. Our method of interview has remained unaltered, though experience has made us more selective, for reasons that I will outline later.

<h2 style="text-align:center">V</h2>

On September 29, 1947, Dr. Wand, Bishop of London, the school's visitor, gave us his blessing as we worked, visiting room after room and using a language so clear and direct that the youngest child could understand and feel the solemnity of the occasion.

And so I had become a schoolmaster, by chance or, to be more accurate, by a devious route. I know something about children, little about the machinery of schools. The reading and the work I had done without any precise objective in my Cambridge days were proving of some value. The one distinct advantage that I had was an absence of any set theory of education. This was an experiment and we had to learn as we progressed. The only thing that we all wanted was to turn out good and well-educated citizens and not to run a dance factory or to make the educational school a mere appendage to the dance studio. Too many dance teachers were throwing in a little bit of education in order to pay lip-service to the new ideas.

Our particular problems were many and still a few remain. The first is in selection. It is obvious that such a school must be for the handful who will be able to take their places in our national ballet. The children are seen by Ninette de Valois, the principal of the dancing staff, Miss Phillips, Miss McCutcheon and myself. They do not perform their little show-pieces, indeed they do not perform at all. Clad in bathing dresses, hair brushed back well over the nape of the neck and well secured, they do a few of the basic movements by which their physique and general aptitude can be judged. Then, if a child is fortunate enough to pass de Valois' critical scrutiny, she is carefully examined by our physiotherapist, Celia Sparger, who has an intimate knowledge of ballet technique as well as anatomy. In addition the candidate receives a general medical overhaul. If all of this is satisfactory, the senior mistress and I interview the parent, talk to the child and put ourselves into touch with her previous school. This parent interviewing is very exhausting work because so much of the child's happiness depends on her mother's attitude from the moment that she is taken into the school, and therefore it is essential to make an impression at this very moment, when the mother already sees her child dancing *Swan Lake* on Covent Garden stage. Before the mother has had a chance of opening her mouth, I start. The speech is more or less a set one.

'Good morning, Mrs. X. We shall be able to find a vacancy for your daughter next term. She deserves the chance to show us what she can do. I must warn you that she is on a year's trial and that, even after that year, there is a risk that something may go wrong. The training is hard and it is a hard career, needing the vocation of a nun and the endurance of a boxer in training. We shall be very frank indeed with you; you in your turn must be frank with your child. You must make her realize the risks, you must help to widen her interests and you must stress the importance of school work. If for some reason she does not succeed, nearly always a reason right outside her control, you must never use the word "failure." Actually from a statistical point of view there is far more chance of being run over at Hammersmith Broadway than of getting on to Covent Garden stage.'

By this time the more exuberant mother seems a little shaken and for the child's sake I want her to be. When the school started I was altogether too jovial and encouraging, with unfortunate results in one or two cases. Now I follow up this talk with a letter in the same tone and with repeats when necessary. Having issued the warning, the interview goes

In class, December 1949

A School Outing, 1949
SADLER'S WELLS SCHOOL

on to practical matters of living accommodation, if they are not Londoners, ways and means, possible grants from the local authority, and so on. Then we have to find out what the child knows. That is special problem number one. Ours has a grammar school programme, but not all of the children are grammar school standard. We take, and rightly so, those that Ninette de Valois picks out. This difference of standard is a headache for the senior mistress; it requires a large staff and a great deal of individual attention, but it is working out amazingly well and, now that we have an even flow of nine-year-olds from the bottom form, it will soon cease to be a major problem though it will always remain a great expense.

From the first we have been exceedingly fortunate in our relationship with education authorities. They have understood our problems and our particular needs and have never failed to give us advice and guidance with, at the same time, the liberty that such an experiment requires. London gives us six scholarships a year, Middlesex is equally generous and most of the authorities give grants to students. So far the only difficulty lies in the conditions of such grants. We have a grammar school curriculum and therefore a basic condition is the passing of the entrance examination to grammar schools. But we require the children before the examination age, and some of the most talented from our point of view fail in the examination. London has allowed some exceptions, but I can realize the difficulties involved. Moreover, from our point of view, it is a risk since it is difficult to place a "failed" child who has not qualified for grammar school. Had we adequate endowments to provide our own scholarships the problem would not exist.

The next problem, a permanent one, is when, after a year, we review the pupil's progress. 'X's knees are not responding to training.' 'B has grown two inches, is over-tall and has outgrown her strength,' and so on but in very great detail.

In my first year this distressed me so greatly that I handled it badly. I thought of the shock to the children and tried to keep them on, concentrating on their general education. In truth, for the child to remain in this atmosphere watching others succeed and knowing that she herself could not was far more dangerous psychologically than the clean break. The longer the decision was delayed the worse it became. At nine, one little girl wants to become a nurse, another a dancer, one boy an engine driver, another a policeman. To say to the normal child a year later, 'It's no good, think of something else,' is merely to cause a temporary, if sharp sorrow; to say so at fifteen when she has worked for five years and hoped for five years is a very different matter. Now I try to guard against shock from the first and it works well. The children themselves often anticipate our decision. Recently for some unknown reason the profession of 'vet.' has been most popular as a second ambition!

I realize that the loss of security involved, even under the best circumstances, is unfortunate, but that is inherent in the profession of dancing.

Our children are very much extroverts and exhibitionists. They could easily become typical stage children and little horrors. Those that have had any connection with dance competitions and the resultant publicity are always handicapped at the start until they have grown out of such experiences. I always know them: they come to our auditions with rows of corkscrew curls that must have kept mother very busy the previous night. In such cases, also, mother is nearly always a thwarted dancer. 'I once learnt dancing and I was very good at it, but times were different and father was very strict. I got married instead, but I am determined that Zoe shall have every chance.' We are careful, therefore, to keep them from public performances, to forbid them the stage door and to see as far as we possibly can that they go to bed early. The longer they remain children the better for them in every way. The interests of the child and the art are identical. I have seen too much harm caused to prodigies and to ballet to have any illusions on that score.

I have always thought that discipline was important in education, and disagreed with the policy of 'free discipline' schools, attractive though they might appear on paper. For a ballet school reasonable discipline seemed more important than ever, since at a comparatively early age the child would have to fit into a complex organization in which tidiness, punctuality and obedience were as essential as in the Army or Navy. I need not have worried in the slightest. Though we have one or two punishments, the most brutal so far being the temporary deprivation of dancing classes, we scarcely ever have to use them. These children are naturally disciplined by their common objective, and by the technique of their gracious art. To me, it is a striking proof of what I mention in another chapter, the value of a disciplined as against a free form of movement in general education. When, one day, I discussed the question of discipline with Form I they were unanimous in thinking it a good thing as long as all the rules were sensible, and the reasons for them made clear. When I asked P., aged eight-and-a-half, why she liked discipline she replied, 'Because I shall have to obey rules when I leave school and if I'm not used to it I shall be unhappy.' No one could have said more.

VI

After we had been going for a year, Miss de Valois decided that we must take boys, and we set to work to enlarge the school for the purpose. It was obvious that we must keep boys and girls apart, both for dancing and much of the school work, since the fifteen to twenty boys that we could take would soon be completely swamped, also overshadowed by the far quicker thinking girls, for from nine to sixteen they work and think at a different pace, especially as our boys are athletes and not potential scholars.

Our boys must be tough athletes. It was no good taking the little boy whose mother had really wanted a girl. Where the boys were concerned we had to offer inducements by way of scholarships. Most of our boys have come from working-class families in the Midlands and the North. They are certainly tough and manly. At the very first audition we asked a small freckled lad with a missing front tooth, 'Why do you want to become a dancer?' He cocked his head on one side, looked straight at Ninette—'Ah've 'eard tell there's money in it.' He is doing very well, for of course we took him.

Much of the future of our ballet will depend upon what we can make of these boys. If the present batch makes good, the prejudice against male dancing will gradually die out and the effeminate dancer, from that very fact a bad dancer, will become a thing of the past.

To me the most interesting thing of all has been to see what we could do with a twelve-year-old who, through unfortunate war schooling, could scarcely read or write. He worked hard and we worked hard. True, there is much ground-work missing, but he is more civilized than most. He now reads Greek tragedy (in translation) with great pleasure—I found by chance that he had taken a whole series out of the library. He can also box reasonably well.

One other lovable boy started as a young hooligan. In one term he has gained easy and natural good manners, retaining, thank goodness, his high spirits.

What is so noticeable is the way in which the classes have mixed and become one. At the end of a few terms it is impossible to tell the coal-heaver's daughter from the banker's. I often get a shock when I see the mother of a 'perfect aristocrat,' and the word 'shock' does not imply snobbishness but the contrary since, given the same chance, the transformation would have happened a generation before.

I had not been schoolmastering long before I found what is the greatest enemy of childhood and of the teacher. Before, I knew of the beastly thing in theory but, thank God, it had been so far removed from anything in my experience, either as a child or an adult, that I took it lightly as 'one of those unfortunate things, nothing much to make a fuss about so long as everyone behaved in a sensible and civilized fashion.' Now I know better.

This is how it strikes. We notice that Z is becoming inattentive, quarrelsome and untidy. She is touchy and cries easily though she has always been a very cheerful child. This is commented on at the staff meeting by all concerned. In America they might say, 'What about a psychiatrist?' Here I remark, 'What about a tonic?'

Soon afterwards I get a letter from Z's mother. 'Will you please send the report and any letters direct to me at. . . . My husband and I have decided to separate.'

We have had twelve such cases in the short life of a small school, each time with an effect on the child that shocked and saddened and left one helpless. Twice mothers have actually told me 'If X's father tries to see her during school hours, please don't let him.' Here is a note from my school diary of a typical case, but one that made a deep impression because the child was above the average in intelligence, very sensitive, and appealed to me for help I could not give.

'X asked to see me this morning. She has been crying on and off for many days and I know it's not because her dancing is not a success. We had all that out and she was calm and logical and had other plans. It might, of course, be delayed action, although it would surprise me in her case.

'She has told me, and I don't know how to cope with such a situation. It is the old story with some additional complications. She ended up by saying—"I hate my father. He is a brute.

I kicked him last night." She wasn't crying when she said that and the adult concentration on a pleasant baby face frightened me. The story that she told—it was afterwards confirmed—showed a degree of selfishness on the father's part that amounted to crime, but nothing that a court of law could possibly notice. I did not attempt to defend her father—I said to her, "I have no doubt that you are right in everything you say, but you must be patient and practical. You are very small, he is large and strong. By kicking him you are being very stupid and justifying in his mind everything he does. You know what grace and dignity mean; kicking is horribly undignified. You are letting yourself down and doing him no harm. The best thing that you can do is to work hard, so very hard that one day you can be quite independent and live your own life. Think of that all the time you are working."'

It was weak as consolation but she was happy that I did not read her a lecture about respect due to parents.

These children have a chance. They have a strong sense of vocation, and they may be all right in the end, although an unhappy childhood must leave its scars and may in its turn prevent a happy marriage. I am certain, however, that others have less chance. If one examined the cases of the rapidly increasing number of juvenile delinquents, one would find—and a probation officer confirms this—that in the majority of cases there was the story of a broken marriage. What makes things worse is the mistaken humanity of the law that enables separated parents to share children. Whatever happens, the sense of security is gone, but in this case there is set up a sense of divided loyalty that each parent either consciously or unconsciously must exploit. A strong sense of loyalty is an essential. We laugh at the Victorian 'Papa and Mamma can do no wrong,' the modern psychologists have found that to love one's parents sets up a mass of complexes with Greek names, but such an attitude does seem the lesser of two evils.

The secret of success in teaching is surely common sense, an intense interest in people, a respect for the individual and an absence of theories and ideologies that try to reduce the pupil to X who must be taught Y. My friend, Professor Cawadias, has stressed that point of view in his brilliant paper on Hippocratic medicine when he underlines the point that there are not a long list of diseases that have their appropriate remedies; there are in fact no diseases in the abstract. There is an individual John Smith suffering from a disease and he can only be cured when the doctor understands both John Smith and his illness. The tendency to call in child psychologists for that slightest deviation from what is, in any case, an unknown normal is both ridiculous and harmful. The good teacher must be a practical psychologist, the general practitioner of psychology, so to speak.

Some time ago there was the case of A, a very talented and highly-strung child. She suddenly became rude to all the staff and very difficult to manage. I knew that she had just had a very upsetting home experience, the usual broken marriage. She had lost faith in people and was dramatizing her own situation by searching for a martyrdom that would enable her to say, 'I am unhappy and everyone is against me.' I sent for her and told her that she had been reported to me for her abominable rudeness. I went on to say that I had not the slightest intention of punishing her as I knew that she was going through a very bad time through no fault of her own. I even told her that she could go on being rude with impunity if it gave her the slightest relief or pleasure, but that I felt she was a little too old for that sort of behaviour. She burst out crying, sobbed for some twenty minutes and left. Since then she has behaved perfectly, worked really well and even looks cheerful at times. Had she been punished she would have felt a martyr and revelled in it: had she been taken to a psychologist she would have become the centre of attention with infinite harm to her character. As things were, a bare minimum of common sense and half an hour of my time accomplished all that could be done. Her very real sorrow and her shattered beliefs can be cured by no one. This shadow of divorce lies over every school.

I write here of what every school teacher knows, but I write with indignation because it is something I have happened on when I already thought I knew the world, and I prided myself on being broad-minded about such things. By reaction one can be far too broad-minded. I have only recently begun to have a decided opinion about the inviolability of the sacrament of marriage and the absolute evil of divorce, but I always knew beyond any doubt that, where adolescents were concerned, except under the positive circumstances of cruelty, the callous selfishness involved amounts to a crime.

Jules Dalou, sensitive sculptor of childhood, during his English exile made a bust of his sixteen-year-old sister-in-law, a work as fine as any of the busts of the French eighteenth century. His biographer calls it *Candeur*. It is always on my desk. This child, who is not particularly beautiful, looks up with an air of naïf astonishment, with wonder because life is so beautiful and exciting, and also with full confidence that she will not be hurt. To me it has become a symbol of happy adolescence. It is an expression to which every adolescent has a right; to remove it prematurely is a sin.

VIII

I have done my share of teaching since the school started, and that is what I enjoy most of all. It is essential if I am to understand these children and pull my weight at the staff conferences. I find I can teach the very young—I would really love a kindergarten—and I can teach the more intelligent and inquisitive student. I have great patience and an infinite interest in people so that I am never bored. I lack the experience and the technique, however, to give routine lessons to the in-betweens who are approaching their examinations.

I always used to wonder if it were possible for a teacher not to have favourites, and the subject always cropped up when I was a schoolboy whenever a 'beak' was under discussion. Personally I find it is impossible to have favourites; one likes A because she is intelligent, B because she has high spirits and is frequently in trouble, C because she is earnest and so very backward and her large cow-like eyes fill with tears as she tries to follow, D because she has just announced that all education bores her and she dislikes learning—the very problem of converting her makes her a favourite, E because she is the type of underdog; and so it goes on. True there is F, nothing very lovable about her. She is sly and I suspect her of being something of a bully. But then, what magnificent material to work upon! She, too, is at any rate a potential favourite with the first pleasing trait that she reveals. I find that all my staff look on this in the same light and that, if we admit to any bias, it is in favour of those who need the most help and who set us the hardest of problems.

It is beyond a doubt the most completely satisfying work I have ever done, or could even imagine. Generally it leaves one exhausted but often triumphant. And when one is at one's most tired at end of term, and the children have gone home, what is more dismal and depressing than an empty, clean, quiet and tidy school building, unless it be a deserted theatre.

IX

A landmark in the history of the school was the visit of Princess Margaret on March 1, 1951. Ballet was born at Court and tradition is a living force in such an art. The Princess Margaret Room in which the pupils now dance commemorates this visit. No one who was there will forget the grace of one whom we regard as 'our Princess.'

CHAPTER NINETEEN

Balletomane's London: Post-War

I

MY work, absorbing as it is, has not made me lose interest in current ballet and in the work of our many visitors. I have always hated artistic parish-pumpery. It is extraordinary how quickly one can lose all sense of values through only watching the work of one company, however good. This chapter forms a pendant to the one on the pre-war ballet and its little world.

What a contrast, the post-war life in the *balletomane's* London! The gracious hostesses who entertained for Diaghileff and were in his councils have disappeared. The prince of hosts, alas, is dead. In any case no one can afford the lavish hospitality of yesterday. When there is a full-dress party it is given by an embassy. But, economic reasons apart, ballet is no longer a novelty, the six weeks' stay of the Russians no longer lends a little colour to the end of the season. There is now no close season for ballet. The company that sets the standard is British, the dancers are not exotics who speak English amusingly and, living in London, they have their family interests and can even, on occasions, be seen pushing prams or queueing for vegetables.

The new ballet public is larger by far and more personal and partisan in its likes and dislikes. Listen to the expertise of the long queue snaking its way round Floral Street: 'The list says Margot but I know that Beryl is dancing tonight. Bobbie was smashing last night. This is the third time I've been this week and my fourth *Lac* this season. Shame that Violetta hasn't got another *Swan Lake*, if I was de Valois. . . .' One night I stumbled on Lady Cunard at the stage door. She was addressing a party of enthusiasts with some heat: 'Mr. Helpmann, not

Bobbie, unless you know him intimately. I have always believed that artists should be treated with proper respect.'

But she was not even a name to these young enthusiasts. And they meant well, even if they kept a hungry artist away from his supper for ten minutes or so.

One can now see men in shirt-sleeves and shorts sitting in the Opera House, the dinner jacket is an exception and on an ordinary night anyone in tails would feel really conspicuous. No wonder, with the performance beginning at seven, pale daylight at curtain-fall, and a scramble home afterwards. This early hour has come to stay. It suits the majority and taps a vast new public. But it does take some of the glamour out of theatregoing.

There are new faces, too, among the critics though many of the old hands have survived their thousandth *Sylphides*, and are bearing up bravely as they face their second thousand. Philip Richardson towers like a lamp-post over everyone in the crush bar, accompanied by his critic, Joan Lawson, old friend of mine of Astafieva days. Cyril Beaumont, hair *en brosse*, takes his seat unobtrusively. Although I have always admired him I used to consider him cold and stand-offish. I was wrong; he is, I think, a shy man. We became good friends in the Tony Mayers' flat over our enthusiasm for things French. Another bond: we received our *légions* together. He is the most knowledgeable and well-balanced of all the critics, a man of taste and real erudition. Caryl Brahms is witty and sometimes cutting as she sidles up to pass a remark on the performers or their audience. James Monahan maintains the *Manchester Guardian* reputation for informed criticism. He is an enthusiast with standards. The music critics are not *balletomanes* and are a little outside the family group. Thank goodness that someone has a watching brief for music. Frank Howes, Dyneley Hussey and Scott Goddard have all made a major contribution to the criticism of ballet. Alas, that none of these writers are allowed the space in which to develop an idea. They can give notices but seldom reviews. There is no doubt that the newcomers are *balletomanes*, a trifle bored with the old stagers and their memories, and very conscious of a mission. It is only with experience that one has doubts. Their doyen, if one can apply the term to anyone so young, is Richard Buckle, witty and an admirable writer, though reckless at times, who edits a paper of great taste and has made sacrifices to do so. I believe he will make a major contribution to ballet. A. V. Coton, P. W. Manchester, Peter Williams, Mary Clarke, and Audrey Williamson complete this group.

After the performance supper habits have altered. This is now a serious meal, gobbled rather than discussed. The main ballet rendezvous now is a certain small café presided over by a Cypriot N., who looks after his customers as if they were his guests. His clientèle consists of those who need healthy nourishment, boxers and dancers. Their photographs adorn the walls. Lee Savold may be seen at one table, Toumanova at another. Each one is capable of eating two rare steaks at a sitting. When there are Spaniards in town the café is completely transformed. Castanets are clicked, guitar strings plucked and heels tap the floor. N.'s favourite cat is Spanish. It was christened Carmen until its true sex was revealed. It is now known as Chico. Customers circulate from table to table gossiping and discussing the performance. Bloomsbury is no longer ballet's residential quarter and those few hummed bars of *Schéhérazade* bring no faces to the window. Our foreign visitors are better paid than the Russians of old and favour Mayfair or South Kensington. The most popular dwelling is a large house in 'Wezzerbee Gardennes,' kept by a delightful Russian couple who love their artists and spoil them even when at times they turn the house upside down.

II

The newcomers who have taken the place of the Russians as 'exotics' are the French. And what a revelation they were, and

BALLETOMANE'S LONDON: POST-WAR

would have continued to be if individuality had not run wild!
Boris Kochno put it to me vividly. 'I have worked with
English, Russians and French. The French are by far the most
difficult. You English have a natural discipline and the famous
team spirit, the Russians are temperamental but even so we
did once have serfs, but the French since their revolution——!'

A French company has original ideas, extraordinary taste,
stars of personality and no *corps de ballet* or cohesion. It is
constantly in the throes of a change of Government.

Our first visitors were *Les Ballets des Champs Elysées*, led
by the twenty-one-year-old Roland Petit, son of a Parisian
restaurant proprietor and an Italian mother. Petit has the most
extraordinary charm, an original outlook and a facility for
choreography that may well make his fortune and prove his
artistic undoing. He is at the crossroads; he will either become
the great producer of grand revues and musicals or the master
choreographer of our period. *Les Forains*, *Les Amours de
Jupiter*, *Les Demoiselles de la Nuit* and *Carmen* are the works of
the master, while *Oeuf à la Coq* and *Le Bal des Blanchisseuses*
have enough zip and invention in them to make the average
American musical look anaemic. It is a pity that the great
success of *Carmen* has not only forced Petit to present it at
every performance but has given him such a keen enjoyment
of success that he may be inclined to work for it deliberately.
Also, since he has formed his own company independently of
Les Champs Elysées he is certainly finding out the difficulties
of acting as director, *premier danseur* and choreographer. I
maintain that it is impossible.

I have seen many close finishes where the costumes were
completed a few moments before curtain-rise but nothing to
equal the case of *Le Rêve de Leonor*, where ten days before the
première the music was not yet chosen and where the final
result was two ballets instead of one.

Leonor Fini had made the costumes and *décor* for a ballet
for which she had devised a crazily morbid scenario, a shop-

285

soiled article, *modèle* 1920. Music had been commissioned, the choreography entrusted to Janine Charrat, and the date of the *première* announced on the bills outside the Prince's Theatre. Three weeks before that date the commissioned music fell through. To anyone else but Petit, urged on by his contract, that would have seemed an insurmountable barrier. Everyone starts feverishly to look for music, music that will fit the swiftly moving scenes of Fini's nightmare. The B.B.C. gramophone library is called into action, the advice of music critics is sought, composers are telephoned and asked if they have anything in stock. The conductor produces idea after idea hammered out on a piano lit by a dim pilot light after the evening performance. Fini turns down most of the suggestions; after all this is her particular nightmare. With the ballet now only a week ahead Charrat wisely throws in her hand and the energetic Petit takes full charge. He has found his music, the *Liebestod* from Tristan, music that has already been worried for Dali's bout of Freudian indigestion; rehearsals are started, they continue half the night and all of one Sunday. Even Jeanmaire is tired though a sudden inspiration by Petit galvanizes her into action and one can hear her little cries of triumph, '*Ça yest, ça yest.*' Yet choreographically, that is if one can divorce choreography from music, this is full of brilliant flashes of improvisation. It is then decided that this has taken a shape of its own and has nothing to do with Fini. It is christened *Pas d'Action* and announced as a new ballet. But now, though there is music and dancing, the *décor* is missing. No matter, there are two or three days to go. The wardrobe is called upon and a brilliant *décor* is improvised with wicker skips and hanging dresses. The work is a success in Paris but a dismal failure in London. Our critics not unnaturally ask, '*Que fait Wagner dans cette galère?*'

Meanwhile Fini's nightmare has been handed over to Ashton with the extraordinarily long period of the fortnight's postponement in which to compose it. He selects Benjamin

Britten's *Variations on a Theme of Frank Bridge*, and produces a passable work obviously below his own high standard. But then it is a little difficult with a bald heroine and a wire-suspended wig whisked across the stage to avoid the ridiculous.

Yes, Petit is brilliant but such improvisation cannot be relied upon except for the last-minute touches of a completed ballet. He worked upon *Carmen* for many months until the pattern and the steps had taken shape; not only the steps but the characters were perfectly realized with Jeanmaire shorn of her curls and *coiffée en gamin*. It was in the final two rehearsals, which I watched fascinated, that he put in the dramatic production touches that made this work so vivid and memorable, the smoking of the cigarette, the wiping of the hands on the curtain, the sucking of the orange, the bird in the cage. His eye for detail is superb; he is a masterly producer as well as an inventive choreographer. The combination is rare. If he is to become the really great figure that he promises to be, he must concentrate on choreography and especially on the musical preparation of his ballets. The enthusiast must learn to plod without sacrificing his enthusiasm. French method must be joined with Italian *fougue*. I owe to Petit some of the most enjoyable hours ever spent watching ballet and I am grateful.

The pedigree of this particular contemporary school of French Ballet is by Lifar out of Kochno. It is a tragedy that their personal differences have not allowed them to work in harness. Lifar, as I have written, made the vocation and trained the dancers, while Kochno provided the ideas and assembled the distinguished collaborators. The theme of a ballet is always a difficulty and since Gautier no one excels Kochno and Cocteau in this. Ideas that look ridiculous on paper come to magnificent life when danced on the stage.

Where the French differ from us is in their use of dancers. We create our ballets and then cast them from a perfectly homogeneous group of classically trained dancers, while they often select a dancer and build a ballet around her personality and physique. In this way we have enjoyed the acrobatic classicism of the elegant stylized Danielle Darmance and have seen Leslie Caron's physique put to magnificent use as the Sphinx. This is the complete denial of classicism and means that the ballets produced are even more ephemeral than usual. When such 'personal ballets' are handled by poets the result is wonderfully exciting. But in the very creation of stars for particular ballets a company inevitably destroys itself. It becomes a case of having so and so on the pay-roll and of having to build a ballet around her. Also it discourages the classical dancers, mainstay of any company.

It is greatly to be regretted that Renée Jeanmaire, Colette Marchand, Nina Wyroubova, Irène Skorik, Nathalie Philippart, Janine Charrat, Ludmila Tcherina, Emile Audran, Vladimir Skouratoff, and the prodigious Babilée have not remained together and that already *Le Rendezvous* and *Les Forains*, so recently created, are memories alongside *Cotillon* and *Jeux d'Enfants*.

I think, were I forced to choose a single dancer, male or female, whom I would like to see at this very moment, it would be Babilée at the top of his form, soaring into the air as the Blue Bird, leaping on to the table in *Le Jeune Homme et la Mort*, hump-backed and sinister in *Le Rendezvous*, mocking and volatile as the Joker in *Jeu de Cartes*.

Off the stage small, stocky and almost insignificant, once he dances he towers at will. Alone among the hard-working French he relies on the mood of the moment, practically jumping from his motor-cycle on to the stage without the saving discipline of a warm-up. He is wayward, mischievous, unpredictable; but since my vague, perhaps exaggerated memories of Nijinsky and my more recent ones of the young Lifar, I have not seen his equal as a dancer. I have one characteristic picture of him in a ballet that is *inédit*.

The scene is London at midnight. Supper is over. The night is hot and it is too early to go to bed. A café would be

At the Tony Mayers', 1948
A gathering of French dancers in London

At my home, 1950
Muriel Smith, Barbara Bocher ('baby' of the New York
City Ballet), Leila McCutcheon

A PAGE OF PARTIES

ideal, but as there is no café in this strange city, a bench in the open is the next best thing. We walk into St. Giles' church-yard and sit down. But Babilée is restless. He sees the children's playground, vaults over the fence and for the next half-hour entertains himself and us with his acrobatic clowning. A very pleasant theme for Cocteau; the graveyard, the playground and the athletic youth. The composer would have to suggest the muffled sound of passing traffic and the chime of a distant clock. The *décor* I would entrust to Brassaï.

III

The 'ballet snobs' in the past were never ready to welcome our dancers. There is this excuse for them: it is so much more amusing to hear some commonplace spoken in a foreign lan-guage. Provided one can distinguish between the performance one has just seen and the dancers one meets afterwards at supper, I can sympathize. I, too, like to watch the behaviour and reactions of a concentrated group of Russians, French, Spaniards or Americans. Ballet is in itself a super-nationality; an English girl who is a dancer has more in common with her French, Russian or American colleagues than with another English girl who is not a dancer. Granted the fact of this balletic nationality, the differences are still many.

The most violently national of all are the French. They adapt themselves less well to conditions and especially to food than any of the others. If there is one French girl in a foreign com-pany, somehow or other when she is present everyone will be speaking, or trying to speak, French. A French company on tour is a complete French community, polite about it but obviously surprised and pained by the habits of the barbarians all around. The tone in the company is not one of sudden dramatic scandals that flare up, then fizzle out *à la mama Toumanova*, but one of continual *fronde*, in which *Egalité* and *Liberté* are very much to the fore.

Here is a picture of Paris in London. The scene, a house in a quiet square in South Kensington. It is the last night of a long season. Our dancers have reached that stage of packing exhaustion when one carries a pile of clothes from one chair to another, wanders aimlessly round the room and then sits down on a trunk and cries (women) or curses (men). I have been invited to dine at nine, have smoked my last pipeful of tobacco and am desperately hungry. As the hours advance I despair of a meal. At one o'clock someone has a bright idea: *'Si on mangeait maintenant?'* But this is to be no snack, no sandwich nibbling. A chicken is produced, stuffed with good things, put in the oven and basted. A salad is made and dressed with skill. *Hors d'œuvres* are invented, raw kipper strips providing an admirable substitute for smoked salmon. Finally someone dives into a cupboard and produces two bottles of red wine. At a quarter to two we sit down to a better meal than any London restaurant could produce, fatigue is gone, packing can wait, the French are vital and happy once again. A heated argument breaks out about the personality of some *maître de ballet*, a scene at the Opéra four years ago is vividly enacted. South Kensington has become Paris.

The next morning and Impresario Leon Hepner has been pacing the platform for a good half-hour; they catch the train to the Midlands by the skin of their teeth.

IV

Other semi-exotic visitors have been the Americans, Ballet Theater and the New York City Ballet. What a rich variety of work they have given us; the Americana of Jerome Robbins, *Fancy Free* and *Interplay*, Anthony Tudor's dramas, *Jardin au Lilas* and *Pillar of Fire*, Agnes de Mille's *Rodeo* and *Fall River Legend*, and Balanchine's doctrinaire eurythmic ballets wonderful at their best. And what vitality in their dancers. Sometimes poetry has been sacrificed to acrobatic efficiency; the classics are best left alone.

It is a truism to say that the Americans represent youth. They are enthusiasts, not only for ballet—all dancers are that of necessity—but for the circumstances of the tour and the places they see. No visitors are easier to entertain or more entertaining in themselves. Never a trace of weariness or boredom as experience crowds in on experience. They are natural and their manners are natural good manners. In giving them hospitality one can feel the warm reflection of their own overwhelming hospitality. They have done more to put America on the map artistically than several hundred miles of Hollywood celluloid, ten musicals, a million dollar crooner and a red-headed comic. I remember the surprise at the very idea of an American Ballet when that pioneer company of Catherine Littlefield's, the Philadelphia Ballet, came to the Hippodrome and delighted us with *Barn Dance*.

It is Lincoln Kirstein more than anyone else who has given a ballet to America. I remember meeting him and having many talks with him in 1933 when the de Basil Ballet came as a revelation. Fokine and others of the great Russians had settled in America and had done very little save enrich themselves. Kirstein dreamed of a school and a company. In Balanchine he found the ideal partner, the one major choreographer not too firmly rooted in the European past. Kirstein sacrificed much of his personal fortune while Balanchine produced a film or a musical a year in order to subsidize the ballet he loved. The American School of Ballet, the American Ballet, Ballet Caravan and finally the New York City Ballet have been born of this idealism.

Kirstein is a man of violent opinions and complete integrity. He once launched a bitter attack on me for having pandered to the impresarios and commercial interests instead of attacking them tooth and nail. I was able to convince him that his heat had been unnecessary and now he has no stronger supporter than the impresario, Sol Hurok. Does he enjoy his ballet? I hope so. All that I saw of him during his Covent Garden season was a tall dark figure with a permanent frown pacing, like Felix the Cat, up and down the back of the grand tier.

America has the physical material in plenty, but how much more difficult the economics than in impoverished Europe. America, as apart from New York, Chicago and San Francisco, is not yet ballet-conscious and the millionaires have not looked in its direction. I remember in 1933 trying to convince people in New York that a certain Agnes de Mille, whom I had been watching closely, had great talent and a highly inventive mind. No one was interested or really believed me. She was labelled as the niece of Cecil B., a girl of some means who was amusing herself in Europe at something strictly non-commercial. It was only when she made a name in a big musical that she was 'discovered,' and it is Agnes de Mille who acted as godparent to Anthony Tudor and launched him in America.

And what a fortune it takes to cope with the terrible expenses caused by the stranglehold of the unions! Lucia Chase has poured money into her Ballet Theatre and yet there are constant crises even after seasons that have been acclaimed by the critics.

But this, thank goodness, is not a volume of criticism or a survey of contemporary ballet but a personal record. Here then is a happy memory of a scene during an American season in London.

It is Sunday—fortunately there is no rehearsal—and we have taken a small party down to Eton where my sons are to act as hosts. Windsor Castle, College, the top-hats, Rowlands and its 'bangers' enchant them. My son points out a tall figure in academic gown and Geneva bands talking to a venerable man in a black coat. 'Those are the Provost and Headmaster.' Great excitement and a general move in their direction while a camera is shoved into my son's hands. 'We'll crowd round them and make a group. It'll make a swell photograph to send home.'

With difficulty and considerable tact a pale and trembling father and sons head them off in another direction, and only breathe again when Provost and Headmaster are out of sight. 'He's very important,' says one of the sons, 'and might not like being disturbed. Would you get President Truman to pose with you?' 'Of course we would,' was the reply.

I think that the Provost and Headmaster could not have failed to enjoy those particular visitors, had we, their guides, not been so lacking in courage.

V

The dancers of the Russian emigration who made pre-war ballet have now become French and *ballet russe* 'is a name that is spoken,' a successful formula but no longer a reality. The *ci-devant* ballerinas are still teaching, but they grow old. There are two Russian teachers of a younger generation, Vera Volkova in London and Boris Kniaseff in Paris. The stars pass through their hands. The only large-scale company created for Monte Carlo but adrift like the others and following the old formula is that of the Marquis de Cuevas. By his fortune—his wife is a Rockefeller—his very considerable charm and a certain flair he has attracted talent from all over the world. His publicity suggests that he is trying to wear Diaghileff's hat, but Diaghileff had a notoriously big head and the hat has fallen over the Marquis' ears. And then Diaghileff had no need of personal publicity; his photo never graced a programme. 'What do you do?' he was asked in an interview. 'Tell your readers that I advise about the lighting.' He was not modest, perhaps even he was too vain to need such publicity.

It is a thankless task to prophesy about the future but one that I cannot avoid, since naturally the subject is constantly in my thoughts both as writer and active participant. Will the great popularity of ballet continue and what form will it take?

Popularity can be a dangerous thing when it is not informed

by proper standards. We have seen that before in the vulgarization of the great romantic movement. The 'Red Shoe' type of hysteria and the various manifestations in great sports arenas, instead of winning a new public as some apologists claim, will only alienate critical opinion. There are signs already that this is happening. In 1949 three great galas were held at the Empress Hall with a superb cast in an attempt to make money for Nijinsky. They were a failure and the unfortunate Nijinsky received a hundred pounds or so. It is true that the artists concerned were over-generously treated in the matter of expenses, but full halls would have given a handsome profit. The public is beginning to learn the difference between watching the athletic performances of isolated stars and a properly balanced ballet. I remember asking Pavlova one day why she troubled to have a large company when she herself was the big draw. She replied quite simply, 'I would not dare appear alone for a whole performance. A dancer can only hold the audience's attention for a very short time.' I have never forgotten that.

When I started my life in ballet I was looked upon as an eccentric; there was not enough work to keep a ballet critic in cigarettes, even at the price that they were then. Now my mail bag averages from twenty to thirty letters a week, the telephone never stops ringing, and wherever I go I cannot avoid the subject. People presume upon the slightest acquaintance to ask me to get them tickets for Covent Garden when I find it difficult myself. I am even waylaid to give autographs to the fans; I may grumble but I enjoy it.

I do not think the present hysteria will last, neither do I think that ballet will fade out except for a month or two a year, although as I will show the risk exists. There should always be a public for the best and, through a reaction from the uncritical attitude of so many, the best will have to be very good indeed. The company hastily assembled by the ambitious dancer and given some such title as the Grand or the Universal or the Grand Universal—and how many of such there have been—

will no longer be able to find bookings. Improved television will set a standard for those living outside the big centres, so that they will no longer be able to tolerate half a dozen tottering swans and eight bedraggled sylphs supporting a utility star.

The future of ballet today belongs to state-supported organizations which alone can afford productions on a sufficient scale and which have a permanent home. Ballet will lose a great deal by this; it will run the risk of academism and complete uniformity. Its rebels will be turned loose as Fokine was by the Maryinsky diehards; but unlike Fokine, they will have nowhere to exercise their gifts. The girl who is an inch too tall or an inch too small for her national organization will have to give up dancing. All state organizations need the competition of a powerful independent international company that can produce the daring and unconventional works not suited to the dignity of an Opera House. *Carmen*, for instance, could never have been put on at the Opéra or at Covent Garden. If this academic sterility takes place, then the public will rapidly fade away even if the subsidized institution runs on. It happened at the Opéra in the pre-Lifar period.

But this gloomy picture, although it must constantly be borne in mind, lies in the future. Today in England the National Ballet is young and enthusiastic, is superbly guided by Ninette de Valois and has its outlet from potential pomposity in its second company.

VI

Any account of the post-war ballet scene in London would be incomplete without some mention of the many dancers outside the ballet tradition. *Balletomanes* are nothing if not conservative and the majority have yet to realize that folk-dancing has always fed ballet and that choreography can be greatly enriched from outside. However, in spite of this we have had more visitors than before.

The problem confronting both Indians and Spaniards has

been to translate their dancing, designed for temple, courtyard and tavern, into terms of the European stage. They must undertake this translation and at the same time maintain their authenticity and integrity. I am not an expert on Indian dancing, I am very sceptical about the claims of most non-Indian experts and the Yogi brigade, but I think that I can tell a good dancer from a bad, and can recognize true classicism even in a foreign idiom. I have enjoyed a long friendship with Ram Gopal, a strong theatrical personality, and was one of the sponsors of Mrinalini Sarabhai's remarkable European tour. I would imagine that Gopal has taken greater liberties with his basic material, but he, more than anyone, even the pioneer Shankar, has created a public for Indian dancing in this country. It is through him that we critics can use certain terms with a façade of knowledge. I have enjoyed these performances within the limits set by my reaction to the music, quite untroubled by learned discussions as to authenticity. Naturally I have felt and understood the Spaniards with greater intimacy because of a knowledge of their music and a love of their country. They, too, have never quite solved the problem of presentation, varying from the extremes of concert atmosphere of the great Argentina, her successor Mariemma and that remarkable couple, Rosario and Antonio, to the inspired and inspiring vulgarity of Amaya's stage show, of which Bérard said, 'I could not touch it without spoiling it.' The Spanish genius is one of individuality and I am grateful to the individuals who have given me such keen pleasure.

The most remarkable post-war visitors to London have been the Katherine Dunham group. Dunham herself is an amazing woman, an anthropologist of repute, a choreographer, the pioneer of a new method and at the same time a popular showman. In England she appealed to the theatregoing masses, in France to the artists, writers and musicians.

Dunham's original contribution to the dance lies in the use she has made of the coloured person's physique and temperament. And here I must break off to talk about colour from a personal point of view, for except in this context I would not have used the word at all.

I have no colour prejudice. That simple statement does not explain my views. Some of my American friends are very blond, others very dark. The very denial of prejudice sounds like a boast that one is broad-minded and therefore that there is something to be broad-minded about. Religion and science are for once in agreement: colour prejudice is without foundation. It is here that some imbecile is bound to chip in with the remark, 'I always pride myself on being very broad-minded' (Pecksniffian smile), 'but one must draw the line somewhere. Now admit you wouldn't like your daughter to marry a negro.'

This is supposed to be a stumper. I always reply, and by no means so politely as in this book, for like 'the-poor-use-their-baths-as-coal-bins' gambit, this makes me very angry: 'There are many millions of white men I would not like my daughter to marry, including Dr. Malan, a handful of Southern Senators and all the Hitler Youth. I would be very proud, however, to claim Dr. Ralph Bunche as a son-in-law. Yet why I should be worried if she married a coloured man is obvious. There are millions of imbeciles like yourself who start by saying, "You can't intermarry with such and such a class of person" and who push the argument so far that they end by sending the whole class to the death chambers. It happened and you know it.'

In Katherine Dunham's case it is relevant and important to underline colour because of the use she has made of it. Coloured physique is not as a rule suited to ballet and one cannot imagine coloured sylphs or swans. On the other hand, coloured folk have a genius for rhythm and for improvisation. They have, almost unknown to them, a very rich dance heritage. They have made a great hit on the stage very largely through being forced to pander as grotesques to the white man's vanity. They have even imitated the white 'nigger minstrels' impression of the typical negro. There are great exceptions such as Marian Anderson and my dear friend, Muriel Smith. But Muriel will have great difficulty in escaping a label and the type of work that entails, in spite of her superb lieder singing and her wide musical culture. As an anthropologist Dunham has gone back to the very sources of the negro dance, and by allying it to the technique of ballet that is suitable, provided it with a grammar or a school. The *décors* by her husband, John Pratt, are remarkably fine and her orchestrations superb. The negro dancer is no longer an ex-slave performer, a clown or a brilliant improviser, but a dancer on an equal footing with others, practising an art with roots and a technique. She has revived and arranged not only primitive dances, but dances of creole origin where African and a highly sophisticated European society met, the junction between Voodoo and Catholicism.

I have sat entranced watching her class, part European part to the rhythm of the drums, and seeing performances she has put on for my benefit, of ballets that she has devised. If her work can avoid becoming commercialized, and therefore advertised as yet another coloured show, its future is immense.

VII

What of my own attitude to ballet in the long interval since I wrote 'the story of an obsession'? Am I still an enthusiast? Yes, but in a different way and for different reasons. I could no longer follow a company around merely watching performances. The thrill caused by the performance itself is far less frequent. It requires the shock of novelty, *Le Jeune Homme et la Mort*, or of perfection, Fonteyn in *Le Lac des Cygnes*, to revive it; then it is as great as ever. My greatest interest lies in the personalities that make up its world, in observing the quick reactions and the sure touch of a de Valois or the artistic development of the smallest of her coryphées. In watching the reactions of the public and the critics and the different approach of the various nationalities involved. Even my committees are richly rewarding; to observe, for instance, Kenneth Clark who has the same incisive Renaissance brain as Keynes, an expertise that is never dry or doctrinaire and the rare gift of communication, or his wife who combines efficiency with the looks of a Pre-Raphaelite beauty, as I heard Michel Georges Michel call her. I am a fervent 'Janeite'. And both believed in our ballet when it was still on 'the wrong side of the river'. This is a world in miniature and I have an excellent vantage-point. There can be no doubt at all, however, that I am in love with my work and the opportunities it gives me, not only to serve the ballet but in a larger sphere. It turned up just in time. There could be nothing more depressing than the sight of an elderly hanger-on of ballet, a lifetime frequenter of *le foyer de la danse*. Diaghileff, on seeing one such figure at late supper with a ballerina, dryly commented, '*L'après dinuit d'un faune.*' I heard this when I was nineteen and have remembered it. 'There but for the grace of God . . .'

CHAPTER TWENTY

Nostalgia

I AM not, I think, a sentimental man, although in any case I would deny the charge, as severe an indictment as being accused of having no sense of humour. It is true that I have committed myself by relating how I wept over Dora's death on reading *David Copperfield*, and Beth's death in *Good Wives* was equally affecting. On the other hand Paul and the wild waves, Nell's and Smike's deaths have left me dry-eyed. Dora and Beth are, therefore, my exceptions though I cannot guarantee not to sniffle when a dramatist piles on the agony. I have said I am 'good audience' and 'good audience' must spill a tear for Marguerite Gautier, *La Dame au Camélias*. In any case where the theatre is concerned I would rather by far have my emotions played on by a Dumas *fils* or a Sardou than my brain stimulated by an Eliot, just as I would rather suffer with Giselle than learn some cosmic truth from Central European or American dance dramatists. Maybe I do not take the drama seriously enough or I take acting and dancing too seriously. I am quite certain that I would have revelled in Sarah and Irving whatever the vehicle they chose.

After watching ballet for over three decades from the Pavlova to the Fonteyn era I may be allowed, sentimental or not, the luxury of a nostalgic chapter, taking out my memories one by one like the faded and beribboned letters from an old escritoire drawer. I have in any case the same weakness as James Agate for the making of desert island lists; what would be the performances I would most like to live again, what are the ideal casts for the classics and so on? Ballet is so ephemeral an art that only memory unaided by any text can prolong its pleasures, even if it cannot communicate them to others. At any rate I shall be self-indulgent. It is a weakness of middle-age, harmless enough if one is strong-minded and refrains from quoting, '*Où sont les neiges d'antan.*'

Agate, of course, would have started any list with Sarah; Pavlova is my Sarah. When I write of her I think of no single great ballet, unless it be *Giselle*, but of a dancer and a *pas de bourrée*. It was sheer magic. There was no impression of bone, muscle and a hard stage, but of a floating movement, a gliding through water. Some fools better employed in watching all-in wrestling or some such obscenity said that she had no technique. They wanted the quantity of the shop-soiled bargain basement. Two turns only, but turns of such perfection that they could even arouse the enthusiasm of a Duncan who had set her face against ballet mechanics. And when she held a pose there was none of the wobble to get adjusted which so many of the modern dancers adopt—'just look at my balance.' Everything was in context, each movement linked with the next. How many of those brief moments I can still see on closing my eyes and humming the trivial melodies that inspired them. *Noël* as she enters in wraps from the wintry street and is greeted by her cavaliers, the folding of the petals in *The Californian Poppy*, the dart of *The Dragonfly* and of course *The Dying Swan*, which she danced some thousands of times, and I saw a hundred times at least and always with some variation in the ending, dictated by the mood of the moment. I would wait for that ending and always be convinced that on this occasion she had reached perfection. As Giselle she caught all three moods, the happiness and unsophistication of youth, the disillusion and '*douce folie*,' and then the spirituality of the last act in which she gave one the impression of mist floating down a moonlit valley.

With the exception of *Giselle* all my memories are of dances that are banal in the extreme when analysed or repeated by others. I once asked Fokine why she used such material. He replied, 'Because she is Pavlova and can transform it.' It was the right reply. She could use her material as a Chardin uses a loaf of bread, a wooden spoon and a jug of milk to produce a masterpiece.

My next memories are of the Diaghileff Ballet, of the perfection of a whole with Karsavina outstanding. What a variety of moods she could evoke and with what a mass of subtle detail! She stands at the opposite pole from Pavlova, the conscious artist as opposed to the instinctive artist. Each one has her rôle to play, but it is Karsavina who stands as the first modern ballerina, as an example to the young dancers of today. An instinctive artist without genius is a disaster. In the mime lecture-demonstrations that she occasionally gives her audiences are not only moved but they can see at work the mind that gave us Tamar and the Miller's Wife, Columbine and the other portraits in that long gallery.

It is not going to be easy to choose a season's repertoire from the fifty or more successes of Diaghileff's twenty years. I would certainly include *Le Spectre de la Rose*, *Les Sylphides*, *Carnaval*, with Idzikovski, the *Dances from Prince Igor*, with Woizikovski; all early season Fokine ballets which, though still in repertoires, grow daily more faded. Next, *Le Tricorne*, *La Boutique Fantasque* with, of course, Lopokova and Massine as the Can-Can dancers. Of a later period, Nijinska's *Les Biches* if only for Nemchinova's blue-tunicked entrance. These Biches were the vicious sylphs of the nineteen-twenties. I would like to see once more Sokolova as Kikimora in *Contes Russes*. She was the one Englishwoman completely assimilated in the Russian atmosphere. Could she have been registered at some dim town hall as Hilda Munnings? And almost the last sensation that Diaghileff gave us, *Le Fils Prodigue* with Lifar as the Prodigal and the serpentine Doubrovska as the siren curled hooplike around his waist.

The famous 'exotics,' sensations of the early years when Paul Poiret dictated fashions and the smart Parisian hostesses gave Oriental parties may not wear so well. Bakst has lost the power to startle us. But what wonderful moments they had; the entrance of the golden slave in *Schéhérazade* when he comes crouching like a panther into the women's quarters, his dramatic death pirouetting on his head as the Sultan's scimitar descends and Zobeïde's final supplication, or in *Tamar* when the curtain discovers her on a couch waving to attract the prince's caravan.

The later company may have been weak in classical dancers, but there was a perfection of production detail not seen since. Also, there was the intense feeling of excitement at a *première*, the feeling that artistic history was being made. One did not go to the ballet to see a dancer, even the greatest, but a collaboration. Sometimes the result would be a manifesto thrown out as a challenge and art and music students would come to blows for or against cubism, constructivism, surrealism. The *première* was a concert and an exhibition of painting and one could be sure of one thing only: Diaghileff would not repeat himself. He might delight you or shock you, he would certainly give you a topic for discussion until the next season came round again, by which time he might well, after a hearty stomach laugh, have discarded the particular work as boring and dated.

It is far easier to be more selective in one's choice of a de Basil repertoire. It would consist of the earlier works before the venture had become commercialized, and when the deaths of Diaghileff and Pavlova, and the Russian *émigré* wealth in the ballerinas' Paris studios, gave him the strongest company I have ever seen. Toumanova and Riabouchinska in Balanchine's *Cotillon*, Riabouchinska and Lichine in Massine's *Jeux d'Enfants*, Baronova, Lichine, Verchinina and Riabouchinska in *Les Présages*, Massine, Danilova, Riabouchinska, Baronova and Shabelevsky in *Le Beau Danube*. How delicate this little work and how ham-footed its revivals have been! Only the classics should be revived and can remain undated; for that reason they do not belong in a chapter of nostalgic memories. This is not invoking the past at the expense of the present, but stating something that is fundamental to the art of ballet. It is for that reason that I can see little practical value in film records and systems of notation. They could not, for instance, recapture the particular fragility of *Les Biches* any more than Nijinska herself could do. *Les Biches* was a commentary on the customs, thoughts and feelings of the nineteen-twenties. The audience viewed it from that angle, felt its subtle allusions. A facsimile would fail for that very reason. The classics may have been produced at a period when the audience was romantically inclined, but apart from the fact that such romanticism is a permanent and basic view of life that has always existed along-side of classicism, there are no subtle emotions, no innuendoes in these works. They are based on a straightforward virtuoso technique that is a direct challenge to the ballerina and that can thrill people at any period when she succeeds in meeting the challenge. Moreover, they suffer constant changes from genera-tion to generation without the slightest damage. Fokine altered *Les Sylphides* many times and spoilt it by his afterthoughts. The particular relationship between dance and movement prevented the possibility of a change. But *Swan Lake* must have been changed far more drastically yet remained the same in spirit. There are many ballet-scientists who leap into print about alterations in *Swan Lake* and *Giselle*. Quite apart from the fact that they cannot possibly know unless they are over a hundred years old and have photographic memories, it really does not matter so long as the fundamentals remain. Each ballerina has her special way of performing an adagio or variation, the way best suited to her physique and temperament, she has her own particular speed and in the case of these ballets this is perfectly legitimate. This is a long digression in a chapter called 'Nostalgia,' but an important and a relevant one, since nostalgia would not exist with such intensity if it were in the nature of all ballets to have a permanent existence. *Revenons à la nostalgie.* . . .

From René Blum's repertoire there is that little gem, *L'Epreuve d'Amour*, in which Fokine returned to his youthful inspiration with Mozart's rediscovered score, Derain's magic

At my mother's, Bath, 1949
A. L. H., Alicia, Vivienne, my mother

Family Group—'The Fourth' at Eton, 1949
Helen, A. L. H., Stephen, Vera, Francis

set and the whole atmosphere conveyed from curtain-rise by
Kirsova's fluttering butterfly.

Although the classics belong to the present there are certain
interpretations that set a standard and that taught one particular
critic his job. First among them, Vera Trefilova in *The Sleeping
Princess*, Alhambra, 1921. The moment that I saw it I felt that
I must try and write of the exhilarating joy it had given me.
The notes that I then took I used six years later for my first
book dedicated to her. She was a purely classical dancer with
dignity, authority and attack. Cold, if you like, but the coldness
was something positive, not just a lack of heat which is what
we generally imply by the word. I was fortunate also in seeing
her dance the one-act version of *Swan Lake* in Monte Carlo.
It was my first. It is strange to think that there was a time when
every movement was not familiar. Then there was the extraordinary Olga Spessivtseva, today, alas, in a New York
mental home suffering and remembering. Many fine judges
place her *Giselle* as the supreme classical interpretation of our
time. I never saw Karsavina's but I would place Pavlova's *hors
concours*, if only for her last act. Spessivtseva had that intense
concentration, that identification with the character that
Alexandre Sakharoff noted in Nijinski as a symptom of escape.
Her Giselle, at its greatest at the Paris Opéra, had the enormous
advantage of Lifar's Albrecht that made of this unfortunate
prince a positive character instead of leaving him a lay figure
from the romantic store-room. Lifar, arms full of lilies, trailing
his long purple cloak, bowed down by grief and remorse, had
really entered a wood in which evil spirits were at large.

Today the classics are in safe hands and Fonteyn has set a high
standard for the dancer and the young critic. Only the very
minor rôles lack attention to detail. There was, in the Diaghileff
Aurora's Wedding, a certain Pavlov who, as master of ceremonies, holding a long ceremonial staff, led the dancers on to
the stage. With what *panache* he acted, what breadth of movement, suggesting from his very entrance that this was the court

305   U

of a rich and powerful King and that the moment we had come to see was one of rejoicing. I do not remember Pavlov in any other rôle, but in this he made a name and earned the high approval of Diaghileff. Yet many of the variations fell below the present standard, that is, after the 1921 production, a key date for ballet in Western Europe.

Among recent events already certain performances have been pigeon-holed as memories. Fonteyn in all the classics, Renée Jeanmaire as Carmen and Babilée in *Le Jeune Homme et la Mort*, both Wyroubova and Skorik in *La Sylphide*. Especially outstanding is my memory of Chauviré's *Giselle*. What a marvel of consistent detail! Here at last is the true peasant girl living in a feudal world. There is no reckless flinging of the necklace, but a sad surrender and even in the joyful moments there is the reminder that Giselle has a weak heart. And then her second act; she is not yet a hardened *wili*, there is the conflict between her still warm blood and her new allegiance. One can feel the cruelty of the inner conflict. Chauviré has a rare intelligence to back her superb gifts as a ballerina.

For me, at any rate, these few memories have been of value, I have rescued Pavlov and his court chamberlain and have left myself in full enjoyment of the present and grateful for the past.

CHAPTER TWENTY-ONE

The Dance of Death: Part II

FIVE years after the war, not only is there no peace but the dance of death accelerates its pace; who now could count on a peaceful span of twenty years? We live in the dark ages of a perpetual pre-war period. This time we are a little more realistic in outlook. We no longer say it cannot happen. We are terrified of the very word appeasement and some honest 'democrats' in their horror of Communism turn Fascist and witch-hunt with enthusiasm.

We are horribly sensitive about the sound of words; 'appeasement,' 'communist,' 'right wing,' 'left wing,' 'reactionary,' but we are not always so very clear as to their meaning. To the diehard even a liberal is a 'dangerous red,' while everyone claims to be a democrat, a word that made our grandfathers shiver as much as 'communist' does an American senator, or 'Trotskyist deviationist' does Stalin, and, God knows, the Kremlin boys have invented a number of very ugly and completely meaningless words to mislead the semi-educated.

Today's undergraduates are more earnest than we were and have a far greater sense of responsibility. There are no bright young people today. They even take 'bebop' in deadly earnest. When we call bathing slips 'Bikinis' and talk of an 'atom haircut,' it is not because we are frivolous or take these things lightly. We are just whistling to keep up our spirits as we struggle through the darkness and the mud.

A violent death is an unpleasant thing for the individual to contemplate but, taken in the light of history, it is of little importance. We are all doomed to die in one way or other before so very long. The Egyptians, Sumerians, Cretans, Greeks and Romans whose work lies on my shelves, are all dead in the sense that we shall be. This time what does matter is the certain destruction of the museums and libraries, the cathedrals—yes, even the myopic Dean's Canterbury—and palaces, the achievements of Michelangelo and Rembrandt, Donatello and Leonardo. Even the intense will to survive of a Cheops is powerless against the A or the H bomb! A fraction of a second can destroy all those God-given treasures that separate man from beast.

What is particularly frightening is the fact that so many seemingly good folk, given the comfortable safety of their own small parish, if such safety were still possible, would not worry in the slightest about such a loss.

Take a look at the 8 a.m. train from anywhere to anywhere. Here are some youths busily engaged in reading a paper with an air of fierce concentration—wait a minute, are they reading? No, they are looking at a series of shockingly drawn scribbles under which there is a text in the jargon or cant of the American underworld. These stories are brutal, dealing with physical violence and strong-arm methods. The women are shown pomegranate-breasted and scantily clad and are deliberately drawn to provoke a snigger. There is not a trace of comedy in these so-called comics, the 'funnies' have not a fragment of real fun. They are mass-produced by tasteless opportunists for the mentally undeveloped. In America we are told that they are taken seriously, that they are able to influence millions politically and morally. They have, we are told—pardon the words— a force in education and their perpetrators are treated with a greater respect than any but the most successful artists. I, too, once read comic papers—they were real comics then—and enjoyed them; Buster Brown, Tiger Tim and, later, the more advanced texts of *The Gem* and *The Magnet* with the doings of Billy Bunter and his friends were something that one awaited with eagerness and read with avidity. I also enjoyed my Buffalo Bill, I was ten years old at the time. When I laid them aside they had given me not only much pleasure, but also the life-long habit of reading. Years before that I had also laid aside my rattle; that too had given me pleasure and had educated my hands.

Let us take a further look at these terrifying grown-up infants; no fear of disturbing them, they are too engrossed in *Superman*. I see them as enormously capable with their hands. They are able to assemble a car, to make a wireless set, but not, of course, to understand anything but the more debased sounds that issue from it. They are symbolized by the synthetic guffaws that greet the more suggestive jests that punctuate the weaker music-hall turns. There is nothing positive about them. They could not be called good citizens; they are too gullible and ignorant for that. They could not be called evil; there is nothing positive about them. They could not be called sportsmen though they read about sport and spend money and time and a little easy arithmetic in filling in their pools.

Let no one say I am exaggerating, taking a pessimistic view of things, attacking a thoroughly worthy section of the community that has as much right to these things as I have to Shakespeare, Jane Austen or Debussy. That is utter nonsense. No one should enjoy certain high-circulation papers with their eight or more comics, and no one should make money retailing such stuff. This is not a plea for censorship, but for education and the resultant self-censorship and for honesty in publishing.

Their womenfolk are superior. They are dealing in something real and worth while. Baby must be fed and washed and taken for a walk—and protected against evil, against a violent death in whatsoever form it may assume. It is more creative to bath a baby than to construct a machine, that is, if constructing a machine is the only way in which the mind is exercised.

And it is not only the humble technician who is a menace, but many of the scientists who construct the blue prints from which he works. Perhaps these scientists, though so much smaller in numbers, are the more dangerous since they pass for educated people. Unless they are spiritually armed they find a purpose in communist materialism or create their machines for the sheer pride in creation. Fuchs is an example, one to be greatly pitied, of the new class, the brilliant and highly capable uneducated. They exist among the doctors and economists too.

That is the great problem of our age; the comic-reading, pool-filling machine-making adult with the mental development of a child of ten. That is at the true root of the problem of the atom and the hydrogen bomb. So far the old universities have stood out against a purely technical training, and have set an example that some of the younger universities are following. But the universities touch far less of the population than the technical colleges and the colleges attached to industry. Moreover, the whole argument that certain children will not benefit by a higher education and that consequently the sooner they are turned into competent wage-earning technicians the better, is a complete fallacy. In the first place the decision is made too early and on insufficient evidence. The teaching profession is so underpaid and overworked that it is impossible for each individual child to receive proper attention. I have had the opportunity, under exceptionally fortunate circumstances, to have charge of some of those children who have failed in the examination that would entitle them to a grammar school education. In many cases I have found that they were no less intelligent than the others. They had merely developed at a later age and needed the special handling that, under ordinary circumstances, they could not receive. Even when they were below the average and remained so, they could still benefit by a higher education before becoming technicians.

To tackle the problem of the young adult by night schools that teach him how to use his leisure hours is an unsatisfactory solution, a mere palliative. Adult education is partly a confession of failure. Cost what it may, the teaching profession must be made so attractive that the very best minds can adopt it without sacrificing the comforts that trade or commerce can provide. I have, of late, met a great number of teachers and since chance has made me a teacher I feel very humble in face of their skill and devotion.

Also, it must be realized that for a long-term policy the teaching of girls is more important and requires more careful study than the teaching of boys. By this I do not mean the teaching of girls for the learned professions, and the top university scholarships, that today is a battle won, but the teaching of the average child who is going to become housewife and mother. It is the woman who can give a sense of values to her family, who has the possibility of continuing the education that she has gained in school. Since by accident I became a schoolmaster, I have realized the tremendous rôle in education that the mother plays, and, although my main object is to turn out girls who will be dancers and I hope artists, I always bear that in mind. I ask myself, can I give Joan or Mary something that she will be able to pass on to her children; a love of reading, the understanding of a symphony or the appreciation of painting and sculpture? Can I awaken in her a sense of awe? It is the mother who largely sets the tone. If I have been able to advance the child one step ahead of her mother, to give her one extra interest, then I have not been an entire failure. I have never seen Miss McCutcheon, our Senior Mistress, usually so unruffled, in such a state of indignation as when one of our mothers asked her if she did not feel that the scholarship children might lower the tone of the school. I am quite sure that after a year or two with us the daughter will not be quite such a snob, yet I hope that she will be a snob, but of another kind, where true values are concerned. And certainly from my highly specialized point of view we will have made a better artist.

It is the word *artist* that is important here. Leaving aside for the moment all specialization, the word artist does not necessarily mean some being set apart, usually a trifle eccentric and with a very special moral code. It is possible to be an artist in one very real sense of the word in every walk of life. The teacher must certainly be an artist. The artistic outlook is not a luxury but a necessity. That, unfortunately, is completely misunderstood by people who use 'highbrow' as a term of reproach and pride themselves on being 'lowbrows.' Horrid words to express horrid ideas; words that can make the adult infant feel virtuous and secure. Was it not one of the Nazi leaders who said, 'When I hear the word culture I reach for my revolver?' The good education must banish those debased words and the ideas that they represent.

But to return to my own seemingly narrow field, and there is much of general application in the experience since the process of education and vocational training is speeded up and can be studied as a whole. As the director of a specialist school my work is twofold, my staff a double one. The vocational staff must train the body, making the sensitive instrument that the artist will one day play upon. There is much nonsense talked about the artistry of children and the danger of suppressing it by a rigid technique. The child may appear to be an artist, little Jane may paint something that does not look to the uninitiated so very different from a Picasso or a Matisse. In reality there is all the difference in the world; the one is instinctive, the other deliberate, the one play, the other hard work. Sentimentalists have written as much rubbish about children's art as the psychologists who look for something significant in every line and colour, ignoring the workings of chance. With dancing the instrument must be made long before the dancer has anything worth expressing. We are concerned with the instrument, the technician and the potential artist in one and the same child. The whole process is there before us. In general early vocational training is a bad thing, but in the case of the dancer for physical reasons it is essential. Therefore it must be controlled, strictly limited to the very few of talent and handled by experts. If, in the early stage, the dancing staff is largely concerned with the making of the instrument, and that statement is not to deny them artistry, it is the educational staff who must give the children the material and the background that they will later translate into terms of their chosen art. The two staffs are complementary, they realize that and they work hand in hand. When they discuss a particular child it is fascinating to see what a complete picture they can build and what results they can achieve in such close co-operation. At first there is no doubt that there was a certain feeling of rivalry, even a latent hostility between the two departments. That soon vanished, partly because of the real wisdom of the two heads, but also because the dancers realized what Miss de Valois knew all along, how very much the educationists can help. It was not just a question of *pliés* and *entrechats*, but of receptive and fully integrated human beings. Latin, French, geography and the rest helped to give a meaning to the mere mechanics.

I write of one small specialized school, of my own job, but what I write has a universal application. A broad grammar school type of education based on the arts and humanities is the finest investment that a country can make. Overcrowded classrooms and a semi-education with one eye on industry and a 'what is the practical use of Latin or music' attitude is more dangerous by far than the complete illiteracy of the masses and the high education of the few that we are so proud of having overcome.

If we are given time our children can be armed against wrong ideas, and it is largely ideas that we are fighting. The soldier who does not know what it is all about makes a poor combatant. Tolstoi has a remarkable chapter on that in *War and Peace*, which is more than ever relevant at the present moment.

I cannot in this chapter escape the controversial subject of religion in education. If I did so, my use of the word education would be misunderstood. There is no problem, or rather there is a different problem in schools of one particular denomination. The problem in those schools lies in avoiding making instruction and devotion monotonous so that once the pupil escapes he never wishes to set foot again inside a place of worship. The problem in the mixed school such as ours lies in taking the line of least resistance; 'its all good from a moral point of view; the Bible is after all a branch of history and literature.' I have heard this said countless times. Yet parents would have a legitimate grievance if one taught, from their point of view, the wrong religion to their child. In a day school the responsibility is largely the parents', but save in the case of the Roman Catholics it is usually neglected. We try our best in practice to see that our Anglicans, Catholics and Jews have the appropriate instruction. That, however, is not exactly what I mean, especially as I am writing of education and not religious instruction. The following episode made a great impression on me; I quote it from my notes.

'A is an exceptionally clever girl, a keen reader and an artist. I found her in the library reading Dostoievsky. She is very interested in Russia. I talked to her about Dostoievsky and his ideas, always a favourite subject, when she suddenly said, "I find it almost impossible to believe in God." When I questioned her she produced some muddled communist ideas. I found out, as I suspected, that in the first place she was thinking of God as an elderly bearded gentleman, a sort of super-conjuror whom science had put to flight. She was trying to tackle this gigantic problem with poor science and no philosophy. We talked for a couple of hours and I lent her some books. She will find them difficult but she has the brain, patience and determination and is not prejudiced.'

This episode confirms me in my view, that all particular religious instruction aside, a school must have an atmosphere in which the conception of God can exist. Religious instruction without that general atmosphere is powerless. It is in the science laboratory, the history and art classrooms that the atmosphere can be created. Faith is for the fortunate few but the feeling for religion in general is a question of the mind. Communism is the opium of the semi-educated. My youths in the 8 a.m. train are waiting to be drugged. The materialist schoolmaster is the most dangerous of all saboteurs, far more to be feared than the man in the dockyard.

In the first part of this chapter I wrote from the spiritual point of view while here I have dealt with education. The two must go hand in hand if we are to be spared to enjoy the many sane and beautiful things that surround us, the pleasures of books and paintings, travel, music and the theatre. It is given to the very few and fortunate to reach a high degree of spirituality by mystic experience and with no education. But the great majority must grope and learn the hard way. They should not be handicapped.

CHAPTER TWENTY-TWO

Final Chapter in the Form of a Dialogue

Intruder: 'I see from the untidy pile of manuscript that you have finished your book. Two years' work delving into the past. Have you altered in those years, grown more meditative or profound?'

Myself: 'I certainly look more profound. I have grown a beard; not one of those sprawling all over the face, aesthetic fringes; they are only for the very young—nor yet a trim Monsieur le Vicomte affair. It is a Protean growth capable of being worn in full dress or in *negligée*, even of being parted in the middle *à la Tirpitz*. In colour it is more white than black.

'I was talked into it one evening at the club by Compton Mackenzie, possessor of a noble beard straight out of the pages of Dumas, sister to that of Monsieur le Cardinal. I had long flirted with the idea; once it shows more white than black it is, like writing an autobiography, a symbol of middle age, a stage in life such as putting up one's hair. Besides I enjoy it, as I enjoy dressing up in my assorted travel trophies. I was tired of seeing the same face in the glass as I shaved. Now with a twist of the comb and the imagination I can see Mephisto, von Tirpitz, Mr. Pooter or "Oom" Paul.'

Intruder: 'And what is the effect on others?'

Myself: 'The family has taken to it remarkably well. My wife in fact threatens to divorce me if ever I shave it. Could such a thing be construed as mental cruelty?

'A beard alters one's attitude to the world. To children it suggests Santa Claus, to their parents it brings a certain authority. Recently in Austria it has resulted in my being addressed as Herr Professor on three separate occasions, waiters become more obsequiously attentive, porters rush for one's baggage and one is no longer expected to surrender one's seat to a healthy young woman. Moreover it will advance by at least ten years my filling the position of the Grand Old Man of Ballet, robbing my friend, Cyril Beaumont, of that distinction. Only a few more years and I shall be telling a group of young *balletomanes* of Taglioni's début, of my *affaire* with the Fiocre sisters and my week-end in the Bavarian Alps with Lola Montez. And they will believe me; no one in England doubts the words of a G.O.M.'

Intruder: 'But enough of looking at yourself in the glass. A bearded Narcissus is intolerable. Even a goat sports a beard and beards are not unknown in the vegetable world; they form the only unpleasant part of the succulent artichoke.

'What I want to know is, how you have developed as a writer, what you have proved to yourself. You said at the beginning that you wrote of necessity.'

Myself: 'I know, and I always have known, that I am not a stylish writer and I have no great creative gifts. I found that out when I tried to write a novel. When I was describing what I had experienced myself it went well enough, but my attempts at fine writing resulted in those very purple passages that I had commented so scathingly on as a publisher's reader. Fortunately in this case the critic took command and the novel reposes in a drawer; I had not the courage to burn it. But in another sense it is my misfortune that the critic is always there to raise doubts; better to let ten purple passages through and to leave one small passage of inspired creative writing in which one can believe. I have a simple mind. I find it difficult to understand the "highbrow" writers on ballet, even with the aid of a dictionary; doubtless I lose a great deal through that. I have no elaborate theories to propound about the dance. I write best and most easily when I feel strongly, either enthusiastically or indignantly, when, in other words, I am writing subjectively and am honest in my recognition of the fact.

'Now for your second and more difficult question: Have I proved anything to myself through the stirring of my memories when writing this?

'Yes; that I have been exceedingly fortunate and exceedingly happy in my father and mother, my wonderful wife and my family, my work and my friends. My only ambition is to carry on as long as possible. I would wish for it all over again but with something added; my good fortune has made me at the same time grateful and afraid. I have planned nothing and it all rests on so little. More than anything I have been searching for a meaning and a secure foundation, for a kind of happiness that no worldly failure can destroy. Writing this has brought me to my goal, especially the chapter entitled "The Dance of Death: Part II." It has brought me safely into the [Roman] Catholic Church. The priests did not "get at" me, I "got at" them first. Some people seek a faith through sorrow. I sought it on account of happiness; a thanksgiving for the life I have described.

'This search for a meaning is the background to all the happy scenes I have described, and it cannot be shut out by living isolated in a little world of music and bright lights.

'Sometimes it makes a violent intrusion, as it did last week when my wife received a letter from an old school-friend. They had not met since Kieff days before the Revolution. This friend writes a story of physical and mental suffering that must be the story of millions today. After the loss of a husband and child, and a hide-and-seek existence between Russian and German bestiality, she is safely in America, married to a regular army officer. And though she is now secure she cannot find peace of mind because she cannot make people understand. She asks her old school-friend, "What has become of you?" Can Vera reply, "I raised a family in South Kensington, I play a little bridge, I go to parties, my husband interests himself in ballet"?

'Two girls sitting side by side on a school bench, worried about their history examination and mildly in love with a handsome mathematics master. And now, after half a lifetime, they can find no common language.

'It is this problem of the true nature of good and evil, also of fear and of the contentment that comes, not from circumstances, but from within that colours everything. Having a good time when possible, doing harm to no one, acquiring tolerance with experience, doing one's work with enthusiasm, performing a charitable deed from time to time, are not solutions. Is it to be wondered, then, that this report of a middle-aged pupil is a poor thing, scrawled over in red ink, "*Not good enough, try harder and still harder next term*"? For that reason I find the title that Nigel Balchin so ingeniously found for me a particularly apposite one.'

NOTES ON THE ILLUSTRATIONS

1. Susie, a grey poodle, was christened Zizi by Renée Jeanmaire but her name has gradually become anglicized.

3. This hitherto unpublished photograph of Pavlova was given to me by the late Ted Tait, a fine man of the theatre and wonderful company on an outing.

4. The balcony of this room became famous; from it Lenin made one of his first speeches during the revolution.

6. By good fortune I met Sir Kenneth Clark in Venice the day before the ceremony and he was able to be present at the memorial service and incidentally to represent the Royal Opera House.

7. Seated in the front row are Toumanova, Baronova, Riabouchinska. In the second row Tchernicheva, Grigorieff, Danilova, de Basil, Mme. de Basil, Massine, Delarova, Woizikovski, Dorati.

   A. L. H. stands behind Dorati and next to Lichine. It must have been a calm day; he is smoking.

9. *Candeur*—Dalou's biographer, Maurice Dreyfous writes of this bust—'*C'est une simple tête de jeune fille de seize à dix-sept ans, tête fine et candide, avec un petit air d'étonnement naïf.*'

   He goes on to say that it is the equal of any eighteenth-century portrait of a young girl.

   It is actually the portrait of his sister-in-law, was made during his stay in London and only cast after his death. I have had it for over twenty years and it has always been to me a symbol of happy adolescence.

10. Photos of the sisters together are rare: these are, I believe, the only two. Vivienne is the only one who did not go on the stage. She became a civil servant. If I had or have a favourite it is Vivienne, perhaps because it was so difficult to get hold of her in those early days. She was delicate and probably this photo was taken between botulism and diphtheria. She is,

thank goodness, tough these days. To me they have altered not at all in spite of the fame of Alicia.

11. Mama looks magnificently placid in this domestic photo.

13. Ninette—Dame Ninette de Valois—dislikes personal applause and being photographed. I had to show this happy scene at which I myself was applauding frantically. It is thanks to her that my work has a *raison d'être*, that there is a national ballet in Britain—*Brava!*

14. The top picture, taken just before Christmas, shows Form I with the author. The crêche on the wall is the joint work of the form; a genuine primitive.

In the photo underneath the author's daughter has joined the school party.

15. A wonderful gathering of French ballet stars at one of the delightful parties at the Tony Mayers'.

Front row: Thérèse Mayer and A. L. H.

Second row: Marie Rambert, Janine Charrat, Yvette Chauviré, Renée Jeanmaire, Colette Marchand, Lycette Darsonval.

Third row: Max Bozzoni, Serge Lifar, J. B. Lemoine.

Back row: Tony Mayer, Georges Reymond, Georges Auric, Constantine Népo, Vladimir Skouratoff, Roger Ritz, Serge Perrault.

Index

Adams, Dr. Coode, 69
Adjemova, Sirène, 55
Agate, James, 74, 300
Aldanov, Marc, 46, 51, 66
Amaya, Carmen, 188
America; ballet companies of, 290–293; impressions of, 173–174; Russian Ballet in, 110–112, 131–135
Amours de Jupiter, Les, 121, 213, 285
Anderson, Marian, 298
Animals, cruelty to, 75, 183–184
Anouilh, Jean, 121
Apollon Musagètes, 42, 220
Argentina, *see* Mercé, Antonia
Argyle, Pearl, 265–268
Arts Council (C.E.M.A.), 99, 251
Ashcroft, Peggy, 255
Ashton, Frederick, 59, 100, 122, 266, 286
Astafieva, Serafina, 42, 117, 218
Astley, Edward, 268
Audran, Emile, 228
Aurora's Wedding, 54, 131, 221, 257, 305
Australia; collection of books, etc., on, 195; impressions of, 139–140, 173
Australia (Haskell), 173
Australians, The (Haskell), 173
Ayrton, Michael, 165

Babilée, Jean, 288–289, 306
Baiser de la Fée, Le, 267
Bal de Blanchisseuses, Le, 285
Balanchine, Georges, 106, 202, 207, 221, 267, 290, 303
Ballet Annual, The, 114
Ballet Club, 101, 202

Ballet Theater, 290
Balletomania (Haskell), 19, 42, 73, 104, 105, 110, 113, 137
Ballets des Champs Elysées, Les, 213, 285
Ballets 1933, Les, 104, 207, 267
Barn Dance, 291
Baronova, Irina, 117, 208, 303
Bate, Philip, 167, 168, 229
Baylis, Lilian, 203, 253, 255–256, 265
Beards, dissertation on, 316–317
Beaton, Cecil, 70
Beau Danube, Le, 303
Beaumont, Cyril, 245, 283, 317
Bedells, Phyllis, 247
Bennett, Arnold, 85
Benois, Alexandre, 62–63
Beriosova, Svetlana, 252
Berlin, impressions of, 39–40
Bernhardt, Curtis, 267, 268
Bernhardt, Sarah, 118, 169
Biches, Les, 42, 302, 304
Black on White (Haskell), 194
Black Swan, 215
Blum, René, 106, 107, 115, 130, 187, 226, 304
Bolero, 205
Bolm, Adolf, 169
Boutique Fantasque, La, 219, 302
Bower, Dallas, 164, 165, 168
Brahms, Caryl, 108, 283
British Council, 119, 186
Brussels, residence in, 37–39
Buckle, Richard, 216, 284
Byard, Theodore, 76, 78

C.E.M.A., 99, 251
Caine, Hall, 82
Camargo Society, 96–101, 202, 257
Cambridge, at Trinity Hall, 67–72

323